KINGS OF THE AIR

French Aces and Airmen of the Great War

Ian Sumner

Pen & Sword
AVIATION

First published in Great Britain in 2015 by
PEN AND SWORD AVIATION
an imprint of
Pen and Sword Books Ltd
47 Church Street
Barnsley
South Yorkshire S70 2AS

Copyright © Ian Sumner, 2015

ISBN 978 1 78346 338 1

Printed and bound in England
by CPI Group (UK) Ltd, Croydon, CR0 4YY

Typeset in Times by CHIC GRAPHICS

Pen & Sword Books Ltd incorporates the imprints of Pen & Sword
Archaeology, Atlas, Aviation, Battleground, Discovery, Family
History, History, Maritime, Military, Naval, Politics, Railways,
Select, Social History, Transport, True Crime, Claymore Press,
Frontline Books, Leo Cooper, Praetorian Press, Remember When,
Seaforth Publishing and Wharncliffe.

For a complete list of Pen and Sword titles please contact
Pen and Sword Books Limited
47 Church Street, Barnsley, South Yorkshire, S70 2AS, England
E-mail: enquiries@pen-and-sword.co.uk
Website: www.pen-and-sword.co.uk

Contents

Maps

Map 1. Airfields of Verdun, 1916

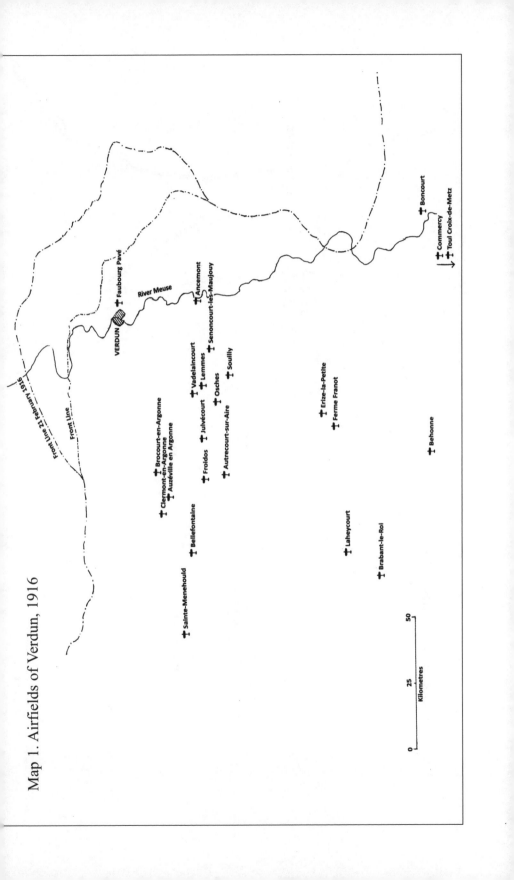

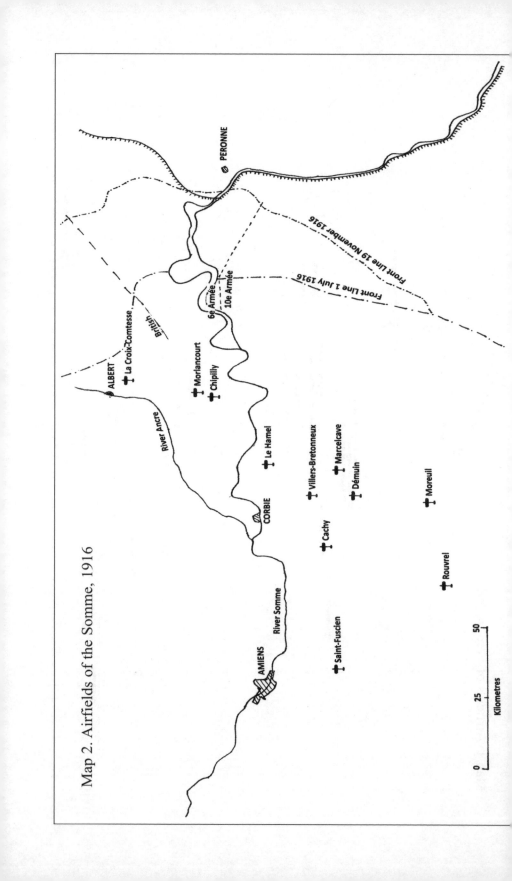

Map 2. Airfields of the Somme, 1916

Introduction and Acknowledgements

When man first took to the air in powered flight in 1903, soldiers and politicians were quick to recognize the military potential of the new technology. Over the next decade aircraft developed rapidly in power and speed, while armies faced the challenge of creating an aviation service, positioning it within the existing chain of command and evolving a doctrine to govern its use. None of these issues had been resolved on the outbreak of war, but over the next four years French aircraft progressed to become a weapon integral to the ultimate allied victory, laying the groundwork for operational developments such as fighters, strategic bombing and photo-reconnaissance, which later became standard in the Second World War.

So novel was the experience of flight that many airmen still regarded their new surroundings with awe: 'This sea of white really is a beautiful sight,' mused Charles Delacommune (C66). 'It's idyllic, seductive, hypnotic. But don't linger. Like the treacherous oceans, it too claims its victims, trapping them in an instant in a cage of frosted glass. The light is worse than night. Hazy, bleached of all colour . . . it burns the staring eyes. The engine drones dull and distant. The mountings wail mournfully. It's like a descent into the void, destined for death. . . . In the world of the clouds you have no desire to violate nature. Discovering perfection, you are gripped by the same feelings of reverence as the explorer who penetrates the mysterious virgin forests or the lonely desert sands.'

The war saw an enormous increase in the numbers of men taking to the skies. By August 1914 only 487 officers and other ranks had gained their military wings; by November 1918 some 16,546 pilots had qualified – the last of them, Adrien Valière, on 11 November. In 1914 some 134 trainees passed through the system; during 1918 no fewer than 6,909 pilots qualified, 40 per cent of them going to fighter squadrons, 33 per cent to army corps squadrons and 15 per cent to bombers. Less than 20 per cent were married, and the majority hailed from an urban rather than an agricultural background, perhaps employed in a manufacturing (often metal-working), commercial or administrative job, or still a student. Most possessed their school-leaving certificate, the *certificat d'études primaires*, the minimum required to pass the obligatory theory test, and a substantial minority had, or were studying for, a higher level qualification – the *baccalauréat* (around 33 per cent) or a degree (around 20 per cent).

Over the course of the conflict 4,745 members of the aviation service and 594 members of the balloon service were reported killed or missing. A death rate of 1 in 28 appears to compare favourably with rates of 1 in 13 for the cavalry and 1 in 4 for the infantry. However, only a relatively small proportion of the service actually saw action in the firing line, whereas virtually every member of an infantry regiment was 'at risk'. By comparison with the infantry, fewer of those killed were officers – 21.6 per cent in aviation, 29 per cent in the infantry – and losses were more heavily weighted towards the later years of the conflict. The infantry suffered the majority of its losses (68 per cent) between 1914 and 1916; in contrast, 80 per cent of front-line aviation deaths took place during the principal set-piece battles of Verdun and the Somme (1916), the Chemin des Dames (1917) and the defensive and offensive campaigns of 1918 – with over half (51.7 per cent) of all losses incurred in the last year of the war.

The purpose of this book is to tell the story of these airmen in their own words. In my previous book, *They Shall Not Pass: the French Army on the Western Front, 1914–1918* (Pen & Sword Books, 2012), I observed that 'Contemporary testimony provides an immediacy often lacking in formal accounts, but it is not without its dangers. Events and emotions remembered years after the event may be recalled imperfectly or coloured by later experience,' and this statement remains equally valid here. In the case of aviation, however, these dangers are compounded by the adulation accorded to aircrew, and to fighter pilots in particular, both during and after the war, resulting in accounts which sometimes prize atmosphere over accuracy. The aviation service represented only a very small element of the French army, so fewer personal accounts were written by airmen. Many interviews appeared in the weekly magazine *La Guerre aérienne illustrée*, first published in 1917, and its successor *La Vie aérienne illustrée*. These contain many useful insights, but it is important to remember that they worked under a censorship regime.

The basic unit within the aviation service was the squadron (*escadrille*), consisting of six aircraft in 1914, ten in 1916 and fifteen in 1917. At the start of the war each squadron acted independently, reporting to an army or army corps commander. In December 1914 a number of bomber squadrons were combined into bomber groups (*Groupes de Bombardement*) of three or four squadrons each. From the spring of 1916 a number of fighter squadrons were placed in ad hoc *groupements* for operational or tactical reasons, and in November 1916 permanent fighter groups (*Groupes de Combat/Groupes de Chasse*) were created. Over the next year or so, provisional *groupements* were created from time to time, combining several groups under a single commander as the local situation required. In February 1918 larger formations, *escadres*, were created from three bomber or four fighter groups. In May of the same year two fighter and two bomber *escadres* plus a reconnaissance group were combined to form the Air Division.

Each squadron was numbered sequentially on its creation, although several renumberings took place during the war, and some units changed their number on more than one occasion. Each number was prefixed by a letter or letters to indicate the principal aircraft type operated by the squadron. One squadron might have a succession of these prefixes – for example, the third squadron changed its designation from BL3 to MS3, N3 and SPA3 as it was re-equipped with different types. The prefixes were not standardized at the time: for example, contemporary usage prefixes SPAD squadrons with either S, Sp or SPA. I have compiled my own standard list and all prefixes employed in this book are given in Appendix 3.

I would like to thank all who have helped to produce this book. The Service historique de la Défense at Vincennes; the Bibliothèque nationale, Archives nationales and Musée nationale des Beaux-Arts in Paris; the Musée de l'Air et de l'Espace at Le Bourget and the British Library in London all provided a wealth of research material from their collections. Christina Holstein was kind enough to elucidate a piece of Verdun topography for me, while reader *extraordinaire* Katherine Bracewell deployed her customary forensic skills. My thanks must also go to Albin Denis and Claude Thollon-Pomerol, whose tireless work has contributed so much to the history of French military aviation during the First World War. The finished work would be nothing without the translating and editing skills of my wife Margaret, to whom I remain hugely indebted.

Every effort has been made to avoid infringing copyright and any omissions are unintentional. If this has occurred, please contact the publisher, who will include the appropriate credit in future printings and editions.

Chapter 1

'Masters of the World'

In October 1897 a small group of senior army officers gathered at the camp
of Satory, near Versailles, to watch French aviation pioneer Clément Ader
test *Avion III*, his latest heavier-than-air flying machine. Also present was
an NCO called Neute (1st Engineers): 'I could see a machine standing
before a largish hangar at the far side of the firing range. It looked
impressive. The bottom half was hidden by a crowd of spectators so only
the superstructure was visible, but . . . [the whole thing] seemed to be
around 8 to 10 metres high. It looked like a huge bat with its wings
extended; it was even the right shade of dark tobacco brown. I never lost
sight of it for a moment. I heard the engine start up and [the machine] began
to roll forward in a straight line. . . . It covered perhaps 100 metres. Then it
climbed very slowly, gained height, and I could see it clearly above the
heads of the crowd. What height did it reach? Twenty metres, perhaps
twenty-five. It was pitching quite heavily as it went along and after some
100 to 150 metres it changed course slightly. The pilot seemed to be having
trouble steering. Then suddenly I saw it fall . . . [and] my pals and I ran
[forwards]. I got a close-up view of the machine . . . [which had] sunk down
on its wheels. I walked right round it. I saw the engines, one right and one
left, and an enormous boiler, perhaps 1 metre wide by 1½ metres high.
Behind it sat the pilot. He had to lean out to either side to see ahead and we
wondered how he managed to steer. I also saw the two four-bladed
propellers. We all returned from the range convinced that we'd just
witnessed something historic. We had clearly, very clearly, seen the
machine above our heads.'

Ader's *Avion III* was the product of government-sponsored research.
Following its defeat in the Franco-Prussian war, France had embraced
technology to counter Germany's clear advantage in population terms – a
strategy that had made it a pioneer of military aeronautics. In the late 1870s
the engineers established a balloon section and, at Chalais-Meudon, the
world's first aeronautical research establishment. In 1880 captive and

dirigible balloons were introduced on manoeuvres for artillery spotting and short-range reconnaissance, and in 1887 a dedicated balloon company was attached to each of four of the regiments of engineers. Ader (1841–1925) was a prolific inventor who in 1890 became the first man to leave the ground in powered flight. His curious steam-driven contraption, christened *Éole*, had quickly crashed and disintegrated, and its underlying stability problems proved intractable; but the minister of war, Charles de Freycinet, was undeterred. An engineer by training, de Freycinet was a notable enthusiast for new technology, responsible during his two periods in office (1888–93 and 1898–9) for introducing the Lebel rifle and commissioning the research that eventually led to the famous 75mm field gun, two mainstays of French armaments during the First World War. In 1891 he offered Ader the significant incentive of 300,000 francs (fifteen times the annual salary of a general) to pursue his heavier-than-air research and produce a viable aircraft, fully controllable and capable of carrying a pilot, plus an assistant or a cargo of explosives, as well as flying fully loaded for at least six hours at a minimum of 55km/h. 'Military aviation was born that day at the behest of M. de Freycinet,' enthused Ader. 'Similar ideas inspired us and we were both very happy.'

The inventor moved his workshop to Satory and six years later proudly unveiled *Avion III*. Like Neute, Ader was convinced his plane had flown that day, but not so the senior officers present. The pilot, they reported, had failed to maintain full control of his machine, which had simply skipped along the ground rather than achieve the sustained flight required. The trial was officially deemed a failure and Ader's funding was summarily withdrawn. The inventor later blamed his own inexperience: 'Designing a flying machine is easy,' commented fellow pioneer Ferdinand Ferber, 'building one is harder, but getting it to fly is hardest of all.'

Ader withdrew from active involvement in aircraft design but continued to lobby on aviation affairs until the end of his long life. He left two permanent legacies, first by inadvertently demonstrating that steam power was a dead end, and secondly by coining the word '*avion*', initially adopted into official usage in 1911 and then more generally into the French language to replace the Anglophone '*aéroplane*'. Ader was also a visionary, one of the first to realize the full military potential of the new technology. As early as 1907 he was recommending that France form an air force, albeit one cast in naval terms, with 'scouts' (fast and lightly armed), 'torpedo aircraft' (heavy bombers) and 'aircraft of the line' (escorts). The enemy, he prophesied, would be boarded in mid-air. Planes would use fortified bases with asphalt runways, temporary landing strips with runways composed of huge rolls of wooden planks, or floating aircraft carriers. And failure to invest in air power would leave great Anglo-German air fleets threatening the capital itself: 'These airborne cohorts will fly methodically over the ten main *arrondissements* of Paris, bombing as they go, sparing neither museums nor historic monuments, and dropping on average four or five bombs per dwelling.' Britain, of course, had been France's ally since the signing of the Entente Cordiale in 1904, but Ader remained unmoved. As Britannia had ruled the waves in the nineteenth century, so she would 'want, nay be forced, to become mistress of the skies' in the twentieth.

In Germany Otto Lilienthal was experimenting with gliders, as were Octave Chanute and Orville and Wilbur Wright in the United States. Meanwhile, in France artillery captain Ferdinand Ferber had taken up the baton, contacting Chanute in 1901 and the following year building his own Chanute-Wright type machine. Ferber in turn inspired a whole generation of French aviation pioneers, among them Louis Blériot, Robert Esnault-Pelterie, and Gabriel and Charles Voisin, all members of the influential Aéro-Club de France (ACDF). Another acolyte was fellow artilleryman Lieutenant Georges Bellenger. 'Ferber was the reason I took up flying,' claimed Bellenger. 'The thorough grounding he gave me helped me to avoid all sorts of mishaps.'

By 1903 Ferber was corresponding directly with the Wright brothers, just months before their historic flight at Kitty Hawk, and in 1904 he was posted to Chalais-Meudon to pursue his research full time. In May 1905 he completed a powered flight of 100 metres – the first European to do so – and that October he received a letter from the Wrights. Wilbur had completed a non-stop circuit of 38 kilometres in the *Flyer III*, and for one million francs the brothers were offering to 'supply their machines under contract, to be accepted only after test flights of at least 40 kilometres, carrying a pilot and sufficient fuel etc. . . . for a journey of 160 kilometres'. But there was a problem: anxious to ensure they alone reaped the profits from their invention, the Wrights had always shunned publicity and would only demonstrate the *Flyer* once the contract was signed.

Most members of the ACDF thought the brothers had exaggerated their claims. Why was so little known about their flights even in the United States? Why had there been no application for the Deutsch-Archdeacon prize offered for the first powered flight? Ferber, however, had no doubts: despite its high price and inability to carry a cargo, the *Flyer* would revolutionize observation work, 'making it possible for the commander-in-chief to track the enemy's marches and counter-marches at all times'.

Overall, he pronounced, it would be 'a prodigious weapon of war'. Colonel Pierre Roques, the director of engineers, also welcomed the offer. 'Despite the secrecy that surrounds their experiments,' he advised the minister, 'all the intelligence available on the Wright brothers and their invention concurs – the[y] appear to have made real progress towards solving the problem of flight.'

The minister was persuaded and in March 1906 a secret mission under Major Henri Bonel was despatched to the Wright workshops in Ohio. After a month of negotiations, Bonel made his final offer: the French agreed to the asking price of one million francs for Wright-built planes capable of reaching an altitude of 300 metres, taking off in winds up to 10m/s, and completing a circuit of 50 kilometres, but in return they demanded a year-long exclusivity clause. The Wrights refused, and Bonel returned home empty-handed.

While Roques and Ferber were enthusiastic supporters of the new invention, many senior officers remained sceptical of its military value. At Chalais-Meudon attention had already returned to proven lighter-than-air technology. Captive balloons were used to report on 'enemy' movements during the annual autumn manoeuvres, and the army ordered a new dirigible, *La Patrie* – with catastrophic results for Ferber and his experimental machine. 'The balloon arsenal was waiting . . . impatiently for *La Patrie* . . . and had been authorized by the minister . . . to remove my plane from its hangar,' he fumed. 'I was forced to leave it outside overnight [where] it was caught unprotected by the storm of 19 November 1906, a month before the dirigible actually arrived.' Ferber's work was completely destroyed in a matter of hours, 'depriving the nation of a plane that the most recent tests had proved to be absolutely ready'.

Beyond Chalais-Meudon, however, aeroplanes were forging ahead. The Wright brothers had finally patented their invention and the Europeans were rapidly making up lost ground, with Paris the main focus of activity. In November 1906 Alberto Santos-Dumont made his first flight – the first in France, and the first to be ratified by the Fédération Aéronautique Internationale – and at Billancourt, just outside the city, the Voisin brothers opened Europe's first aircraft factory. The Wrights now crossed the Atlantic hoping to breathe new life into the French contract. They offered to concede exclusive rights for six months – but the French now demanded three years. Besides, the value of the *Flyer* had diminished somewhat: French aircraft were beginning to appear on the scene, offering more powerful engines, greater stability, and wheels instead of skids so they could take off unaided.

Backed by private capital from a group of industrialists, Wilbur Wright returned to France in May 1908 and stayed for almost a year. At Le Mans, Auvours and finally Pau, where he opened the world's first flying school, he broke records, trained pilots and introduced a number of wealthy and important passengers to aviation, among them future prime minister Paul Painlevé and future president Paul Doumer. Other manufacturers opened their own flying schools, and commercial sponsors such as the Michelin tyre company and the *Daily Mail* funded prizes to stimulate research and attract publicity. Aviation was also beginning to attract wider political attention. In November 1908 both houses of parliament formed aviation groups, the senate unanimously voting 100,000 francs 'to encourage the development of aviation in France'. Senator Paul d'Estournelles de Constant, a pacifist who believed aviation would help prevent another war, spoke in favour of the motion. 'Aviation development is hugely important to the defence of the nation,' he proclaimed. 'It is clear that in the not too distant future . . . we will have a completely unexpected resource in dirigibles and aircraft.'

Le Matin adopted a more strident tone. 'Let's get French military aviation up and running,' it thundered. 'Let's do it quickly and on a grand scale. It will bring us security now and power in the future. If world domination once was gained on land, and now is acquired at sea, tomorrow it will be won in the air.' Clément Ader entirely agreed: 'Aviation is the arm-of-service capable of defeating the enemy with the fewest number of casualties! . . . Whosoever is Master of the Air will be Master of the World.'

Throughout 1908 and 1909 records for height and endurance were broken repeatedly by an increasingly famous group of civilian pilots. In July 1909 Blériot became the first man to fly across the Channel – a feat of great symbolic importance attracting huge public interest; the following month saw the first international air meeting, a week-long affair held at Bétheny, near Reims, attended by all the leading planes and pilots of the day, as well as by thousands of spectators; and in September the first Paris Air Salon also pulled in the crowds: 380 exhibitors and 100,000 spectators packed the Grand-Palais, with Blériot's plane the main draw. A group of officers was present at Reims to evaluate the planes on show, and within a matter of weeks the minister of war, General Jean Brun, had asked the engineers to establish a military aviation service. The ministry allocated 400,000 francs for the purpose, volunteers were sought for pilot training, and five aircraft were purchased for assessment at Chalais-Meudon: two Farman biplanes, one Blériot 11 monoplane and two Wright *Flyers*.

Now military politics intervened. Introducing new technology to the army of the period was never a straightforward process – and aircraft would be no different. Fearful of a new military strongman after a century marked by coups and revolutions, the constitution of the Third Republic had placed the army firmly under political control. It had also established a deliberately labyrinthine command structure: the notional commander-in-chief was the minister of war, who also allocated the budget, while the chief of the general staff held overall command of operational formations and was also the designated wartime commander in the field. However, the latter exercised no authority over the generals heading the separate service departments of infantry, cavalry, artillery and engineers, and also had to compete with them for funding. General Joseph Joffre, who occupied the post from 1911 to 1916, later complained that the staff 'existed in total isolation from the various departments within the ministry, who [in turn] knew nothing of the requirements agreed by the council [of the general staff]'. Meanwhile his department was 'just one among many, without the authority needed to ensure all the myriad sections of the ministry worked together effectively'.

The problems of a divided command were compounded by the chronic political instability of the Third Republic. Coalition governments came and went at regular intervals, and with them ministers of war. Funding decisions, and the technological advances they financed, could thus be rather quixotic, owing much to the power and opinions of individual directors and the shifting sands of French parliamentary politics. The politicians felt themselves entitled to intervene at any time, and the system provided fertile ground for internal military rivalries to be played out on a very public stage, in the press and in parliamentary debates.

Against this background, the French now faced the enormous challenge of creating a new air service, positioning it in the military hierarchy, and formulating doctrines to govern its use – all while adapting to a rapidly evolving technology; and over the next decade, in peacetime and in war, different factions with rival concepts of the role of air power competed for supremacy. No sooner was the ink dry on the contracts for the first five aircraft than the artillery was vying with the engineers for control. Parliament immediately voted the gunners 240,000 francs for aviation purposes, and in early 1910 General Brun gave in to the pressure and created a separate artillery aviation section under Lieutenant Colonel Eugène Estienne, the dynamic former head of the Grenoble artillery school. 'Planes could seemingly be used straight away to meet the specific needs of the artillery,' Brun later explained, 'but further development was clearly required before [the engineers] could employ them for general military purposes.'

Fortunately, Estienne was no narrow partisan. Basing himself at the main artillery establishment at Vincennes, he invited a select group of officers from all arms of service to train as pilots and work together to develop doctrine, test aircraft and assess their military potential. Among them was a fellow gunner, Lieutenant Georges Bellenger. 'All with the minimum of bumf,' recalled Bellenger. '"Don't be afraid to show initiative and imagination," the colonel told me. "All I want from you are results."' Six aircraft were purchased – two Wrights, two Farmans and two Antoinettes – and Estienne and his team set to work. Next door was the new Pathé film studio, guaranteeing some rather exotic lunch companions in the local restaurants: 'Our motley uniforms could one day be found alongside the court of Louis XIV; the next, cowboys and Indians, even a tame panther brought back from Abyssinia by one of the directors.'

Brun had in effect created two parallel aviation services: one concerned primarily with long-range reconnaissance and development, the other with target identification and shell spotting. But his decision aroused furious opposition and on 11 June 1910 he reunited both services under the control of the engineers. By now aircraft had progressed sufficiently for use in long-range reconnaissance, a possibility amply demonstrated just two days earlier when Lieutenant Albert Féquant and Captain Charles Marconnet broke the world distance record in flying their Farman 158 kilometres from Châlons-sur-Marne to Vincennes. 'I made my decision because the current situation differs markedly from that envisaged when I formulated my original proposals,' argued Brun, in an effort to counter the strong artillery lobby within the Chamber of Deputies. 'Nine months have passed since I first considered giving the artillery joint control of aviation. What has happened in the meantime? Aeroplanes have made enormous, and completely unexpected, progress. I structured the service on the premise that [aircraft] would be useful only to the artillery, i.e. to investigate the battlefield proper. [However,] the magnificent run undertaken by Captain Marconnet and Lieutenant Féquant shows [they] are capable not just of covering a few kilometres over the battlefield, but 160 kilometres and more.'

The engineers demanded the immediate transfer of Estienne's artillery aviation section lock, stock and barrel to its own facility at Chalais-Meudon. But on 21 June Georges Bellenger received good news: 'the Vincennes establishment will continue under its [current] CO. Although now under the control of the engineers, it will become the independent military aviation laboratory, charged with research into the military use of aviation . . . We can breathe [again].'

Siege exercises held at Châlons and Verdun in July 1910 showed planes in action, operating effectively with the artillery by pinpointing targets invisible from the ground and adjusting fire accordingly. 'Even in its present state of development,' commented Major Fetter, in charge of the exercises, 'the aeroplane is a very useful tool for seeking out and identifying targets ... visually and photographically.' However, Fetter did sound one note of caution: underpowered planes flying missions at low altitude were clearly vulnerable to ground fire.

Two months later the annual autumn manoeuvres, held in Picardy, offered the first large-scale opportunity for pilots to practise alongside ground troops, with thirteen aeroplanes (plus four dirigibles) taking part. Despite poor weather, Bellenger's trials of a Blériot monoplane persuaded Estienne that such a light, easily transportable type could feasibly accompany all kinds of unit on campaign, while Adjudant Victor Ménard and his observer Lieutenant Marcel Sido flew several long-range reconnaissance missions, spending forty-five minutes in the air each time and returning intelligence so precise it forced the staff to change their dispositions. Orders were subsequently placed for twenty Blériot monoplanes and an equal number of Farman biplanes, including some two-seaters. 'Aeroplanes are as vital to armies as guns and rifles,' commented Pierre Roques, by now a general. 'We must be willing to accept the truth of this or risk being forced to do so.'

On 23 October 1910 General Brun recognized these developments by according aviation permanent status as a branch of the engineers, the first step on the road to an independent service. The energetic Pierre Roques was appointed inspector of military aeronautics, charged specifically with preparing the army's aircraft and balloons for war, and he immediately announced a grand *Concours militaire* to be held at Reims the following year. Despite their achievements in the autumn manoeuvres, the current generation of planes were primarily sporting machines, and the competition was specifically designed to produce military aircraft, with entry restricted to French manufacturers and engine-builders, and guaranteed orders and substantial cash prizes for the winners. 'The races and meetings organized thus far have really been tests of speed,' remarked Roques. 'The *Concours militaire* has a rather different focus: power.'

A detailed specification was drawn up – 'a little too stringent', according to manufacturer Henry Farman. 'Nevertheless,' he continued, 'it will have the fortunate effect of setting aviation on a different course. Speed will no longer be the only criterion; planes will also be asked to lift a load of almost 300 kilos. And, if war comes, you can do an awful lot of damage with 300 kilos.' Indeed, Roques had chosen this figure as the minimum required to give a plane an offensive capability, carrying weapons 'to combat any aerial opponent trying to prevent it from completing its mission', or bombs 'to destroy and particularly to demoralize [the enemy]'. Entrants also had to be three-seaters; simple to maintain, dismantle and transport by road or rail; and capable of operating from rough ground, climbing to 500 metres within 15 minutes, covering a 300-kilometre circuit non-stop, and reaching an average speed in excess of 60km/h.

Seventy-one planes from forty-two different manufacturers eventually entered the competition in September 1911, but all had struggled to fulfil the requirements of the specification, particularly with regard to load. Fewer than half could get off the ground, only sixteen passed the preliminary stage, and accidents – two fatal – were legion. After six weeks of trials, just eight planes – built by Nieuport, Breguet, Deperdussin, Farman and Savary – completed the course, with the Nieuport 4G monoplane pronounced the winner. Nieuport received orders for ten planes and 780,000 francs in prize money; the runner-up, Breguet, orders for six planes and 345,000 francs; and third-placed Deperdussin orders for four planes and 218,000 francs. However, the final rankings had still been determined by speed, and in general the competition failed to produce the types envisaged. 'Of course, my crate handles like a flat iron,' one unnamed manufacturer told Estienne, 'but it's fast and I'm desperate for the money. It should do well enough with an ace in the cockpit.' Sadly, his optimism was ill-founded. 'Although ten of the beasts were built,' reported Estienne, 'not a single pilot was prepared to go up in one.'

A supply and repair organization was set up to provide an effective logistical tail for the new planes, and Roques also addressed himself to pilot training. Specific qualifications for military pilots and observers were introduced in February 1911, followed by one for mechanics, and the service grew from just 43 qualified pilots in October 1910 to 152 by December 1911, with another 122 pupils under instruction. The pilots' course was more intensive than its civilian equivalent, and soldiers, reservists and civilians alike were encouraged to apply. Until then military and civilian pilots had all qualified through the ACDF. Some had simply bought an aircraft and taught themselves to fly – a potentially hazardous undertaking, as Roland Garros discovered to his cost: 'There were two types of aeroplane at the time, big ones costing around 20,000 francs [ten times the annual income of a miner] and the famous [but] tiny Demoiselle, which was available for a relatively modest sum. My only option was to go for this little machine. I bought one and set off for Issy-les-Moulineaux to teach myself.' Garros eventually coaxed the engine into life and began to taxi: 'After scarcely 30 metres a huge biplane came in to land, piloted by Maurice Clément. I hadn't seen him [at all]. I was concentrating too hard on the job in hand, wondering how on earth I was going to get off the ground. I couldn't get out of his way and he landed right on top of me, cutting my machine in half and reducing it to matchwood. By some miracle I escaped unhurt. So ended my first flight.'

Despite this inauspicious start, Garros soon obtained his wings and went on to become one of France's leading pre-war pilots – a multiple record-holder and, in 1913, the first man to cross the Mediterranean.

Estienne's research team was also hard at work. Bellenger successfully trialled a plane equipped with a camera: 'My machine made a terrific observation post,' he later commented. 'Photographs taken from an aeroplane provided much more detail than those taken from a balloon tethered some way from the target.' Wireless telegraphy was introduced to improve liaison with the ground, Captain Brenot and Lieutenant Victor Ménard demonstrating its potential reconnaissance use by transmitting a signal 50 kilometres from Rambouillet to the Eiffel Tower in July 1911. And aircraft were also investigated as bombers. 'I conducted a few trials at Vincennes with half a dozen bombs . . .', recalled Georges Bellenger. 'During the final one a bomb got trapped by its cord beneath my fuselage and dangled there while I circled above the racecourse . . . It happened to be a race day. Colonel Estienne was watching from the ground as I headed for the course with a bomb trailing behind me, tearing his hair out at the thought of the potential catastrophe if it fell among the spectators. He was even more worried when I landed and he saw the bomb had disappeared. But as we listened anxiously for any sounds from the racecourse, a gamekeeper turned up, complaining that a plane had dropped an incendiary in the woods . . . What a relief . . . Colonel Estienne declared it was the last time he would test live munitions in such a spot.'

The autumn manoeuvres of 1911, held in eastern France and the Ardennes, provided another opportunity for joint exercises with ground troops, a total of forty-seven planes taking part. 'Aircraft have undoubtedly made themselves useful,' concluded the official report. 'Very considerable progress has been made since 1910. The machines have shown that in future they will be of real tactical value. The aeroplane provides a complementary means of gathering intelligence that . . . allows the more economical and effective use of the cavalry. Its existence should be recognized and our troop movements concealed by marching at night or under the cover of trees, but its importance should not be overstated. It in no way vitiates currently agreed tactical doctrine.'

However, the report also included some words of warning: 'Aerial observation for military purposes demands specialist training, plus skills not as yet possessed by the great majority of our pilots,' it cautioned. Nor could the pilot double up as the observer: he was too busy flying the plane. And, despite successful 'attacks' on infantry formations, the vulnerability of unarmoured planes to ground fire was again confirmed. 'An unarmoured aircraft is very exposed,' commented Estienne in 1912. 'There's an even chance a pilot will be hit by a 10,000-round volley, the kind of thing he'll face in an hour over enemy lines as soon as he learns not to flinch at fire from the rear.'

The autumn of 1911 also marked the aeroplane's debut in action. On 23 October 1911, during the Italo-Turkish war in Libya, Captain Carlo Piazza spent an hour above Turkish lines in the world's first reconnaissance mission, followed in November 1911 by the first bombing raid, and in March 1912 by the first night mission, both flown by Giulio Gaviotti. Meanwhile, in the aftermath of the Agadir crisis the French sent a detachment to Morocco, where it performed useful work guarding the approaches to the port of Mogador.

At the Vincennes research establishment Georges Bellenger had been joined by former dragoons officer Lieutenant Charles de Rose, the first man to gain his military wings. Convinced that air-to-air combat was inevitable, the pair had begun to investigate means of arming aircraft, despite the opposition of senior officers, particularly among the staff, who feared it would lead to pilots abandoning their mundane reconnaissance or spotting duties to go haring after the enemy. In ground and air testing they demonstrated the potential of a 37mm Hotchkiss revolving cannon – but, recalled Bellenger sadly, his report to the minister 'succeeded only in putting to sleep those it was intended to rouse', and a proposal to arm aircraft, placed before parliament in February 1912 by Deputy Adolphe Girod, was defeated.

De Rose was also mulling on combat tactics: 'Will aeroplanes destroy each other?' he pondered, addressing a group of officers at Lunéville in March 1912. 'It remains a moot point. From personal experience I know how hard it is to spot a plane flying below you, especially with the current dark-toned canvas. A nearby aeroplane can often pass unseen. I conclude that a plane making an attack must therefore be faster [than its opponent] and approach from behind and slightly below.'

On 29 March 1912, after eighteen months of rapid development, the aeronautical service was finally awarded formal legal recognition as part of the army – and as a branch of the engineers. But the artillerymen were restive: in their opinion the essential work of shell spotting was being neglected. 'The main role of aviation is to work in tandem with the guns, identifying a target and directing fire upon it,' insisted General Victor Cordonnier, a former instructor at the staff college, the École de Guerre. 'We must never grow tired of repeating this.' Estienne, too, was convinced the artillery needed its own planes. 'An artillery unit entering battle without aircraft is inevitably heading for disaster,' he argued. 'The artillery has seen no technical advance comparable to that offered by the aeroplane . . . since the gun . . . In a war of movement, one aeroplane can often be worth more than ten guns. . . . What we need above all are eyes, eagle eyes; we're crying out for them like the giant Polyphemus, formidable but blind.'

For the minister of war, the time had come for the two warring parties to bury the hatchet: 'Aviation belongs neither to the engineers nor to the artillery,' he declared. 'It belongs to the army. It belongs to the nation. All must work together, renouncing sectional interests and conscious only of the public good.' On 22 April he ordered that squadrons be formed, their aircraft all marked with a red, white and blue cockade, so marking the birth of the first five squadrons of the future French air force, each six machines strong and based around a different aircraft type. Then in August 1912 the various aircraft and balloon units were allocated to one of three geographically organized Groupes Aéronautiques, each with its own training and maintenance facilities: Versailles, with bases at Chalais-Meudon, Douai and Étampes; Reims, with bases at Châlons, Verdun, Toul, Épinal and Belfort; and Lyon, with bases at Avord, Pau and Biskra (Algeria). Two months later the Vincennes establishment was downgraded and Estienne exiled to command 3rd Groupe Aéronautique at Lyon: 'Artillery aviation buried with full military honours,' grumbled Bellenger.

Pierre Roques, the inspector of aviation, received no chance to enjoy the fruits of his labours. In April 1912 he was appointed to lead an infantry division and was replaced by fellow engineer Colonel Édouard Hirschauer, the former commander of a balloon company, who soon announced an ambitious four-year procurement plan, targeting a strength of 1,832 planes and 2,730 engines by 1916. This was an expensive prospect when each plane cost on average 25,000 francs, plus 10,000 francs in annual maintenance and 4,000 francs to train a pilot – and in late 1912 a national appeal fund was launched, *'Donnez des aéroplanes à la France'* ('Aeroplanes for France'). With vociferous press support, a network of national and regional committees raised over 6 million francs during the next two years, funding the construction of airfields and the purchase of some 200 machines.

Seventy-two aircraft took part in the autumn manoeuvres in Touraine and Poitou in 1912, most controlled at army level, although some were placed with army corps on an experimental basis. Aircraft and dirigibles both demonstrated their worth: the aircraft, the two-seaters in particular, in strategic and tactical reconnaissance roles; the balloons 'attacking' troops on the march. Two months later Hirschauer issued instructions for the organization and deployment of his squadrons. Describing military aircraft as 'essentially tools of reconnaissance for army commanders', he outlined their strengths and weaknesses: '[They] provide a means of gathering intelligence quickly. [They] also outperform cavalry reconnaissance in [their] ability to identify enemy columns en masse and to bypass physical obstacles and the enemy outpost line. However, the aviator only gets a glimpse of the enemy at a single point in space and time, and while he can determine the composition of a unit, he cannot identify it. Reconnaissance aircraft struggle to maintain contact [with the ground], particularly when faced with a number of scattered targets; and finally they cannot operate at night, giving the enemy a chance to modify his situation. The established methods of intelligence-gathering (spying, cavalry, vanguard . . .) remain important but will be even more useful if employed in tandem with aerial reconnaissance.'

A revised technical specification drawn up in the spring of 1913 also focused on reconnaissance and offensive deployments: 'As the aircraft will be flown by pilots of no more than average ability they must perform well. They must be stable in wind and turbulence and respond quickly to the controls. It must also be easy to take off and land. Further to these general requirements, each of the three main categories of military aircraft will display its own characteristics: aircraft designed for long-range reconnaissance and potential attacks on ground targets . . . minimum two-seater . . . with sufficient space around the observer for wireless telegraphy equipment, a weapon capable of attacking ground targets or a firearm suitable for air-to-air combat; aircraft designed for air-to-air combat . . . armoured, good air speed . . . capable of carrying a load of c.75 kilos; light aircraft, easy to dismantle, transport . . . and reassemble to accompany troops whenever and wherever required . . . [as well as] capable of taking off and landing on any type of ground and in very confined spaces.'

However, the supremacy of the engineers was increasingly contested. The artillery had never abandoned hopes of controlling aviation, and new voices demanding greater autonomy for the rapidly expanding service had also joined the debate. On 16 April 1913 a new aeronautical department was created, putting the aviation and balloon services on the same footing as the infantry, cavalry, engineers and artillery. 'The era of trial and error negotiated with such difficulty suggests [this reform] is needed,' argued Deputy Paul Bénazet. 'Over this long gestation period, many decisions have been taken and decrees and orders issued ad hoc, and the need to bring some order to our aeronautical affairs has become apparent. The new arm of service requires a director reporting directly to the minister, with the same powers and responsibilities as [his peers].'

At the same time command of the aeronautical units was transferred from the inspector of aviation to the local fortress and army corps commanders, marking the genesis of a new quarrel between the partisans of an independent air service and those who wanted to integrate the squadrons within ground formations. The minister ordered a leading representative of the artillery lobby, General Félix Bernard, to conduct an enquiry into the future of military aviation, and in August Hirschauer resigned, the victim of a smear campaign accusing him of collusion with the aircraft manufacturers. The post of inspector was abolished and Bernard assumed command of the newly independent service as director of aviation.

The vulnerability of unarmoured spotters had been proved in action by the recent Balkan Wars, and Bernard's immediate priority was to produce a specification for an armoured spotting machine. Fortunately, his demands proved impossible to fulfil: contemporary engines were as yet insufficiently powerful, the few prototypes produced were all too heavy and difficult to manoeuvre, and a potentially disastrous re-equipping of the service on the very eve of war was only narrowly avoided.

Preoccupied by artillery spotting, the new director of aviation showed no interest in arming aircraft: 'The[ir] only function is to operate wherever telegraph wires make it difficult to raise a captive balloon,' he maintained. 'They do not therefore require weapons.' Meanwhile the experiments conducted by de Rose and Bellenger had reached an impasse. They had proved that firing forwards was the most accurate method, mounting the gun on the fuselage in front of the pilot, within easy reach for reloading; but the fast, highly manoeuvrable planes suitable for combat use all had a front-mounted engine, leaving the pilot in danger of shooting off his own propeller. Trials conducted by Bellenger in a Deperdussin with the observer firing over the propeller from behind a screen were inconclusive, while a prototype synchronizer gear developed by Raymond Saulnier was ignored by Bernard. De Rose and Roland Garros were working on a different plan

– to armour the edge of each propeller blade – but war intervened before it could produce results, and in August 1914 French aircraft took the field unarmed.

Twenty-five squadrons were mobilized on the outbreak of war (twenty-three serving with the five armies, plus two attached to the independent cavalry corps), employing a total of 132 aircraft from a dozen different manufacturers. Yet despite the best efforts of GQG, opportunities for senior officers to work with aircraft had been few and fleeting: the grand autumn manoeuvres lasted only a fortnight and involved just a third of the army each year, and war broke out before the 1914 exercises could take place. 'Too many senior officers lacked confidence in aviation,' argued journalist Henri Mirguet after the conflict. 'In their view, the birdmen were mere entertainers or acrobats, unlikely to achieve anything worthwhile.' This is perhaps a little unfair. In an army short of machine guns and heavy artillery, aircraft could be considered something of a luxury: they were fragile and expensive, hampered by unreliable engines and dependent on good weather. The relatively small number of machines also seemed unlikely to affect the outcome of the conflict, particularly when compared with the firepower of the infantry and artillery. Yet even the engineers, it seemed, shared something of Mirguet's view. 'In response to the growth of heavier-than-air, plans are now in place to train a number of pilots,' read a circular seeking volunteers. 'You appear to have just what is needed to succeed in *this attractive sport*' (author's italics). The most famous of the sceptics was General Ferdinand Foch, then commander of the École de Guerre. 'Aviation is a sport,' he famously declared after the 1910 manoeuvres. 'Militarily, it's no use whatsoever.'

On Sunday, 2 August 1914 General Bernard and his peers entered battle expecting a short, decisive conflict, with no significant role for the aviation service. Bernard immediately closed the military flying schools at Avord and Pau and returned the members of the Chalais-Meudon establishment to their regiments. As for Colonel Eugène Estienne, his experience and expertise were completely ignored: he was sent directly from 3rd Groupe Aéronautique to assume command of an artillery regiment.

Chapter 2

'A Full Apprenticeship' –
1914–15

'Ill-disciplined acrobats' – the war begins

When Germany declared war on France on 3 August, Lieutenant Pierre Perrin de Brichambaut (MF8) was stationed close to the border, at Nancy. The following day he received orders to make a reconnaissance around Château-Salins. Better still, he was given permission to go armed: 'Marvellous words. Thrilling. I really did jump . . . for joy. Into the fuselage, alongside my mechanic, went my good old .351-calibre hunting rifle, my automatic pistol and a box of (the rather ill-named) 'Bon' flechettes. We took off armed to the teeth, full of enthusiasm. Just think, our first real taste of action.'

Crossing the lines at 1,400 metres, 'a pretty incredible height . . . for the time', they soon ran into trouble. 'Sapristi, they're firing up at us, sir!' called the mechanic/observer as holes began appearing in the fabric of the wings. Perrin showed no hesitation: he promptly let off a few shots from his carbine, dropped his flechettes on to the Germans below and emptied his pistol at them. With that, the pair flew off, 'very pleased with [them]selves'.

Within hours sensational reports filled the newspapers: Roland Garros had rammed a German Zeppelin on the French side of the frontier, pilot and airship both lost! No, the pilot was Marcel Brindejonc des Moulinais! No, Brindejonc had blown up an enemy arsenal with a huge number of casualties! The reality was somewhat different: Brindejonc, a celebrated pre-war flyer and long-distance racer, was stuck in the barracks at Saint-Cyr. 'I've just devoured some "monkey" [i.e. ration meat],' he wrote to his friend, journalist Jacques Mortane. 'I'm sitting on my bed. We're sweeping up so I'm covered with dust from the crumbly cement floor and it's making me sneeze. I can't bear the thought of having to live like this for the next two years – no freedom at all and too tired each evening to venture one step beyond Saint-Cyr. There are sixteen of us sharing the room [and] my mechanic is available whenever I want him. It's much better than ordinary infantry quarters but some things are still pretty dire. Life's much harder in 3rd Company than 1st because the last lot ruined things for us by taking liberties. I'd like a few minutes to study or read. But no. All I can do is take snaps of barracks life [and] that's no fun at all. . . . I'd like to make myself useful now I've learned how to handle a gun and perform an about-turn. I'm a bit brassed off. Still, that's progress. Last month I was totally brassed off. Did you see that I've looped the loop four times as a passenger? It's capital!' Fortunately for Brindejonc, his posting came through quickly. By mid-August, 'overjoyed to be at war', he was serving with DO22, attached to Fourth Army in the Ardennes.

At the start of hostilities French planes outnumbered German. However, the limited experience gained on manoeuvres had done little to prepare the squadrons for the realities of war and they performed poorly in the first weeks of the conflict, hindered by inadequate planning, training and tactics. 'It's a pity . . . we couldn't have delayed the outbreak of war by six to twelve months,' commented one pilot on 7 August. 'Our role could have been that much greater. We might have planned the air war instead of making it up as we go along.' Roland Garros, soon to be posted to MS23, thought France had failed to make use of the experience of its civilian pilots. On 21 July, with international tensions mounting, he and several other stars of the pre-war aviation circuit had met with Jacques Mortane. 'If only they'd listened to us and consulted us in peacetime we'd be completely au fait with military aviation by now,' argued Garros. 'We could have been extremely useful. Instead we'll have to start from scratch.'

One vital area of operations was aerial reconnaissance. Despite the lessons of pre-war manoeuvres, peacetime opportunities to rehearse observation skills had been few, compelling aviators and army staffs alike to learn on active service. In consequence, aerial reconnaissance had little impact during the battle of the Frontiers. Staff officers struggled to coordinate the activities of their squadrons, leaving much to individual initiative, and lacked confidence in the often conflicting and fragmentary reports produced by pilots battling to identify the enemy below. 'The movements reported by our pilots do not allow us to conclude the enemy offensive has begun,' opined Joffre, at news of enemy soldiers marching through Belgium in unexpected strength and of large troop concentrations in the Ardennes.

In Alsace the six squadrons attached to First Army remained underused in difficult terrain, while in the Ardennes Third and Fourth Armies simply blundered into the advancing Germans and were badly mauled. Brindejonc des Moulinais (DO22), by now a corporal, could find no sign of the enemy on a reconnaissance flight on 17 August, and it was another five days before he finally spotted a battle line: '[It] seemed to run between Virton and Robelmont. Towards Rossignol we caught sight of a long column of cavalry coming out of a forest. The mist was hampering us a little but we could still make out all the twists and turns of the firing line.' Sadly, his sighting was too little, too late: the battle line belonged to 3rd Colonial Infantry Division, marching to near-annihilation. At Morhange in Lorraine Captain Paul Armengaud (HF1) managed to give warning of German intentions: 'I could see all the guns behind the revetments, the lines of trenches, the abatis in the woods, the hidden reserves; it had every appearance of a trap set for our army and the left of the neighbouring army.' However, GQG simply refused to believe him: Second Army duly advanced and was repulsed with heavy losses.

Sergeant Eugène Gilbert (MS23/MS49) focused on the army's failure to practise cooperation work. 'We made a big mistake by not thinking about aircraft working in tandem with the other arms,' he insisted in July. 'Our soldiers aren't familiar with us and mistakes over aircraft nationality are inevitable. We should have established an aviation element within each army corps and had them perform joint exercises.' Gilbert's fears were soon vindicated. Although French aircraft were clearly designated with their red, white and blue roundels, aeroplanes were such a novelty that most ground troops mistrusted any machine flying over their heads, whatever its markings. The long, hot retreat that succeeded the battle of the Frontiers brought a member of 119th Infantry close to Esternay: 'We were following a narrow road that zigzagged across a broad plain. Far ahead, the column was painfully strung out, and several stragglers were cutting across the fields to rejoin their units. Our section was in pretty good shape and had fallen in behind to scoop them up. Just then an aeroplane . . . passed some 200 to 300 metres over our heads. French or German? A roundel or a cross? Difficult to tell. But a couple of men ahead of us stopped and fired in the air like a hunting party shooting at pigeon or partridge. Nevertheless the plane carried on south and disappeared from view behind the nearest hill. A few hours later – when we were all back with the column – we passed a group of soldiers loading a plane, minus its wings, on to a big lorry. An adjutant stood alongside it, at the edge of the road. He had his arm in a sling and we regarded him with interest as we passed by. "Quite so!" he shouted, quite without rancour. "Take a good look, you set of ***! You almost did for me there. Try not to mistake me for a Boche next time."'

The same evening an order arrived expressly prohibiting 'firing on [our] aeroplanes' – to little avail. 'Our troops are still firing up at us whenever we fly over them,' complained Lieutenant Alfred Zapelli (D6) on 4 September. The following day he decided further action was needed. 'I've had my roundels repainted four times bigger,' he claimed. '[Now they're] 2 metres wide.'

French aircraft were performing little better as artillery spotters, a point rammed home to one group of resentful airmen by General Franchet d'Espèrey, the newly appointed commander of Fifth Army: '[The general said] our results have been fine from a strategic point of view, but tactically we're lagging a long way behind the Germans because they're so good at artillery spotting,' noted one pilot in his diary on 3 September. 'Then . . . [he] spouted some nonsense about the way the Germans adjust their fire (two aircraft crossing over the target). Most of us are only here to fly reconnaissance missions. It's not our fault if the rest of the squadrons aren't up to the mark. Blame the brass-hats. They don't believe [in aviation] so they don't give us enough support. And they're not willing to learn how to use us to best advantage.'

In the fortress city of Montmédy, a group of hard-pressed artillerymen would certainly have backed the general. Around 3.00 pm on 23 August one of their officers was heartened by the arrival of three French planes: 'A bit late, but an opportunity not to be missed. I went looking for one of the pilots. Sadly, their machines weren't powerful enough to carry an observer. So be it. But the [pilots] swore that if required they'd be back the following day in armoured two-seaters. On that note, off they sauntered.' Two days later, with no sign of the promised spotters, the officer turned in despair to the governor of Montmédy: 'I asked him to call Stenay. Could he get them to send a machine capable of carrying an observer and a pilot, emphasizing this last point in particular? About two hours later, much to our delight, a French biplane appeared. I hurried over to say hello. "Can you carry an observer?" [I asked]. "No," [came the reply], "the squadron only has single-seaters." What a let-down! I was sorry to have brought this poor pilot on a wild goose chase, but I'm starting to understand why we see so few French planes. There can't be that many to start with and they must all be occupied on long-range reconnaissance duties. We can't have enough left over to spot for the artillery like the Germans.'

Flying his Dorand DO.1 over Luxembourg, Corporal Brindejonc des Moulinais was feeling very jumpy: 'I was gripped by a crazy desire to get away, to make a rapid turn back towards the airfield. Honestly, anyone who's ever experienced the sensation that thousands of pairs of eyes are following you, thousands of rifles pointing at you, while bullets clatter past, sometimes hitting a wire or a rib, will understand what I'm talking about, and why I might have been feeling on edge. Then the artillery joined in.' Sergeant Lucien Finck (HF7) knew exactly what he planned to do if he came under fire: 'Several pilots had persuaded me that you can't be hit at 1,200 metres. The Moroccan campaign [1911–12] had proved it. Suitably reassured, I took off with every confidence. I climbed to 600 metres over Verdun and headed straight for my target. At 1,200 metres over Conflans, I realized my mentors might have been better advised first to acquaint themselves with our front. Rifle and machine-gun fire surrounded me on all sides. It all looked pretty chancy.'

Finck struggled up to 1,800 metres, where he found 'things pretty quiet apart from the odd shell'. But even then he didn't quite have the skies to himself, seconds later spotting 'a German that very politely drew aside to let us pass'. And he quickly discovered that altitude could pose its own problems. 'My engine cut out at 1,800 metres,' he reported on 10 August. 'I dived to 1,200 metres to stop my propeller jamming. My Gnôme [engine] started up again as soon as I pulled back on the throttle. Condensation in the carburettor had formed two blocks of ice in the air intakes.'

Sergeant Auguste Métairie was serving with the Camp Retranché de Paris (CRP), the Paris garrison, under the command of General Gallieni: 'Our machines afforded us no more than relative safety, very relative indeed. The lines changed completely from one day to the next, so we had no idea where the opposing sides were. You had to keep your eyes open all the time. We were operating at altitudes which seem risible today, starting our reconnaissance missions at 2,000 metres and ending somewhere between 1,100 and 1,500 metres. Luckily, the Germans were lousy shots.'

Métairie and his squadron were equipped with the Farman HF.20, whose 'pusher' configuration, with the engine behind the pilot, gave the crew a good field of vision over the countryside below. On 2 September, with the French in full retreat across the Marne, Gallieni ordered six reconnaissance sorties. One plane turned back with engine trouble, but four all spotted German columns moving south. The sixth and last sortie was flown by a 160hp Gnôme-powered Breguet AG.4, piloted by the aircraft's designer and manufacturer Corporal Louis Breguet, with balloon officer Lieutenant André Wateau as his observer. They left the airfield at Vélizy at 3.30 pm. 'Groups of cavalry and infantry moving . . . through the Automne valley,' they reported. 'Spotted fires in the forest of Compiègne . . . Saw nothing in the Ourcq valley.' It seemed to Wateau that the German armies were turning south-east, away from Paris.

From their base at Écouen REP15 and MF16, the two squadrons attached to General Maunoury's Sixth Army, were scouring the same area. At 8.00 am on 4 September Lieutenant Émile Prot (MF16) and his observer, Lieutenant Edmond Hugel, set off in fine weather in search of the German advance guard, expecting to find it moving south-west towards Paris. 'To my utter astonishment, the road [between Nanteuil-le-Haudouin and Gonesse] was completely empty,' noted Prot. 'First German troops [spotted] at Nanteuil. They had passed the village but were [further east] close to the Brégy–Meaux road. The advance guard was over towards Sennevières. Lots of movement on the Nanteuil–Crépy and Nanteuil–Lévignen roads. Troops resting. Parks of all kinds. Apparently some kind of logjam. Another column at Lévignen; the head of the column already entering Betz.'

Prot and Hugel had confirmed Wateau's findings. So too did further sorties flown the following day: von Kluck's First Army had definitely swung away from Paris. However, the staff of Sixth Army had little confidence in their squadrons. Arriving hotfoot from Alsace, aviation commander Captain Georges Bellenger had received a brusque welcome from the chief of staff, Colonel Guillemin: 'I can't be bothered wasting my time with pilots,' barked the colonel. 'They're nothing but ill-disciplined acrobats.' Unfortunately, some of the reports produced by Bellenger's crews had been confused and contradictory, and Major Duthilleul, the head of intelligence, refused to believe any of them.

'The enemy columns march by while VI Army washes its linen in rivers all over the region,' fumed Prot. 'I went to [HQ at] Le Raincy to make my report. Pointed out a flank guard, its exact position mapped from first to last.'

Duthilleul had dismissed it as nothing more than an outpost line.

'They're not outposts,' insisted the horrified pilot. 'They're whole columns.'

'My men are despondent,' reported Bellenger on 6 September. 'They're performing their duties half-heartedly and I no longer dare exceed my orders.' However, by quietly slipping the relevant reports to his CRP counterpart and a British liaison officer, the feisty Bellenger had made sure the crucial information reached General Gallieni. Sixth Army was ordered to attack the German flank and the mood was transformed: 'The faces of my aviators lit up at the news and this time they took off full of vim.'

Auguste Métairie (CRP) soon had a narrow escape: 'My mission was to fly as far as Lizy-sur-Ourcq and reconnoitre the battlefield. It was all so strange and confusing that – I admit – I began to dawdle. . . . Everything was on fire. Eventually I stumbled across the heart of the battle. It affected me badly [and] I stopped checking my watch. Suddenly the engine started missing, then nothing. It was dead. Out of fuel. Damn it! Was I going to end up in the hands of the Boches? Ahead I could make out Meaux [and] to my right the Eiffel Tower. I had to descend. Between 1,800 and 1,600 metres I was very apprehensive. I couldn't even summon up any sympathy for the burning villages. All I could think about was myself.' Then Métairie spotted a Maurice Farman spiralling down. Was the pilot crazy? Or could it be a captured machine? Métairie followed the plane down and quickly realized the troops below were French: 'What a sight for sore eyes! Everything's fine! I can see some red monoplanes: they're REPs, they're French. I won't be taken prisoner [after all].' He landed, begged a little petrol and eventually flew home as calmly as possible.

On 8 September, near Triaucourt-en-Argonne at the eastern end of the battle line, information provided by two French spotters – one piloted by Lieutenant René Roeckel of HF7, accompanied by Lieutenant Mingal of 46th Artillery, and the other by Sergeant Joseph Chatelain – brought Third Army a significant success which finally persuaded GQG that aviation might have a role to play. 'I helped our artillery destroy half the German batteries opposite,' wrote Roeckel. 'I carefully reconnoitred the enemy guns in the morning before directing our fire upon them. Then I had the pleasure of watching from the air as the shells from our 75s fell among the German batteries. We destroyed two caissons in under a minute. People can talk of nothing else.' Two days later Roeckel was back in action, this time directing artillery fire on to enemy columns around Vaux-Marie, with heavy casualties again the result.

'Good sight and a robust constitution' – recruiting aircrew

In August 1914 qualified civilian pilots rushed to volunteer for the aviation service, temporarily overwhelming the Paris recruitment office, and Jacques Mortane was roped in to help sort the wheat from the chaff. The 31-year-old Mortane, real name Jacques Romanet, then volunteered for aviation himself, but his first posting came as something of a shock: 'Life in the Dijon depot is certainly not without incident. They've started me off as a stevedore. I go to the station to unload drums of petrol and caustic soda (350 kilos!) from the trains. It's hard going without specialist training in les Halles. The NCOs don't understand that I wasn't born a market porter. I speak to them like a civilian and they threaten me with a court martial. A fine start! . . . I'm serving my apprenticeship with recruits from the class of '14. I feel young again. I'm learning how to salute, perform an about-turn – why? – and march. I've never taken so much exercise in my life.'

Although Mortane was accepted for the service, the celebrated pre-war pilot Maxime Lenoir (C18/N23) was not. Lenoir was famous for his aerobatic displays, a specialist in looping-the-loop, and was recalled to the army on mobilization fully expecting to be directed into aviation. But no: 'When I mentioned my pilot's licence to the recruiting officer, I might as well have been talking about my school certificate. "Oh," he said. "It's you, the pilot. Aviators are lunatics. You'll have to change, lad! Can't be doing with mavericks in wartime. You can join the cavalry [instead]!" As a former cavalryman [with 7th Hussars] I was offered a superb mare. So I got a ride of sorts, if by no means the one I wanted. And the poor beast awarded the supreme honour of transporting me soon fell victim to one of those random accidents so common in wartime: she was shot out from under me.'

The volunteers included a number of well-qualified female pilots, none of whom were allowed to join up, despite the enthusiastic campaign led by Marthe Richer, a pre-war pilot and general secretary of the newly formed Union Patriotique des Aviatrices. 'We can perform any task demanded of us – despatches, liaison, patrolling the skies over towns and cities, transport or testing,' she told the press in 1915. 'We're volunteering our services, to France or to her allies. We're not asking to be sent to the front because as women we couldn't undertake active duty. But we do think we could play a support role in the rear and so release a number of military pilots for more useful employment.' Jeanne Pallier was another willing volunteer. 'Tall, strong, loose-limbed, regular features, forceful and frank in her speech, [she] . . . has held a pilot's licence since 1912 and taken part in several flying competitions in France and abroad,' wrote journalist Andrée Viollis. 'She made herself available to the aviation service as soon as war was declared, but while the Russian, Serbian and Italian armies have contrived to create a special role for their female aviators . . . the French authorities have shown no inclination to welcome our own.'

No amount of favourable press coverage could produce a change of heart: Pallier became an ambulance driver, while Richer turned to espionage. And yet . . . Marie Marvingt, who had gained her pilot's licence in 1910, was rumoured to have flown her own ambulance aircraft, taken part in bombing raids, and served in the trenches with a battalion of chasseurs à pied. Although it seems unlikely that an unqualified female pilot could turn up and join a raid, the citation to her *Légion d'honneur*, awarded in 1935, is unequivocal: 'Authorized by M. Millerand, Minister of

War, Mlle Marvingt took part in two bombing raids on Frescaty aerodrome.'

France had gone to war with 487 qualified military pilots, but many more were needed – with no immediate source of supply, following General Bernard's decision to close the flying schools. By October GQG was scouring the armies for suitable candidates: 'To ensure recruitment into this category of personnel, I ask you to identify those among the officers, NCOs and men under your command eager to become a member of aircrew and capable of making a useful contribution without delay. Only those candidates with previous pilot training, good vision and a robust constitution should be put forward.' With the war of movement rapidly giving way to trench warfare, volunteers were sought particularly among the under-used cavalry, including reluctant horseman Maxime Lenoir, who soon obtained his transfer to aviation and gained his military wings in December 1914. During 1915 more men transferred from the cavalry than from any other arm, but from then on first the infantry and then the artillery took the lead.

Some commanding officers proved extremely reluctant to lose their best men. 'They selected candidates among those with any kind of technical background, or men and officers whose wounds rendered them unfit for active service,' complained Jacques Mortane. 'It took a while to make certain [COs] understand the importance of producing pilots for France. Some chose applicants with no aptitude whatsoever, while others jealously guarded soldiers who were perfectly suitable. How many of our [future] aces had to apply up to eight or ten times [for a transfer]?' The spy scares rife on the outbreak of war also left their mark. 'It has been reported that, in our haste to recruit on mobilization, a certain number of dubious individuals may have infiltrated our aviation personnel,' warned a circular dated 26 October 1914. 'In a service as sensitive as [this], it is vital that only men of proven reliability or at least of known background are employed as NCOs or other ranks so we can keep a close watch on others as required.' A model form was attached, to be completed for each volunteer, including a column headed 'Secret Information Supplied by the Police'.

Regulations laid down the minimum standards for admission: candidates for flying personnel were supposed to be in perfect health – with a maximum clothed weight of 85 kilos for pilots and 75 kilos for observers, bombardiers and gunners – and physically fit, although slightly less rigorous standards applied for balloon crews. Dr Guilbert, MO at the Le Crotoy flying school, felt 'that trainees recruited among the sick and the wounded should be checked . . . even more strictly than the rest'. But not everyone shared his view. Raymond Berthelot (VB119) qualified for night bombers in 1918 after heart problems had forced him out of the artillery, while cavalryman Jean Renoir transferred to aviation in 1916 after developing gas gangrene in a leg wound suffered while serving with the Chasseurs Alpins in the Vosges. Initially passed fit for the observer role, he was eventually posted to a bomber squadron, where he continued to press for pilot training. 'Would be happy in a fighter,' stated his application. 'With his leg wound would find flying a light aircraft less tiring. Would prefer to start training at Buc or Juvigny [sic] or close to Paris because would like to see his invalid father [the artist Pierre Renoir] occasionally.' Renoir was accepted at his second attempt, but struggled to gain his wings. While probably not much of a pilot, he enjoyed his time with C64 until an injury sustained in a bad landing in November 1917 forced him back to the cavalry. After the war he became a celebrated film director, and his masterpiece *La Grande Illusion* is based at least in part on his own experiences.

Strict application of the admission criteria would also have excluded a number of fine aviators. Lieutenant Paul Tarascon (N3/N31/SPA62), for example, had been fitted with a prosthetic foot after a pre-war accident, but finished the war with twelve victories to his name. Sous-lieutenant Marc Bonnier (VB102) needed glasses, Lieutenant Roland Garros (MS23/SPA26) was so short-sighted he wore spectacles beneath his goggles, and Captain François Coli (N/SPA62) flew on despite losing an eye after crash-landing into a hangar in March 1918. Coli refused all medical assistance until he had dictated the following order: 'The CO apart, no member of the squadron is to enter his plane into a hangar by any means other than the doors expressly designed for the purpose.'

In late 1915 Parisian doctors Jean Camus and Henri Nepper tried to create a more scientific basis for aircrew selection by developing a way of testing the potential airman's reactions to a range of visual, auditory and tactile stimuli, including a revolver fired immediately behind the head! Hooked up to a machine that measured breathing and heart rate, suitable candidates would display 'little or no change in their respiration, no trembling – either before or after [the shot] – no constriction or dilation of the blood vessels'. Those unsuited to the work would, unsurprisingly, 'tremble slightly before the shot and uncontrollably thereafter, with the blood vessels typically narrowing'. Yet in April 1917 Charles Biddrich (N73) found himself in 'a dark little place with barred windows adorned with numerous cobwebs, on each side of the main room a rough bench, and in the corner a huge old-fashioned barrel stove. The examination was not severe, none of that business of shooting pistols off unexpectedly that we used to hear was part of an aviator's preliminary examination.' William Wellman (N87) was given 'heart tests, after I had hopped about the floor a few times; eye tests by reading a few letters across the room; balancing on one foot with my eyes closed to prove that I had a fair sense of equilibrium; and a few other balancing tests, during which I was whirled around on a piano stool with eyes closed and then requested to walk a straight line, with them open. Weight and measurements followed, and it was all over.'

By February 1918 the regime at the basic training school at Dijon-Longvic had undoubtedly become lax: 'A recent inspection . . . showed that a substantial number of trainee pilots transferring from the front have received an inadequate medical check-up regarding eyes and heart,' noted a report to the ministry. One of those trainees was André Duvau (BR29), who, like Jean Renoir, had reapplied using contacts within the army after he was rejected by his original medical board. He was sent for a further examination to Dijon, where the doctor passed him fit without even looking at him. 'He literally shoved me out of the door,' recalled Duvau. 'True, it was aperitif time and he seemed desperate to swap the camp for the café.'

Many of those who volunteered for the aviation service were lured by the undoubted glamour and excitement of flight. 'I was in my late teens in the years before the 14–18 war,' recalled André Luguet (C18), later one of France's leading film actors, 'the time of the first long-distance flights. I got to know several pilots who had a licence already and naturally it sparked my interest. I knew men like [Hubert] Latham, [René] Labouchère [and] Louis Chatelin, who all became close friends of mine. Latham and Labouchère were pilots for Antoinette . . . I spent a lot of time on the airfields, [including] Mourmelon, where I watched the Wright brothers making their early flights. Since I had aviators to take me on to the airfield at Villacoublay, I witnessed the first trials conducted by the so-called "flying men" before they were renamed aviators.'

Young Robert Sarkis (SPA84) was also bitten by the bug: 'I used to spend my holidays in a delightful little spot called Ris-Orangis [where] I made friends with . . . the son of an aviation pioneer called Delagrange. We would take our bikes from Ris-Orangis to Juvisy and spend the whole day there watching an aeroplane rolling along the ground, sometimes hovering a couple of metres above it, for a distance of about 500 metres. What a show! We went every day and that's when I swore I was going to be a pilot.' On his call-up in 1917, Sarkis was directed first into the artillery, but he lost no time in transferring to aviation. Gabriel Pallier (SPA15) also requested a transfer from the artillery, aged just 20, in 1917: 'I fancied myself a knight of the air,' he later recalled, 'a swashbuckler like Fanfan la Tulipe.' But others had more personal reasons for joining. Paul Waddington (SPA154), a Frenchman of Irish extraction, volunteered after his brother James was killed while serving with VC116. 'Asks to replace his brother shot down and killed in aerial combat,' noted his CO on his application. Waddington was accepted for pilot training without delay.

In 1915 René de Lavaissière de Lavergne was serving with 17th Artillery in Champagne, physically unharmed but psychologically fragile: 'I'm sick of the rage I feel at everything separating me from my loved ones. I've had enough of it and I'm hoping to bring them closer by getting a transfer to a mobile unit (armoured cars, self-propelled artillery). Their billets are further to the rear, so it would be easier to meet up with my wife. . . . I'm getting more and more depressed, and I'm starting to hate all the members of my family who preach patience and resignation. They say I should ask for a medical that might lead to a spell in the rear, but I'm too proud to put myself through that charade, and it might have unintended consequences.'

De Lavergne failed to obtain his transfer to armoured cars, but reapplied for aviation and in June 1916 became an observer with C11: 'Personal initiative and self-motivation now became the crucial factors in a life-or-death struggle. If you ran a risk or took a knock, you could immediately do something to defend yourself. Blind resignation was replaced by individual action with a clear outcome. . . . I found it exhilarating [and] despite the danger it restored my morale. By adding a sporting dimension to warfare it transformed my state of mind and gave me a life completely at odds with my experience in the artillery.'

A journalist in civilian life, Jean Daçay was serving as an artificer sergeant with 65th Infantry when he decided to volunteer in 1914: 'It looked like I'd be spending [my] war on manoeuvres, behind a screen of younger combatants, on defence works, on a treadmill without glory and without danger. At least the air service would provide an element of unpredictability and combat.

'"Méry," [I said]. "Can you get me in to see the CO?"

'General uproar. "You must be mad."

'[But] I persisted and, as night fell and the roads grew dark, the pair of us headed for the villa in the woods that housed the officers' mess.

'"Volunteer for aviation, Sir."

'"Eh! Who?"

'"The artificer sergeant."

"'I've known him for twenty years," chipped in the adjutant, an old school friend and my erstwhile rival in English classes. "He's a journalist, so you'd think he'd know down from up. But it really is a stupid idea.'"

Despite his enthusiasm, Daçay does not appear to have realized his dream of front-line service. He eventually returned to his previous career, writing for Jacques Mortane's *La Guerre aérienne illustrée* and other contemporary publications.

Foreign volunteers entered aviation via the Foreign Legion. They were initially scattered throughout the service, but in April 1916 the Americans among them were brought together in a dedicated squadron, N124, later better known as the Escadrille Lafayette. Kiffin Rockwell (N124) and his brother Paul had both joined up on the outbreak of war, and others followed their example. 'Now, I do not want you to worry about me,' Kiffin told his mother. 'If I die, you will know that I died as every man should – in fighting for the right. I do not consider that I am fighting for France alone, but for the cause of humanity, the most noble of all causes.'

James McConnell (N124) had started out as a volunteer ambulance driver: 'All along I had been convinced that the United States ought to aid in the struggle against Germany. With that conviction it was plainly up to me to do more than drive an ambulance.' McConnell 'made up [his] mind to go into aviation' precisely because he was unwilling to be labelled a shirker, but as the war ground on, aviation was increasingly characterized as something of a refuge. 'War isn't an entertainment, nor is it a business,' commented Jacques Mortane in 1917. 'I'm sorry to say that some of our pilots teeter over enemy lines like Blondin crossing the Niagara Falls on a tightrope. Recent hard knocks [the Chemin des Dames offensive] have certainly affected them, but . . . they still have time to recover some of their old "pluck". There's still plenty for them to do. . . . [But] we must choose carefully. For some, aviation is less an arm of service than a means to an end. They joined half-heartedly, expecting the war would be over before they reached the front. . . . We should no longer tolerate anyone who fails to carry out his orders in line with the most stringent definition of duty.'

Alfred Rougevin-Baville, latterly CO of SPA99, also reckoned that the quality of applicant had declined over the course of the conflict: 'To start with . . . they were chaps who wanted to fly. But by 1918 we had opened a lot of flying schools offering a refuge to a number of fellows who didn't want to risk their neck in the trenches. They were types who lacked go, who crawled from school to school until the day they were finally packed off to the front. After a full eighteen months' training I was considered an experienced pilot and one day I found myself commanding a squadron composed mainly of chaps unwilling to follow me into action. The patrol leader waggled his wings. The message was clear: "Close up on me, we're going to attack." Instead, they climbed to gain height or "take a balcony seat" as we used to say. It was utterly stupid. The Germans were well trained and already flying "stepped up", so they invariably picked off any stragglers. I took some losses and looked on with sorrow as my lily-livered good-for-nothings got themselves killed. The spirit was different at the beginning; they were chaps who were eager for the fight.'

Over the war as a whole, the majority of aircrew were in their early twenties. 'Young men,' said Marcel Jeanjean (MF/AR/SAL33), 'just lads for the most part.' In 1914 the typical officer – most squadrons had four or five – was in his late twenties or early thirties, with around four years' service, while the CO, a lieutenant, tended to be slightly older, in his mid-thirties. The NCOs were a mixture of long-service personnel in their late twenties and conscripts from the current classes (1911–13). Many had transferred to aviation within a month of their call-up, while others had entered direct. But such was the level of casualties that by late 1918 officers and men were typically much younger: by then, nearly all aircrew were conscripts from the wartime classes of 1914 to 1918 – so aged between 18 and 20 on call-up – while the CO was just a couple of years older than his men.

One of the youngest of all was Corentin Carré. Fifteen-year-old Carré had adopted the identity of an older refugee in 1914, volunteered, and found himself in 410th Infantry. Mature beyond his years, he was quickly promoted to adjudant, but nevertheless decided to transfer to aviation: 'I'm leaving the infantry not because of the troubles and hardships we endure in this arm of service, but because responsibility for the fifty men under my command has weighed rather too heavily on my young shoulders. Farewell, my stout-hearted poilus. I'll try to show aviation what a lad from our regiment can do.' After training at Étampes and Avord, Carré joined SOP229, an army cooperation squadron attached to Second Army, on 17 December 1917. He was shot down and killed just three months later.

Of course, applying for the aviation service was just the beginning. Every volunteer needed training before he could take up front-line duties, and the war effort demanded a constant supply of aircrew in unprecedented and ever-increasing numbers. In 1914 the most urgent priority was to reopen the flying schools: their ill-timed closure in August had cost General Bernard his job, leaving Édouard Hirschauer, now restored to favour as director of aviation, to face the challenge of building a system virtually from scratch. The two pre-war schools at Pau and Avord were reopened within weeks; the three manufacturer's schools – Farman at Étampes, Caudron at Le Crotoy and Blériot at Buc – were pressed into service in February 1915 and later militarized, and over the next seven months five more new military schools were created. In September 1915 the system assumed its final form, rationalized and streamlined by the newly appointed inspector of schools, former senator Major Adolphe Girod. All candidates for aircrew underwent basic military training at the Dijon depot before proceeding for their initial pilot training to one of nine schools: the five older establishments plus the more recent creations at Chartres, Ambérieu, Juvisy and Tours (the last two replaced by Istres and Biscarrosse after their transfer to Belgian and American control respectively in January 1917).

Pilots who gained their wings then moved on to advanced training specific to the types they would be flying at the front: artillery spotters to Châteauroux; observers and gunners to Cazaux; bomber pilots to Avord, which also housed a night-flying school; and fighter pilots first to Pau to develop their aerobatic and combat skills, then to Cazaux (or later Biscarrosse) for extra gunnery training. Only then was a qualified member of aircrew sent to the pool – the Groupe des Divisions d'Entraînement (GDE), situated in and around Plessis-Belleville, north of Paris – to await his posting to a front-line squadron. By 1918 the whole process normally took six months.

The flying schools were situated far from the front, often in sparsely populated areas. Le Crotoy, for example, lay at the mouth of the Somme estuary: 'At the end of the sandy road, the beach seems vast and grey. Planes fly back and forth, motors whine . . . pot-bellied Bessonneaux hangars crouch sleepily in the dunes. It's the school. Out there, on the horizon, something which might be the sea . . . it's retreated so far you wonder if it will ever return.' Even after Girod's reforms, the facilities could be somewhat rudimentary. Marcel Jeanjean was certainly unimpressed by his first experience of Avord: 'Everywhere a complete shambles. Ghastly huts. Rotten mattresses laid on the ground. The CO shouting "What do you expect me to do with this lot?" at the latest batch of trainees.'

The huge demand for front-line aircrew also made it hard to ensure a supply of good instructors. The Istres school trained pilots on Caudrons, using single- and dual-control machines. '[It] operated like a factory, churning out a whole series of pilots,' recalled one instructor. 'We didn't have enough instructors, especially in the early days, when to our sorrow three of our comrades were killed.' All instructors had front-line experience, but some were posted as much for respite from the front as for any perceived training ability: 'During his time with the squadron, from 3 August to 1 October 1916, X was unable to perform effectively as a pilot, lacking either the self-confidence or the physical qualities required,' a CO wrote of one of his subordinates. 'He has been transferred to the schools as an instructor. I hope he will be able to make himself useful there and do his best to dispel the unfortunate impression he made with the squadron.'

Training consisted of a mixture of theoretical lectures and practical work. Passed fit despite his heart problems, Raymond Berthelot arrived at Ambérieu on 29 June 1917, making his first flight, on dual control, some two months later. During that time he was kept busy attending lectures on a variety of subjects: 'cross-country flying, navigation, brakes and landing, mechanics, intelligence-gathering, aerodynamics, the Voisin aircraft, stability, accidents, engines, carburettor, lubrication, magnetos, flight safety, faults, the airfield, topography, compass work and meteorology'.

The theory lectures at Le Crotoy took place in a hangar, with the trainees gathered around a flimsy instructional airframe: 'an instructor stands in front of a plane prepared by the mechanics and picks apart [their] dream: a bit of steel, wood, canvas etc. – nothing terribly solid. . . . "Calm down, my friend[s]," he says. "These things weren't built to fly."' Meanwhile practical training began on the 'penguins', Blériot monoplanes fitted with small 20hp engines and with wings cut down to keep them on the ground. 'They are rather difficult to handle and are designed to teach the men to steer straight,' reckoned Charles Biddrich (N73). 'At first you go sideways and twist around in each direction except the one in which you wish to go. After you catch on to them, however, you go tripping along over the ground at some 35 or 40 miles an hour.'

From the penguins, the trainee transferred to the 'rouleurs'. More Blériots, airworthy this time, but the novice still had to stay on the ground and concentrate on steering a straight course. Next came the 'décolleur' class, where the student was allowed to reach the height of a metre or so before cutting the engine and returning to the ground. With every successful attempt, the flights increased slowly in height and distance, all under the watchful eye of an instructor.

Pupils were then encouraged to progress at their own speed in a series of machines with ever larger and more powerful engines: 'Since Saturday,' reported Charles Biddle (SPA73), 'I have passed through four classes so you can see that we are moving right along.' Marcel Travet (C212) described these classes as follows: 'The 50s class, the first step to the stars. Then the 80s, cross-country flying and the pilot's licence'. At Le Crotoy the 80s class became known as the 'clown flight' due to the 'unintentional acrobatics of the trainees on the day of their first solo flight'. Marcel Jeanjean described that momentous occasion: 'The trainee, rather pale, heeds his instructor's final words of advice. "Listen! This is a racehorse you've got in your hands now, not a 'penguin'. Don't push too hard on the joystick or the plane will dive straight into the ground. And don't pull back too hard either or you'll start to climb steeply and suffer a fatal loss of air speed . . . Make sure you never cross-control or you'll end up in a spin. And take real care when you're banking. Feel very gently for the controls or you'll go into a barrel roll.'

'That's it! I've flown!' reported Philippe Connen, a pupil at Étampes. 'Not that I particularly enjoyed the experience. I stepped on to the fuselage of my MF.12 at 8.25 am, with a north-easterly blowing at 5 or 6m/s. The pilot was Lepeintre. "Mind you strap yourself in," he shouted. But I didn't know how, so I was most unhappy. "Watch your helmet!" he called, when it was taking me all my time to stop the propeller wash snatching it off my head. We bumped along. I felt the shock in my stomach and knees every time we hit the ground. But I still managed to spot another aircraft in flight – probably de Marcieu – a flock of crows and a farmer in his field. Our route took us round a little wood east of the hangars. Half an hour later, Lepeintre took me up in a 50hp MF.1. This time I took the controls. But I'm not as happy as I expected. I need more practice.'

Future ace Georges Guynemer (MS/N/SPA3) completed the rouleur phase at Pau on 1 February 1915, making his first flight six weeks later. 'He was very nervous,' recalled his instructor, Paul Tarascon. 'But he loved it. All he could talk about was flying. He'd been bitten by the bug.'

The final stage consisted of a 'serpentine' and a 'spiral'. 'Both were methods of losing height without gaining distance, i.e. to land on a spot under you,' explained Charles Biddle (SPA73). The final test consisted of two flights to a given location and back, staying aloft for a specified time, and then two triangular routes, each 225 kilometres long. Raymond Berthelot (VB119) received his wings at Ambérieu after 12 weeks of training, 39 hours flying time (10 hours solo) and 139 landings.

But bad weather could soon bring everything to a halt. 'The weather [at Étampes] has been pretty lousy for the past couple of days,' complained trainee pilot 'Eugène'. 'Miserable days like these seem to drag on for ever. Time passes more quickly when it's fine. The airfield's lively; the planes are out of their hangars, all the trainees are milling about, you're coming and going, the hours seem to slip by more quickly. Nothing new to report, except for a new captain in charge of the school. He's been here for three days already and I've still not had a close-up view. They say he's not as good as his predecessor, but I've seen such a procession of them. . . . I've just put some lime tea into boiling water. It's the only half-decent moment of the day. In half an hour I'll be in bed.'

Pupils unable to master the Blériot solo went off to train on dual-control Caudrons or Farmans at Le Crotoy, Avord, Châteauroux or Istres, the schools specializing in turning out pilots for the two-seater squadrons. Marcel Travet described the experience of one such trainee at the Caudron school at Le Crotoy in 1916: 'Helmets in hand, all the chaps in his class wait on the beach for their turn. . . . The instructor lands: "Your go, new boy. Don't touch anything, whatever you do." In front of him are the dual controls linked by a steel rod to those of the "chief". He'll be careful not to go anywhere near those. A mechanic gives the propeller a turn, the wind whips into his face, the ground zooms past, then suddenly it's slipping further and further away. He's airborne. A few sharp turns. Unashamed, he holds on tight. Everything is all jumbled up. As the plane banks he can first see the sky, then the beach, then the sea again. The engine cuts out. Suddenly it stops. The plane dives, the cables whistle, the sand draws closer and closer. It looks like they'll hit it face first. The "ace" feels distinctly insecure. What's next? Nothing. A sure hand has straightened up the kite and now it's rolling along once more. That's it. Rather pale, the new initiate climbs down. It's grand to be back on terra firma. Bit by bit, these initial sensations evaporate. A few more flights and he can navigate the controls. He takes over in the air. If "it" banks, a sharp punch in the back recalls him to duty. The chief lets him try his hand at taking off and landing. Then one day he says, "That's fine. Tomorrow you start on the 50s." The trainee couldn't be happier ...'

Maréchal des Logis Louis de Diesbach (N15) found the move from basic training to more advanced types rather a challenge: 'I'd earned my licence at Chartres on an old Farman, so at first I was flummoxed, like the rest of my comrades. Flying a fighter is nothing like piloting a machine as slow and stable as a Farman. . . . [However,] I soon managed to progress to other much faster planes, like the Morane or Nieuport. At that time we used to lubricate the rotary engines with vegetable oil, castor oil especially, which had a very particular aroma. I loved that smell and I loved being in that atmosphere, with planes all around me, and some fine comrades as well.'

Simple aerobatic manoeuvres – loops, spins and rolls – were taught at Pau. Initial instruction again took place on the ground; but when the time came to put theory into practice, the pilot was on his own. 'In the hangar stood "The Cowkiller", a plane stripped of its fabric, upon which [Sergeant Alfred] Fronval made us rehearse the manoeuvres we had to perform,' recalled one trainee. 'Lieutenant Simon [the school's CO] used to stand on the landing strip and track the progress of the pilots through his monocle. They normally passed over at 1,500 feet. He kept his eyes trained on the sky. "I knew it, I knew it!" he'd shout. "He's going to crash." And without fail some poor sod smashed into the ground . . . You have to remember the Pau school suffered plenty of fatal accidents. A guard of honour was permanently mustered for burial duty.'

André Steuer (N103) was surely aware of this reputation when he arrived at Pau in 1916: 'This is a pretty momentous day as I'm about to embark on aerobatics. I'm not remotely afraid but it seems a good idea to prepare myself to die. I'm not indestructible. If the worst comes to the worst, you may be sure I went with a clear conscience.' Although Steuer survived his training, he didn't enjoy his time at Pau: 'They've put me in a [Caudron] R.4, which I don't like at all. Abandoning my Nieuport Bébé is a real wrench after all we've achieved together. I feel like a rich man turned pauper or an artist turned painter and decorator.'

The Pau school also tackled other aspects of fighter operations. 'In the combat school,' said James McConnell (N124), '[the pilot] learns battle tactics, how to fight singly and in fleet formation, and how to extract himself from a too dangerous position. Trips are made in squadron formation and sham battles are effected with other escadrilles.' Charles Biddle (SPA73) trained there in 1917: 'One thing that bothers me a little,' he complained, 'is that the machine-gun instruction and practice has been much reduced. The reason for this seems to be in order to save time in turning out pilots, but to my mind it is very poor economy. . . . Many of the men here know nothing about shooting and think that all you have to do is to shoot straight at what you want to hit, which is of course the surest way to miss it. There is a machine-gun school near Bordeaux [Biscarrosse] where the men used to go. A friend of mine . . . got there by putting in a special request on the grounds that he didn't know one end of the gun from the other.'

As a famous pre-war flyer, Jules Védrines (DO22/MS3/N3) felt no need for further training. 'It's pointless sending [me] on a course at the Air Gunnery School,' he responded tersely. '[I'm] familiar enough with machine guns [already].' His reward? – fifteen days for insubordination. But Louis de Diesbach (N15) took a very different view of the place. 'Obviously, shooting from a plane is very tricky and you need lots of practice,' he wrote in 1916. 'It was all rather specialized. First they released small balloons in front of us and got us to fire carbines at them. Next they put us in a dinghy with an outboard motor and made us fire at small balloons floating on the water. Then we picked up speed and, of course, we missed. It's very tough. Finally, we had to use a machine gun to familiarize us with taking actual and relative speed into account. They'd even built a big target from white stones at the far end of the lake for us to shoot at from the plane. We used a type of gunsight called a collimator, invented by Engineer [Lieutenant de Vaisseau] Le Prieur. But it's not easy when you're on your own and you have to think about flying [the plane], watching your speed, and keeping an eye on the collimator, all the while peering over your shoulder to make sure no one is creeping up behind you. You often miss.'

'Finally,' concluded James McConnell (N124), 'the pilot is considered well enough trained to be sent to the reserve, where he awaits his call to the front. At the reserve he flies to keep his hand in, practises on any new make of machine that happens to come out or that he may be put on in place of the Nieuport, and receives information regarding old and new makes of enemy airplanes.' The 'reserve' was the pool of qualified pilots at Plessis-Belleville. In 1916 the CO had his HQ in the chateau of the fabulously wealthy Radziwill family at nearby Ermenonville, while Carroll Winslow (MF44/N112) had to make do with a billet in the village: 'There are four separate camps, one for each branch of aviation, and there are over one hundred machines in each camp. We were practically our own masters, and could make flights whenever we wished. The idea is that the pilots here have an opportunity of perfecting themselves and that, if they do not fly, why, then it is their loss.' Adjudant Jean Carayon (SAL16) found it 'extraordinary, '[a] colourful shambles . . . accidents on a daily basis, a crazy carnival of a place, spahis mingling with colonial troops, everyone poking fun at a uniform with a sweater that almost came up to your ears, but a very pleasant atmosphere'. Future film director William Wellman (N87) was less impressed: 'It was in reality a good deal of a dump.'

After three weeks at Plessis-Belleville Winslow was classed as 'available' for posting to a squadron and received orders not to stray too far from the airfield: 'I must say that I experienced a curious sensation, waiting around in this way, not knowing where I would be in a week. You never know to what sector of the front you are going until your orders are handed to you. Three days after my name had been posted on the bulletin-board an order came detaching five pilots to the "Armée de l'Orient" at Salonika. My name was sixth on the list, so I missed by one being among them. That evening, however, my turn came. This time the direction was Toul.' After two days' leave in Paris, Winslow found himself serving with MF44.

Raymond Berthelot took longer than most to reach his squadron. Having gained his wings, he left Ambérieu on 21 September 1917. A month's advanced training on the Caudron at Avord was followed by a month at Istres, then a return to Avord for night-flying training. In January 1918 he moved to the bombing school at Le Crotoy and finally reached his squadron, VB119, in June 1918 after almost a year in training.

Potential observers followed a different route. A training school was established at Plessis-Belleville, but qualified artillery observers were deemed in little need of further training. They were quickly posted to a squadron and could be operational very soon thereafter: in 1915, for example, René de Lavaissière de Lavergne took to the air just three days after he was posted to C11. 'Most of the observers were staff officers,' commented Auguste Heiligenstein (MF5/MF44/C106/229), 'graduates of the Polytechnique or engineers from the [École] Centrale [university-level institutions specializing in technical subjects].' But not so Heiligenstein: 'Those of us who'd come up through the ranks were at the foot of the table . . . seldom admitted to the endless late-night games of bridge or poker. We weren't exactly cold-shouldered but we never felt we were [quite] on the same side.'

Some observers, Heiligenstein included, eventually became pilots. In 1915 Captain de Saint-Quentin, aviation commander of Second Army, reported that his observers were growing increasingly concerned at the quality of pilot turned out by the schools: 'If this situation is allowed to persist I fear the best observers will ask either to train as pilots themselves or to return to their batteries.' But many observers were content to stay in the passenger seat. 'Although I'm familiar with flying a plane,' claimed Georges de Ram (MF8) in 1917, 'I've always refused to train as a pilot on the grounds that it's more useful for a specialist photographer not to abandon his trade. I think the day will come when I'll be able to act as both pilot and photographer. It would be grand if the dangers of my missions no longer had to be shared with my friends.' Captain Walser of 4 Squadron, Royal Flying Corps saw this continuity as a real source of strength. 'The Observers are all Officers and carry out practically all the work,' he commented after attending a training course for French observers in December 1916. 'A large majority are artillery officers. Observers can seldom transfer to Pilot and thus many Observers have a great deal of experience. These Officers on the whole appear to be very keen on their work and are continually discussing possible improvements on their system. They appear inferior to ours in: i) Original training – this is very scanty and an Observer has to pick up wireless, machine gunnery and knowledge of observation, as best he can; ii) Discipline – very lax compared with the RFC; iii) Flying in bad weather. On the other hand, owing to the fact that their Observers are permanent, they take a greater interest in their work, and study the theory of battle tactics, topography, photography, etc., more than ours do.'

Most bomb-aimers were also ex-artillery officers. The aimer had to take a number of variables into account when manipulating the bomb sight – course, altitude, speed and wind direction, as well as the weight of the bomb – and mathematical knowledge was considered essential. Observers and bomb-aimers alike were sometimes forced to act as gunners to defend their aircraft, but the service also had room for specialists in this field. 'An aristocracy . . . always has its haves and have-nots,' grumbled one of their number. 'We machine-gunners are the untouchables, the lowest of the low among the warriors of the skies.'

Operational training in front-line conditions took place in the squadron until 1918, when the Centre d'Instruction pour l'Aviation de Combat et de Bombardement (CIACB) was established at La Perthe to 'give pilots, gunners, gunner-bombers and observers, according to speciality, all the theoretical and practical training they require to fly operational missions as soon as they reach their squadron'. Aircrew progressed from the GDE to the CIACB and thence direct to their squadrons, and the first CIACB-trained aircrew were arriving on the front line by the autumn of 1918. The CIACB was also used to train squadron leaders, to retrain personnel who had spent time away from the front, and as a conversion unit. On 2 August 1918, for example, the pilots of VB114 arrived to train on the new Farman F.50 prior to their conversion to F114. An associated night-fighting school, the Centre d'Instruction pour l'Aviation de Chasse de Nuit, was opened at nearby Pars-lès-Romilly in November 1918, but by the time the armistice was declared it was still not fully operational.

In addition to aircrew, each squadron also included a number of mechanics. Men with any kind of engineering or electrical background were supposed to be directed on call-up into one of the 'technical' arms of service, such as aviation. Or that at least was the theory. In August 1914, according to Georges Bellenger, one recruiting office in the Seine département, home to several aircraft manufacturers, was directing all self-professed 'aircraft riggers' into the cavalry, whence it was impossible to obtain their transfer to aviation. Potential mechanics were examined on their general level of education, their specialist knowledge of soldering, welding and the internal combustion engine (theory and practice) and their overall reliability. Having completed their basic training at one of three aviation depots – Saint-Cyr, Dijon or Lyon-Bron – successful candidates then progressed to more specialist training on topics such as engines or rigging, often at a manufacturer's facility.

'English or Italian squadrons are awash with mechanics, clerks, etc.,' complained *La Guerre aérienne illustrée*, 'but French units operate with an absolute minimum of effectives, each specializing in a different, but extensive, list of duties. The days are seldom long enough for them all to complete their tasks. From . . . the quartermaster sergeant to the sergeant mechanic, from the storekeeper to the armourer, all work like Trojans so the pilots, observers and gunners can take off as soon as they get the call from the sector or group commander. Meanwhile the mess corporal might limp slightly from the shrapnel he received in the artillery; the armourer proudly shows off the palm he won as a bomber; and the old territorial who passes the plates in the mess speaks movingly of his three years in the trenches.'

For Lieutenant Jean Pastré (BR7), flyers fell into three categories – would-be, active and retired. 'Before the war would-be pilots were recruited among civilians; afterwards they'll come from the military. It's easy to assume their only ambition is to fly upside down over the reconquered territory. But no . . . the real attractions are the tailors' adverts and the prints in *Vie parisienne*. They want a belted mac, boots with complicated laces, a tender-hearted pen pal [*marraine*] with indecipherable handwriting. They join up in search of this imaginary paradise [and] find themselves closer to the real thing. Never mind: they're doing it for France.

'Active flyers come in two categories: observers and pilots. These two sets of fly-boys refer to each other as "parcels" and "taxi drivers" respectively. They're both wrong: they're all idiots. Nose in the air and hand outstretched, they live in hopes of a welcome shower from on high. When at last they feel the long-anticipated droplet, they affect a kind of weary sadness completely at odds with their inner satisfaction. The observer of the species (*Observatorius aviator*) is a particularly strange bird. He talks in logarithms, walks around festooned with a mass of complicated communications equipment, and will talk to the artillery staff only via the telephone or a bizarre assemblage of kit known as a TSF [*télégraphie sans fil*/wireless] – exact meaning: *toujours s'en foutre* [always buggering it up]. And still he can't make himself heard. All he thinks about is becoming a pilot. Never mind: we'll get 'em!

'Meanwhile retired flyers exist in seventh heaven – the one with no turbulence and no clouds. Seventh heaven consists of a nice office, a secretary and a pair of slippers – Honour on one, Country on the other.

These demi-gods have firm opinions about aviation and share the motto of the official government suppliers: "Keep on Flying". But they're quite happy to leave the actual work to others. It's thanks to their enthusiasm and their inestimable advice that we can shout it from the rooftops: French aircraft are the undisputed masters of the skies!'

'Indispensable' – the fight for acceptance

Aircraft had demonstrated their worth at the battle of the Marne in both artillery spotting and reconnaissance roles: Roeckel's success at Triaucourt and Vaux-Marie confirmed all the hopes of the pre-war artillery lobby, while the identification of von Kluck's change of direction provided information crucial to the decision to engage the enemy. 'The staff gained an overview of the situation by combining the fragments of intelligence produced by aerial reconnaissance and cavalry patrols,' commented Joffre. 'But aircraft, and especially those of Sixth Army and the Camp Retranché de Paris, undoubtedly took the lead on this occasion.'

Joffre made no immediate move to build on these achievements, but everything changed on 25 September 1914 when he appointed Major Édouard Barès, the aviation commander of Fourth Army, to the new post of aviation commander at GQG. Originally an infantryman, Barès had gained his military wings in 1911 and, as an official observer during the Balkan Wars, was the only French aviator to have seen aircraft in action. He had concluded that squadrons would need to specialize and, like fighter pioneer Charles de Rose, he was convinced that they could play an attacking role. 'Aviation is a weapon, and clearly an offensive weapon, whether in air-to-air combat or by bombing enemy troops, camps and fortifications,' he advised Joffre in November 1914. 'It can operate independently at long or short range, or attack in liaison with other troops. [Types with a long operational range] are also capable of destroying or blocking enemy railway lines some 200 to 250 kilometres behind the front. . . . To reap maximum reward from future generations of aircraft, we must plan ahead, broaden our horizons and extend our ambitions.'

On 10 November 1914 Joffre issued a note heavily influenced by the ideas of his new aviation commander: 'The aviation service is not simply a reconnaissance tool as originally supposed,' he wrote. 'It has become, if not indispensable, then at least extremely useful in directing artillery fire. It has shown itself capable of conducting long-range missions, working in liaison with other troops, or acting as an offensive arm by dropping powerful projectiles. And its task is also to seek out and destroy enemy aircraft. . . . The organization of aviation within [each] army must henceforth accord with these new roles. Squadrons must specialize, at least to some degree.'

Barès was also convinced of the need for independence, with command of all aviation resources concentrated in the hands of GQG to allocate according to the demands of the strategic and tactical situation. But here he failed to carry the day: ground commanders refused to part with their squadrons, Joffre was unwilling to press the point, and GQG received direct control only of the specialist bomber force created in November 1914. Consequently, army and army corps squadrons remained an organic part of their parent formation, committing the greater part of the aviation service to liaison with ground forces and limiting the role of GQG to the resupply of men and materiel.

Barès envisaged a force markedly different from that devised in pre-war expectations of a short conflict. By the end of January 1915 the number of squadrons was planned to grow from 25 to 65, composed of 16 army squadrons, 30 army corps squadrons, 16 bomber squadrons and 3 cavalry squadrons, and requiring 390 aircraft, including 96 bombers (more than any other belligerent at the time). Army squadrons and army corps squadrons were to act essentially as cooperation squadrons, operating in liaison with the ground troops: army squadrons would focus on long-range reconnaissance, contact patrols, air-to-air combat, tactical bombing and photographic missions, while army corps squadrons concentrated on short-range reconnaissance, artillery spotting and contact patrols.

During the artillery preparation phase of an offensive, army corps squadrons were to deploy observation aircraft scouring enemy lines to identify targets invisible to the balloons, whose maximum operational height limited their view to just 6 or 7 kilometres, while spotters in wireless contact with the batteries corrected and controlled the fire of the guns. During the assault itself the planes would overfly the leading troops on contact patrols, using wireless telegraphy to update HQ on enemy dispositions and the progress of the attack. Wireless contact, however, was not two-way. Aircrew were equipped with Morse transmitters, but ground troops were confined to more traditional methods of signalling: a wave, portable battery-powered lamps, strips of cloth laid on the ground or Ruggieri smoke pots.

Fighters were to protect army corps aircraft operating over the front, pursue enemy aircraft reconnoitring and spotting over French lines, and conduct long-range reconnaissance missions where their speed could be used to advantage. Meanwhile bombers would strike at key locations (railway stations, villages, bivouacs) during the preparation phase of an offensive and target key enemy strongpoints during the attack.

Over the winter of 1914/15 Barès worked hard to replace many of the obsolete aircraft types then in service. The Blériot 11 – slow, heavy, and offering the observer virtually no downward vision – was quickly withdrawn, and other types soon followed it on to the scrapheap: the Breguet AG.4, the Henri Farman HF.20, the 80hp Gnôme-powered Voisin L, the Dorand DO.1, the Deperdussin TT and the REP N. Although each had performed well enough in manoeuvres, all had struggled in action. The Blériot, Deperdussin and REP – monoplanes that were manoeuvred by changing ('warping') the angle of the wing – proved particularly unsuitable for reconnaissance duties. The pilot needed to maintain a firm grip on the control column at all times and as a result was left unable to handle a map.

Barès was aiming to standardize on a smaller number of types: three biplanes – the Maurice Farman 7 for reconnaissance, the Voisin 3 for long-range reconnaissance/bombing, and the Caudron G.3 for reconnaissance/artillery spotting – plus one speedy monoplane, the Morane Saulnier L 'Parasol', for reconnaissance and potential combat use. The Farman and the Voisin were pushers offering a good field of forward and downward vision – a distinct advantage – but pilots and observers remained very wary of the rear-mounted engine. Many airmen chose to undo their seat belts when faced with a crash, preferring to risk ejection rather than stay put and be crushed. In a series of accidents the Farman also revealed an alarming propensity to catch fire, hence its macabre nickname 'The Crematorium Oven'. Meanwhile the rotary engines powering the Caudron and Morane made these planes extremely awkward for the novice. Indeed, some pilots claimed the 'MS' of the Morane trademark actually stood for '*Morte Subite*' ('sudden death').

By the spring of 1915 the aviation service comprised 51 squadrons and 4,350 men, including 500 pilots and 240 observers, enabling Barès to increase the size of each squadron from six aircraft to ten over the summer. Each army was allocated two squadrons, one equipped with the Caudron and the other with the MS L Parasol; each army corps was given one squadron (sometimes two in tactically significant sectors) plus a balloon company to cover its 4- or 5-kilometre section of the front; and each heavy artillery regiment received a balloon company. On the recommendation of Barès, the French also began to implement a new expansion plan, aiming to more than double the size of the service to 119 squadrons by the following year.

'It's one reconnaissance flight after another, no let-up,' grumbled

Brindejonc des Moulinais (DO22/N23), once so enthusiastic for the fray. 'I'm throwing myself into it to try and keep my spirits up. I'm more than happy to do my duty. I don't have much to report [although] I did have one fright on 22 November while I was spotting for the artillery with Sous-lieutenant de Dampierre. There aren't many batteries prepared to hurl vast numbers of shells at us, but a couple of them [decided] to take us on. We couldn't scarper because we didn't want to funk it, so I stunted around a bit to confuse our attackers. We completed our mission and came home safe and sound, but with several holes in the fabric.'

Despite the initial reconnaissance failures, the first weeks of the war had also produced some promising developments. The most important reconnaissance task of any army corps squadron was reporting on the enemy's defensive arrangements: identifying trenches, wire entanglements, machine-gun nests, artillery batteries, pillboxes, and any shelters capable of concealing reserves before a counter-attack. 'Reconnaissance flights undertaken by officers equipped with a camera have produced very good results,' reported First Army's aviation commander on the opening day of the conflict. 'It could well be worthwhile to extend their use throughout aerial reconnaissance . . . They constitute a very effective method of investigation which allows us to produce immediate, exhaustive and incontrovertible intelligence.' Joffre approved the idea and advised the minister to authorize the purchase of cameras. Georges Bellenger, too, was enthusiastic, but Barès was harder to convince: 'If you want to take photographs from a plane, I don't see any harm in it,' he told Bellenger. 'But that's no reason for the government to buy you a camera. There are some excellent Kodaks in the shops for [just] 100 sous.'

Techniques and procedures – as so often in the early days of aviation – had to be devised from scratch: 'No one had yet worked out how to make the best use of aerial intelligence, at least as regards infantry dispositions,' claimed Paul-Louis Weiller (MF22/MF40/C21/BR224). In late November 1914 Bellenger clashed with General Berthelot, recently appointed commander of 5th Group of Reserve Divisions in the Soissons sector. Faced with a series of aerial photographs of the German trenches, Berthelot refused to believe them. 'Until now, Sir,' fumed Bellenger, 'I thought cameras captured exactly what's in front of them. You have just taught me they record things that don't exist. My compliments, I'm most grateful to you.' He then stormed out of the room, leaving the red-faced Berthelot banging the table in rage. However, the general went on to re-examine the photos and established procedures for their interpretation which were quickly adopted throughout the army. In December 1914, on Joffre's orders, each army HQ received its own aerial photography section, with mobile developing lorries and specialist photographic interpreters to handle the exposed film, and over the next four years improved aircraft, cameras and interpretation techniques allowed photo-reconnaissance crews to fly further, higher and more safely, capturing a wider swathe of countryside with no loss of detail and providing greater foreknowledge of enemy plans and dispositions. Meanwhile the number of photographs soared – from 48,000 photos in 1914/15 to 293,000 in 1916, 474,000 in 1917 and 675,000 in 1918 – but Berthelot cold-shouldered the insubordinate Bellenger from that day on. Within months he had been transferred out of aviation, spending the rest of the war in the artillery and a variety of staff posts. 'It's always wrong to be in the right when dealing with the staff,' sympathized General Charles Christienne, later the first director of the Service Historique de l'Armée de l'Air.

The information contained in the photographs was transferred to the staff and artillery maps so essential in preparing attacks, discerning enemy build-ups and planning the barrages that preceded and accompanied each set-piece offensive. Aerial photography was also used to revise the maps themselves: the pre-war maps issued by the Service Géographique de l'Armée (SGA) had soon been revealed as obsolete, and Paul-Louis Weiller realized cameras offered an easy and effective way of updating them. 'I noticed the staff map was inaccurate,' he recalled, 'and proved it by using my Kodak Vest Pocket camera to take photographs of [the site of] woods and individual trees that no longer existed.' The results convinced the SGA that action was necessary, and from Weiller's simple Kodak grew a huge but vitally important operation: 'From early 1915 our reconnaissance aircraft were entrusted with the huge task of creating the photographs needed to produce maps of the front and smaller-scale trench maps. Once complete, the trench maps gave an accurate picture of the terrain and identified every target. The aviator and the gunner could at last jointly agree their objectives, something previously impossible. Commanders could see the whole of the enemy defences and evaluate their strengths and weaknesses. In short, they could get a clear picture of everything lying before them.'

The photo-reconnaissance crews, both pilot and observer, faced an enormous challenge. To stop vibrations spoiling the image, the pilot had first to stall his engine and then restart it – a task requiring great skill and no little sang-froid. Meanwhile the observer had to lean out over the side of the aircraft, buffeted by the slipstream, holding the camera with its long, heavy lens – 26cm, 50cm and eventually (for balloons) 120cm in focal length. Fixing the camera to the side of the fuselage helped a little. So too did the replacement of glass plates by roll film in February 1915: each mission could now take 300 pictures instead of 12, vital in those sectors of the front line, Artois and Champagne, scheduled for offensives that spring.

In Artois control of the fortress-village of Carency was rapidly wrested from the Germans, but the attack soon bogged down. 'Is there any point recounting my aerial adventures in Artois?' mused Major Guy de Lavergne (C6). '[All] I can say is that every day Billard and I flew our new twin-engine Caudron over La Brayelle aerodrome, near Douai, and dropped our six 40mm shells. "Our squadrons have bombed the enemy airfield at La Brayelle," boasted the communiqués. "Our squadrons!" . . . One plane . . . and as for bombing, six shells, not all of which exploded.' Beset by anti-aircraft fire, de Lavergne found a novel way of fighting back: 'the anti-aircraft battery at Lens fired hundreds of rounds at us en route and we were flying through cotton-wool explosions fore and aft. I kept myself busy with the wireless set, automatically retransmitting "Sh*t to the Kaiser" to annoy the German operators. The moment we crossed the front line we said goodbye to the guns. I dropped my shells and enjoyed watching them explode near the hangars.'

After the spring offensives had ended in failure, a huge effort was made to prepare for a simultaneous assault in the same sectors in September. In Champagne the army group commander, General de Castelnau, sought all practicable means of gathering information. Between 15 March and 24 August twelve separate missions were flown behind German lines to deposit agents, often customs officers displaced by the invasion, to collect intelligence or commit acts of sabotage, particularly against railway lines. The task was a dangerous one and one senior officer did little to sugar the pill. 'I need a volunteer,' he told one group of customs men. 'Frightful job. One-way trip. Anyone game?'

The pilot par excellence for these special missions was Jules Védrines (DO22/MS3/N3). 'Sheer determination was all that was needed,' he recalled after the war. 'The crucial factor was to quell the desire to turn tail and run. As in all my risky missions, thoughts of my children helped me to take off cheerfully [enough]. They comforted me. I thought admiringly of the poor bugger next to me . . . now he really did have nerves of steel. Comparing our respective lots stopped me dwelling too much on the dangers ahead. Our plan wasn't a bad one. I would fly over the lines at normal height and head straight for the drop, while simultaneously trying to confuse any enemy observers. If I spotted any kind of nearby activity, I'd ensure I landed behind a copse, giving my plane a better chance to remain unnoticed and my passenger to take cover quickly. I made damn sure I was clear to depart, did my best to check my "parcel" was OK, then opened the throttle to the maximum and returned to my previous height, leaving no sign of my point of take-off.'

On 23 September 1915 a group of a dozen planes took part in a coordinated operation to land agents. 'Special mission,' noted Georges Guynemer (MS/N/SPA3) in his logbook. '3.00 am. 3,000 metres.' That morning all twelve pilots returned home safely, but just six weeks earlier Eugène Mô (MS12) had met a very different fate: 'He was captured by the Germans during an intelligence mission in the occupied zone near Attigny in the Ardennes, imprisoned at Rethel and eventually shot at Amagne-Lucquy on 6 August 1915. Spurning a blindfold, he [reputedly] spat in the face of the commander of the firing squad and shouted "Vive la France" before he fell.' The agents were routinely left to make their own way home, usually via Belgium and the Netherlands, but after the arrest of Edith Cavell on 15 August 1915 the Germans managed to roll up many of the intelligence networks operating in occupied France and Belgium and 'special missions' were put on hold. For Guynemer at least, the end could not come soon enough: 'I swore I'd never do it again. . . . [Flying] special missions really is a filthy job.'

The Artois/Champagne offensive in September 1915 marked the first organized attempt to deploy all the spotting and photo-reconnaissance experience accumulated over the preceding twelve months. During August 1915 alone 121 photographs were taken of the Champagne front and 1,704 reproductions distributed to the infantry and field and heavy artillery, and over the following month the numbers increased again: 'A few days prior to the attack,' reported Fourth Army's photographic section, 'each infantry unit received sufficient good photographs of their respective sectors (first and second positions) to supply every captain (in front-line and support units). Photographs of their respective sectors were also provided to the artillery, balloon [and air] squadrons. Between 1 September and 24 September 5,232 prints were distributed: 3,015 to the infantry and 2,217 to the artillery.'

Once identified, enemy emplacements had to be destroyed. By mid-1915 all spotter aircraft were equipped with Morse transmitters, to such good effect that the Germans were forced to start camouflaging their batteries. However, certain French artillery commanders remained harder to convince. 'Some artillerymen were pig-headed about using planes,' observed Alfred Zapelli (D6), 'but they were powerless without our help.' Both pilot and observer needed steady nerves for this vital work, which required them to maintain an exposed position within both wireless range of the French battery and visual range of the target. In 1915, over Tilloy near Arras, Lieutenant Perrin de Brichambaut (MF8) turned his Maurice Farman into the strong westerly wind blowing at 2,500 metres and throttled back his engine, leaving himself almost stationary in the air. From this vantage point Perrin and his observer were able to spot for their batteries. Surrounded by 'huge bursts from 105mm shrapnel shells, streaked white and greenish yellow, by pink wisps from the 77s, by the grey and black blotches emitted by the other shells, [the observer] never flinched, taking notes and working the telegraph as calmly as if he was in his office,' marvelled the ebullient Perrin. But even he found this particular bit of airspace fast becoming untenable. A 105mm shell suddenly exploded right in front of his aircraft: 'a jolt, then a sudden violent pain in my stomach had me doubled over the controls, struggling for breath. My mind went blank, my strength deserted me and my reactions slowed. A terrible plunge [awaited us] and a speedy, sure, inevitable death. It was an awfully difficult moment. My observer tapped me on the shoulder. "What's up?" he asked anxiously. That was all it took to bring me to my senses and snap me back into action. I was at 2,500 metres with a comrade to save. I pulled myself together. "Nothing," [I replied]. "I'm fine."'

Although Perrin's aircraft was in a bad way – a longeron split, a wing strut severed, rigging wires broken, bomb rack shattered, three control cables snapped and 180 holes in the fabric – he managed to land without further incident. Nevertheless, he admitted, 'once I'd climbed down from the plane that day I couldn't hang on to my much-abused breakfast any longer.'

Maxime Lenoir was posted direct from the Caudron school at Le Crotoy to C18, where his pre-war aerobatic skills at first seemed unnecessary: 'We were put down for artillery spotting as soon as we got there. It was no joke, I can tell you. No joke at all. We had to spend hours on end in the cold and snow, spotting [enemy] batteries and reporting the fall of shells to our own. No other form of entertainment, apart from watching the "coal boxes" trying to shoot us down. The odd bombing raid gave us a bit of a break. That was more interesting and enjoyable. And sometimes we saw a bit of aerial combat as well.' But on 5 June 1915 Lenoir at last got a chance to deploy his talents in the skies west of Verdun: 'Lieutenant Rivier and I had set off on reconnaissance [and] I was busy checking my height over the sector when all of a sudden I spotted shell-bursts in the distance. I raced over and soon found a magnificent Boche taking photographs. We were joined by Captain [Louis] Quillien [MS/N37] – a real hero, now dead. A few short metres from the enemy, my observer opened fire. [The Boche] certainly didn't lack courage. Far from running away, he made a half-turn and opened up with his machine gun . . . I manoeuvred in reply, turning repeatedly like a hunter circling his prey. And so did he. If our lives hadn't been at stake, it would all have been rather droll. With Captain Quillien working alongside us, the stubborn Boche eventually dived, plummeted, completed one magnificent loop and smashed into the ground behind our lines.' The unfortunate German, an Aviatik C, became the first of Lenoir's eleven victories.

André Quennehen (MF5) – famous pre-war flyer, fencer and rugbyman – was also determined not to be cowed by German ground fire. '[I was] flying low over the Boches at 1,100 metres amid a hail of bullets,' he reported after a reconnaissance mission on 8 September 1915. 'When that didn't work, they chucked at least two hundred 35mm revolver cannon rounds at me. The shells all passed overhead, with a few narrow misses. The Germans thought they could bully me. I went back a second time to show them French planes never flinch. They tried to get to me again, with greater success. Then I bade them farewell by cutting my engine and pulling off a few stunts over their heads.'

Yet despite its dangers, the essential work of the spotter went largely unappreciated. 'The public hears nothing about artillery spotters,' complained *La Guerre aérienne illustrée*. 'The stars of this speciality never receive a mention in despatches. . . . Although they run the full gamut of risks, spotter aces are routinely neglected. Weather conditions, guns, machine guns, rifles, planes and shells German and French all conspire to bring them down. The spotters climb into the slowest planes, those least able to defend themselves. Their task requires unfailing courage, utter indifference to death and a particular talent for flying – whatever the conditions, whatever the altitude. When the spotters can't fly, the troops on the ground are paralysed. In the present conflict, with its emphasis on long-range shelling, a battery without aviation support is blind. Planes identify targets, scour the ground, identify the enemy guns and report their findings. Then the shelling begins and the plane again assumes control, correcting and adjusting fire.'

'That's the way to tackle German aviators' – the first aerial combats

For Sergeant Joseph Frantz (V24), the airmen of both sides shared a certain esprit de corps in the early days of the conflict: 'At the start, we aviators were a little more, shall we say, chivalrous than the other arms of service . . . we raised a hand in greeting when we met another plane, even an enemy one.' Lucien Finck (HF7) encountered one such German flying a Taube over Thionville. '[The plane] was 100 metres ahead and a little below me,' he recalled. 'The pilot's muffler was flapping in the wind. He turned round, spotted me and gave a hearty wave. Then the [Boches] were too polite to go armed, now they're too well-armed to be polite. I'd have had trouble doing him much harm, though. My only weapons were an old-fashioned standard-issue revolver and a box of wind-resistant matches.' But this gentleman's war was short-lived and pilots and observers like the young Jean Navarre (MF8/MS12/N67) were soon taking potshots at their opponents: 'the enemy came towards me, banked, flew parallel to me and waved his hand in greeting. He was on his own, too. By way of response I fired my three rounds . . . He dived quickly, without waiting to find out what came next. . . . I flew home, pleased as punch.'

French planes had gone into the conflict unarmed, leaving aircrew to provide their own weapons well into 1915. Many men chose a pistol and carbine, but some had rather different ideas. Émile Reymond (BL9), a doctor and pre-war chair of the senate aviation committee, had learned to fly as a hobby and volunteered for aviation rather than the Medical Corps. 'My mechanic/observer turned up just before take-off, armed with a Lebel [rifle] and a bayonet,' he noted in his diary. 'I'd the devil's own job getting him kitted out with a shorter, more portable carbine.' Flying as an observer on a reconnaissance mission over the Meurthe valley on 5 September 1914, Reymond soon got a chance to use his guns. 'We spotted our first Aviatik to our left,' he recorded in his diary. 'It was coming towards us and climbing. I fired from my right shoulder, aiming straight for the pilot. The plane dived and lost height. . . . [the pilot, Lieutenant Albéric] de L[amberterie] pulled at my sleeve. On our right, another German plane was approaching fast, much closer to us [and] almost at the same height. I lifted [the gun] to my left shoulder, targeting the centre of the propeller. I missed. Abandoning the carbine, I withdrew my revolver and took careful aim. The pilot's position in the Aviatik meant he could only shoot through the propeller, so I let him close in. At around 80 metres I squeezed off all six rounds, one after the other. The plane dived away, banking sharply.'

Pilots soon tried to grab hold of a machine gun, among them Jules Védrines (DO22/MS/N3). His pre-war reputation had won him a special role intercepting airships rather than flying routine reconnaissance missions, but his self-confidence and independent spirit often put him at odds with his superiors, particularly his squadron CO, Captain Paul Leclerc. On 2 September, flying the ungainly, heavily armoured Blériot 36bis two-seater he had nicknamed '*La Vache*' ('The Cow'), Védrines engaged a Taube over Suippes. Observer/mechanic Corporal René Vicaire used his Hotchkiss machine gun to fire three 25-round strips at the German, eventually bringing him down, smoking and leaking oil, on the French side of the lines. The ground troops opened fire, but the pilot and observer escaped, rejoining their own lines after a 48-hour manhunt.

Védrines claimed the victory but it went unconfirmed. Vicaire pinned the blame on the CO: 'At a time when aircraft didn't carry insignia, painting a nickname in big letters on the fuselage was bound to rile a stuffed shirt like Captain Leclerc. Standing up to the captain made Private Védrines unpopular with his superiors and they had him transferred to 2nd Reserves in Tours.'

Joseph Frantz had also managed to acquire a machine gun – a Hotchkiss. He asked the squadron mechanics to mount it on a tripod and used it to gain the first confirmed air-to-air combat victory. About 9.30 am on 5 October 1914, flying a Voisin 3, Frantz and his observer Louis Quenault brought down a German Aviatik at Jonchery-sur-Vesle. If he came across an enemy aircraft, Frantz planned to follow de Rose's advice: 'The only answer was to come up behind the target and get close enough in to give yourself a moving target. We managed to do just that, with some luck [on our side] because I reckon our plane was perhaps 10km/h slower than the Aviatik we attacked that day. He was returning from the French lines when I spotted him. We were flying at a height of around 2,000 metres – in fact, I reckon exactly 2,000 metres – when he appeared 200 to 300 metres below us. We'd been dropping bombs on the enemy and hadn't noticed him earlier. . . . I flew closer and realized none of our planes had that kind of fuselage. I dived and reached a terrific speed, certainly around 125km/h by the time Quenault fired the first round, and managed to get right on [the German's] tail and cut off his retreat. Of course, he saw us and tried to get away. He fired three or four shots from his machine gun, banking left and right. He tried to regain his lines but I stayed on his tail all the time, following him as closely as possible. After forty-seven rounds [sic] I said to Quenault, "[The gun's] jammed again. Try to clear it." Then I had to shout because you couldn't hear a thing above the noise of the engine. Just then the Aviatik shot up in front of me and Quenault tapped me on the shoulder.

'"Look out," he said. "He's turning inside."

'"Oh no [he's not]," I replied, and dodged him with a sharp right turn . . . he flipped on his back and fell to the ground behind our lines, trailing a great plume of smoke.'

The struggle had quickly attracted attention on the ground – military and civilian. The stretcher-bearers of III Corps were looking on anxiously 'as the two machines fought in the air, like two birds of prey locked together. The German seemed the faster and tried to escape using sudden changes of height or sharp turns. But the Frenchman was more nimble. He manoeuvred himself into the best position to take a shot and emerged the victor.' Sous-lieutenant Marcel Jobit also had his eyes glued to the scene: 'A turn appeared to give [the Aviatik] the upper hand, but shortly afterwards it dived a little too recklessly, flames appeared [and] it plunged to the ground. I jumped on a bicycle to reach the crash site, deep in the trees, immediately to the south of a pond that had undoubtedly lured the aviators.'

Frantz and Quenault followed the German down, landing in a nearby field of stubble, but the enemy crew – pilot Sergeant Wilhelm Schlichting and observer Oberleutnant Fritz von Zangen (FA18) – were both dead. A number of sightseers had also appeared: 'My mechanic and I drew closer,' recalled Frantz. 'A crowd had already gathered. One woman handed me a bouquet [and] another brought a pheasant. It was all very upsetting because we didn't normally see bodies in the aviation service.' Then Jobit spotted more onlookers arriving by air: 'About 11.00 am two Farmans and another biplane passed overhead, drawn by news of their comrade's deeds. No doubt about it, that's the way to tackle German aviators.'

While Frantz had sought out his opponent's blind spot by attacking from the rear, René David (HF13) preferred a frontal approach. 'I attacked an Albatros with my Henri Farman and a Lebel rifle,' he reported after an encounter on Christmas Day 1914. 'My gunner was Lieutenant M. The Boche accepted combat straight away. He throttled back and fired his machine gun. We replied with six rounds. He banked and made off. To close with the Germans in our old "crates", you had to fly towards, and some 50 metres below, them. Once in position, you turned so you were travelling in the same direction and fired. With its front-mounted engine, the German plane was completely blind.'

Another star of the pre-war aviation circuit was Sergeant Adolphe Pégoud (MF25/MS37/MS49) – the first man to loop-the-loop, and the first to descend by parachute from a plane. Like Védrines, Pégoud perhaps enjoyed a wider choice of mission than his comrades, and his reputation had certainly brought him a better plane. While the rest of his squadron had to put up with a sluggish Maurice Farman 7 or 11, Pégoud had a fast Morane-Saulnier, which he put through its paces one clear February morning in 1915: '9.35 am. Took off in the Morane [from Sainte-Ménehould] with [my observer/gunner] Lerendu for a two-hour flight reconnoitring German aircraft and escorting our own. At 2,000 metres over the Grand-Pré sector, a Taube appeared, heading towards me. Turned the machine gun on him from approximately 50 metres below. He made a half-turn; [I] followed at a distance of around 100 metres, still firing. A minute later the Taube – quite clearly hit – side-slipped to the left and plummeted down, its nose enveloped in smoke and flames, wing canvas shredded. It disappeared from view south of Grand-Pré. Almost immediately, I spotted two Aviatiks, one overflying the area south-east of Grand-Pré, the other north-east of Montfaucon. Turned my machine gun on the closer of the two, the one near Grand-Pré. At the first rounds the Aviatik dived full throttle; [I] charged down after him, firing the whole time. Aviatik quite clearly hit by machine-gun fire. I watched him dive until he disappeared from view, [then] levelled out at 1,500 metres, climbed again and set off in pursuit of the second Aviatik, now directly over Montfaucon. Turned the machine gun on him from about 40 metres below. The Aviatik fought on for some fifty seconds, returning fire with an automatic rifle. The Aviatik realized he'd been hit, turned and dived. I swooped down after him, firing all the time. Spotted the Aviatik's tail and wings quite definitely hit by machine-gun fire. Watched him disappear into the void, [then] levelled off at 1,400 metres, enemy shells all round, small and large calibre. 1.45 pm landed at Sainte-Ménehould.'

At a time when downing any enemy aircraft was still unusual, destroying three in one day was an extraordinary feat, and Pégoud was the hero of the hour. Returning his aircraft to the hangar, he collided with another plane, putting both machines out of action, but the authorities ignored the mishap. 'Congratulations from everyone at HQ, from the commander and his staff,' he wrote the following day. 'General Julien, the commander of the engineers, came to say well done and invite me to dinner this evening. Then came the commander of the lines of communication and several officers who asked me to dine with them the day after tomorrow. Made my report: compliments right along the line. Dressed for dinner with [the] general. Arrived 7.00 pm at the Hotel Saint-Nicolas, where he dines with all his staff. Around forty at table. Introduced to them all. Most delightful meal, no ceremony, no fuss, very chummy. Congratulations all round. Everyone wanted more details. All withdrew at 8.30 pm. Most agreeable. Came home and went to bed.'

While Barès had swiftly managed to secure official recognition for the role of the fighter, producing an appropriate machine was a different matter. Aircraft were still unarmed, and many senior officers – front and rear – continued to dismiss the whole idea of specialist fighters as impractical nonsense. An army commander could block any local initiative taken by his aviation commander, and GQG was preoccupied with bombers. However, de Rose and Garros were undaunted. Resuming their pre-war research in November 1914, they decided to test a lightweight Morane-Saulnier G single-seater, selected for its speed, manoeuvrability and rate of climb, fitting a light Hotchkiss machine gun to the fuselage just in front of the pilot and fixing a steel deflector plate to each of the propeller blades. Their experiments proved the system viable: 90 per cent of the bullets cleared the propeller, and the Hotchkiss was easy for the pilot to handle one-handed. The gun only fired 25-round strips, but this was no problem as their preferred tactic was to close in and fire from point-blank range. All the pilot had to do was point his aircraft at the target and shoot.

The heavy deflector plates had one obvious disadvantage: they reduced airspeed by some 10km/h, yet Garros was confident that his modified plane could still outstrip the enemy Aviatiks and Albatri. The plates were fitted to a number of machines on an experimental basis, and Garros took to the skies over Flanders, scoring his first victory on 1 April over Westkapelle: 'I'd taken off alone to drop 95 kilos of shells on a German station. Arriving over the target, 10 kilometres from our lines, I saw a plane in the middle distance, around 500 metres above me. Our batteries were firing at it. I reached the correct height, made my approach and came under attack from the batteries. I opened fire from 30 metres: the Teuton replied with his rifle and I reloaded my machine gun three times. After several rounds the enemy fled in disarray, descending at full speed. I stayed right on his tail. The combat lasted ten minutes and finished at a height of 1,000 metres. Riddled with bullets, the Albatros burst into flames and spiralled down. It was [a] tragic [end], appalling.'

Garros downed two more opponents in subsequent flights. Then on 18 April disaster struck during a bombing run over Courtrai, when engine trouble forced him down behind enemy lines near Hulste. He had just enough time to set fire to his plane before being taken prisoner, but the Germans found enough among the ashes to grasp the significance of his modifications.

In the meantime, de Rose, by now aviation commander of Fifth Army, had also decided on direct action. With the support of his army commander, General Franchet d'Espèrey, he turned one of his two-seater reconnaissance squadrons into France's first fighter squadron, aiming to convince the doubters that planes could first seek out enemy machines, then pursue, catch and destroy them. De Rose replaced the Nieuport 6M with six new MS L Parasol two-seater monoplanes: a high-winged, aerodynamic aircraft offering good all-round observation and a rapid rate of climb – and the only contemporary French aircraft faster than its German opponents. He and his deputy, Captain Auguste Le Révérend, personally selected and trained new pilots and observers, including future aces Aspirant Georges Pelletier-Doisy and Corporal Jean Navarre. And at Jonchery-sur-Vesle on 1 March 1915, N12 became MS12. The crews were still armed with just a carbine, so pilots were advised to make surprise attacks, flying high and concealing themselves in the clouds or the sun before swooping down on the enemy. With only four rounds to play with, the pilot had to get as close as possible to the enemy so the observer could fire a head shot, but five victories were gained in April alone.

However, the plane's rotary engine made it notoriously difficult to fly. 'The pilots still aren't completely won over by the [Parasol],' reported one aviator. 'You have to position yourself very carefully into the wind on take-off and landing. In normal flight the elevators seem ultra-sensitive and the ailerons slow to respond. As soon as you dive, especially at full throttle, the elevators and ailerons both seize up and become hard to shift. If you kick at the rudder bar without banking, the control column moves the wrong way and you can't retrieve it. In turbulence, [the plane] has a peculiar sideways movement which may initially be disconcerting.'

In consequence, the Parasol was normally reserved for experienced pilots, but future aces Georges Guynemer (MS/N/SPA3) and Lieutenant Alfred Heurteaux (MS38/N/SPA3) insisted on learning to fly it while training at Avord. The instructors thought the pair were getting above themselves. 'Volunteering to fly the Morane didn't exactly make us flavour of the month,' recalled Heurteaux. 'I remember the first time we took one up, the little low-winged 18-metre type. We nagged the chief pilot and he gave in. "Brace yourselves," he said to us. "Here you are, two of them. Jump in and do your worst."' In the adjoining hangar, mechanic Jacques Viguier was servicing REP aircraft. 'The group next door included Guynemer, Sanglier, Barnier and Lemaitre,' he recalled. 'All four had already made a name for themselves in training. They'd nicknamed Guynemer "*Le Môme de Fer*" ["The Iron Kid"]. He wore leggings with leather trousers that weren't boot-cut. He was a real long streak of piss in these enormous trousers. He was saucer-eyed and thin as a lath, a real trial! He just had to fly! . . . "Viguier!" he used to shout across to me. "Come and get her going." I started the engines for Guynemer, Barnier and the rest of them, but for Guynemer in particular. He just had to fly!'

On 8 June 1915 the young Guynemer arrived at Vauciennes, where Adjudant Jules Védrines welcomed him to MS3. First impressions were distinctly unfavourable: 'This 20-year-old kid looked a bit of a toff,' recalled Védrines. 'Elegant, nay refined, in appearance. And, I admit, he really got my back up. I'd seen quite enough of these chocolate-box observers! . . . [His] first flight definitely didn't turn out as planned: he crashed on landing. Some of the chaps made a bit of a joke of it. He was a boy among men, never opened his mouth – and he wasn't particularly well thought of. Major Brocard had to tick him off a few times, and I just didn't know what to make of him. [He] took another plane up and subjected it to exactly the same treatment. His stubbornness was starting to worry us: we couldn't let him smash all our planes. Quite understandably, the CO flew into a rage and told the "crate-wrecker" he never wanted to hear his name again. "The Nipper", as we called him, came out of the squadron office, pale and distraught. He looked like a little girl lost: all the teasing and animosity had reduced him to an absolute bundle of nerves. So he decided to confide in a man who although rough and ready also seemed the most kindly disposed towards him. He came looking for me. "You don't know me," he said, "but if only you knew how much I want to succeed!" His words belied his youthful appearance. So determined, so manly, so convincing was his voice . . . so capable did he seem of correcting his faults . . . that I promised to speak to [Major Brocard]. . . . Brocard, who knew his men, accepted my proposal – with just one proviso. "If he hasn't made the grade in a fortnight," he added. "I'll show him the door."'

Fortunately, Guynemer soon found his feet. On 19 July 1915 he and Private Charles Guerder took off in their Morane – their mission to intercept an enemy Aviatik flying over French lines. Guynemer caught up with the German and Guerder fired off a complete drum, but their Lewis gun jammed and their opponent flew off unharmed towards Laon. Then a second Aviatik appeared. 'We followed him,' reported Guynemer, 'and dived as soon as he was over our lines, putting ourselves 50 metres below him, behind and to his left. On the first salvo, the Aviatik swerved and a fragment of the plane broke off. The German fired his carbine in reply. One bullet hit the wing; another grazed Guerder's hand and scalp. On the final salvo, the pilot slumped in the cockpit, the observer lifted his arms and the Aviatik plunged in flames between the trenches.' The German crashed behind French lines: Guynemer landed beside it and promptly broke his propeller. Both pilot and observer were awarded the *Médaille militaire* for their exploit.

However, this would be Guynemer's last victory for some months. Anthony Fokker had perfected a synchronizer gear that used the turning of the propeller to control the firing of a Maxim gun, and from July 1915 the new Maxim-equipped Fokker Eindecker gave the Germans several months of uncontested air superiority. 'Wonderful!' exclaimed Sergeant Auguste Métairie (CRP) in May 1915, when he heard of his posting to MS49. But joy soon turned to disillusion. 'My comrades and I weren't as well armed as we would have wished,' he recalled in 1916, 'or as well as our adversaries. Machine guns were few, compelling us to go to fight the impeccably armed Boches with a carbine. Some [pilots] resorted to taking a brick with them to drop into their opponent's propeller.' When Métairie came under attack from a Fokker while escorting a raid on Dornach on 31 October 1915, he had to rely on his flying skills to lure his opponent away from the bombers: 'I was trying to draw him back over our lines before engaging him in combat and was manoeuvring to stop him firing. I pulled out all my stunts and reckon I gave him a hell of a headache. Every time he thought he had me in his sights and all he had left to do was fire, I darted into a turn or a spin and forced him to start all over again. He didn't appreciate that at all and moments later left the field.'

Over the summer of 1915, MS12's victories persuaded other army commanders to form their own two-seater fighter/reconnaissance squadrons, but de Rose knew the next requirement was a specialist single-seater, and in June he despatched Captain Léonce de Dreuille to compare the new Morane and Nieuport prototypes. Both machines were fast and manoeuvrable, but the Morane N relied on wing-warping, making it much harder to land and handle at high speed. De Dreuille advised that it was suitable only for the most experienced pilots, so de Rose opted instead for the smaller Nieuport 11 – nicknamed the 'Bébé' – a fast, highly manoeuvrable lightweight design developed from pre-war competition racers, whose ailerons made it the better all-rounder.

De Rose worked with the company to modify the original design, particularly to reduce the excessive vibration set up by the engine. He also abandoned the heavy deflector plates, now revealed to compromise the propeller's aerodynamic performance as well as cutting airspeed. Sergeant Robert Alkan, an MS12 mechanic, was busy working on a synchronizer gear to match Fokker's system, but in the interim de Rose had a Hotchkiss or a Lewis machine gun fixed to the Bébé's upper wing, firing over rather than through the arc of the propeller. Each plane carried three 25-round drums or strips for the Hotchkiss, or three 47-round drums for the Lewis, but reloading was a tricky operation that put both pilot and plane out of action for a dangerously long time. 'You had to swing the weapon down by pulling a lever,' explained Captain Georges Thenault (N124), '. . . and the wind brought it sharply backwards at the risk of cracking your skull if you didn't keep your head well down. It was far from an easy job to substitute a full drum for an empty one with your fingers frozen and hampered by thick gloves, and one needed quite a lot of practice to do it properly, especially as one had to use one hand for piloting the ship for fear of getting into a spin.'

Neither the Hotchkiss nor the Lewis gun could match the German Maxim, but de Rose had always preferred to operate from close range, and forward firing allowed the French to begin to counter their opponents. Nevertheless Philippe Féquant (VB101/N65) continued to bemoan the disparity in firepower. 'In 1915 we were so obsessed by bomber development that the only fighters we produced were a few 80hp Gnôme-engined Nieuport Bébés,' he remarked. 'The Bébé [certainly] handled better than the Fokker, but its only weapon was a Hotchkiss machine gun, slowly firing its 25-round strip, while the Fokker's Maxim rapidly spat out several hundred rounds.' Jacques Mortane also highlighted the imbalance: 'How many losses are caused by this? The [enemy] can open fire at 200 to 300 metres, but our pilots are forced to wait until they're just 30 metres away. They have to get close to avoid wasting bullets. In a duel to the death at 3,000 metres, the man with a thousand rounds to burn must always hold all the aces.'

On 4 January 1916 the newly promoted Adjudant Auguste Métairie (CRP/MS49) was despatched to Paris to pick up his new aircraft: 'I didn't waste much time [there], eager as I was to catch up with the cocky Boches in my little fireball. I got back to Belfort after a marvellously quick trip that demonstrated all the potential of my new machine.' Machine gun mounted on the wing, and trailed by a number of anti-aircraft bursts, Métairie took off in pursuit of an Aviatik: 'I was going flat out, climbing steeply to reach the enemy in time. At 2,500 metres I found myself at the same height as the intruder. I raced towards him at 150km/h. But when he spotted my tiny aeroplane, the thoroughbred of the skies, he preferred to refuse combat. He turned tail and scarpered as fast as his legs would carry him.'

'Approaching the target' – the bombing campaign begins
The first bombing raids on enemy territory were flown as early as 14 August 1914, when Lieutenant Antoine Cesari and Corporal Roger Prudhommeaux (MF16) decided to drop modified 155mm shells on the Zeppelin hangar at Metz-Frascaty. According to the official report, the pair left their Verdun airfield at 5.30 pm and flew directly to Metz: 'They arrived over the line of forts, the corporal in the lead at 2,200 metres, the lieutenant above and behind at 2,500 metres, to be met by a sustained barrage that literally blanketed them with explosive shells. They

maintained their course. Corporal Prudhommeaux dropped his bomb and checked it had released correctly. Smoke from the enemy shell-bursts hid the exact point of impact, but he is sure it landed on or very near the target. Lieutenant Cesari's engine stalled just before he reached the airfield. To make sure he didn't go down before completing his mission, this officer simply glided towards the hangar and dropped his bomb from a height of 2,000 metres. Just then his engine started up again. Like the corporal, Lieutenant Cesari was unable to see the point of impact due to the smoke. Nevertheless, he reckons it landed just a few metres from the hangar.'

Under a political and strategic imperative to drive the German invader from French soil, GQG was quick to embrace bombing as a means of carrying the war to the enemy on the battlefield and beyond. Dirigibles were the proven technology and the seven machines available in August 1914 were soon called into action, the *Adjutant-Vincenot* and *Fleurus I* venturing as far as Sarrebourg and Trier. None could match the enemy Zeppelins, and with a top speed of 52km/h they were slower than the newfangled aircraft, but they could carry a bigger load (up to 300 kilos), operate at a higher ceiling (2,300 metres) and cover much greater distances. Only six weeks earlier the *Vincenot* had set a new endurance record with a flight lasting 35 hours 19 minutes.

On 20 August 1914 the *Dupuy-de-Lôme* set off from its base in Maubeuge to raid the Belgian university town of Louvain, but three days later friendly fire brought it down over Reims. When news came through that the Germans had also lost four Zeppelins since the start of the war, GQG immediately grounded the remainder of the French fleet. Missions eventually resumed on 2 April 1915, but only at night, effectively confining the dirigible to a bombing role. The *Commandant-Coutelle* and the *Alsace* were added to the strength in 1915; the *d'Arlandes*, the *Champagne* and the *Pilâtre-de-Rozier* in 1916. None could equal the Zeppelins, but the last three did represent a huge advance in performance, with a top speed of 70km/h and a payload of 1,200 kilos. The majority of their raids were directed against railway lines and other infrastructure targets.

Airship commander Captain F. led one successful raid into enemy territory. 'The Boches were using us for target practice but to no great effect. Nothing was whistling past our ears, so I stuck my head out to get a better view of the spectacle . . . Our target was now visible off to port. Another half hour and we'd be there. I pointed it out to the [crew] but they had already spotted it. We'd thought of little else for days now, the name always on our minds even if never voiced out loud. . . . I took the wheel, in line with standing orders, and handed over to my bomb-aimer. A mechanic arrived to join the pilots. We armed the bombs and shells and placed them in position. The shelling got heavier as we came closer. [Then] a pair of lights suddenly appeared below and slightly ahead of us – brighter than the rest and flashing frequently at regular intervals. Now we were directly overhead! The time had come. The officer at the bombsight gave the signal. I caught the smell of the burning fuses and counted down a few seconds in my head. A single flame, followed by several more; then nothing except will o' the wisps. The airship had shed part of its load and was continuing towards its second target, not far away. Time to prepare for another drop. Again all sense of danger evaporated and an indescribable feeling took hold of me: an acute appreciation of the power I held in my hands, a sense of frailty and . . . a secret and intensely human desire to spare all the little children and anxious wives. The airship slowed, turned and headed back towards the first target to complete its work of destruction. Slowly, very slowly, it made ground into a headwind, the two huge eyes of the beast below shining brightly. I passed directly above them. How angry they seemed! One last load of bombs . . . yet more flames . . . the muffled echo of a blast drowning out the engine noise . . . and the mission was over.

'[Back at base] the pilots descended from the gondola one by one, walking rather stiffly in their heavy clothing and after so long without moving. We gave our pals a bit of a scare – our faces were covered in sand and streaked with the sudden sweat produced on landing – but our laughter quickly reassured them. The flight crew departed. Then, in the quiet of the night, all you could hear was a hissing sound: the airship was betraying its wounds.'

Indeed, dirigibles remained intensely vulnerable. In late 1915, within months of entering service, the *Commandant-Coutelle* was written off after a crash-landing and the *Alsace* was destroyed on the ground. In June 1916 the *Adjutant-Vincenot* was brought down over Verdun, and eight months later the *Pilâtre-de-Rozier* was shot down in flames over Alsace with the loss of the entire crew. GQG once again grounded the fleet, and in March 1917 the remaining dirigibles, plus their crews and the school at Saint-Cyr, were transferred to the navy for anti-submarine work.

The first two specialist bomber squadrons, V14 and BR17, were created in late September 1914, and V14 was soon involved in a daring attempt to end the war in a single stroke. On 1 November information came in that Kaiser Wilhelm was visiting the Belgian town of Tielt and would be leaving for Courtrai between 1.30 pm and 2.00 pm. Several bombers were immediately dispatched from Dunkerque with orders to 'hit the Kaiser's convoy as it left [the town] or even while it was still [there]'. But they were too late: the Kaiser had departed an hour earlier and the French missed their man.

The winter of 1914/15 saw the creation of four bomber groups – Groupes de Bombardement GB1 to GB4 – all under the direct control of GQG. Each group was initially three squadrons strong and equipped with the latest French bomber, the Voisin 3. Armand Viguier (VB107) was fond of the plane: '[it was] a huge biplane, fitted with a 130hp Canton-Unné sited behind the cockpit . . . Despite having only one magneto and one spark plug per cylinder, this stout engine still powered the aircraft with great heart. For protection we had a Hotchkiss machine gun mounted on a tripod above the pilot's head, well within reach of the bomb-aimer seated behind him. It fired 34-round [sic] strips. . . . To cover the rear we had . . . a cavalry carbine. . . . It had a 3-round magazine but could only fire single shots. . . . The bomb-aimer climbed on the dickey he used as a seat, braced himself against the upper wing, and fired "in reverse" from this position, trying his best to avoid the arc of the propeller, which extended 30 centimetres above the wing.'

The early bomber squadrons did not carry bombs as such, but modified shells. The Voisin, for instance, carried six modified 90mm shells, each held in a tube fashioned by the squadron mechanics and secured to the outside of the nacelle by a cord cut with a knife once the plane was over its target. Beneath the nacelle it also carried an extra 120mm or 155mm shell fitted with a contact fuse that could only be armed as the plane was approaching its target – the task facing American volunteer Victor Chapman (VB101) en route to Dillingen in August 1915: 'The lieutenant jogged me to make a sighting so as to get our speed for dropping the projectile. Placing the sights successively at the spots marked for the height we were (2,400 metres) I took two views of the same object, keeping the time with a stop watch (31 seconds) and by this means got spot on the curve of my projectile for that height. We must be approaching the target for the Lieutenant motioned me to load the projectile. This is by far the most difficult operation, for the 155 shell with its tin tail looking like a torpedo four feet long, is hung under the body and, without seeing its nose even, one has to reach down in front of the pilot, put the *détonateur* in, then the *percuteur* and screw it fast. After which I pulled off a safety device. You may imagine how I scrambled round in a fur coat and two pairs of leather trousers and squeezed myself to get my arm down the hole. I really had a moment's nervousness that the *détonateur* would not stay in the hole but fly back into the *hélice*. However, all went well and the Lieutenant handed me the plan of the town of Dillingen . . . Right underneath us was a great junction of railway lines, tracks and sidings. "That's a go," I thought, and pulled the handle when it came in the sighter. A slight sway and below me the blue-gray shell poised and dipped its head.'

Georges Kirsch (V29) was also nervous when handling the shells: 'The things always scared me to death. It was [a] clumsy [business] and there were several serious accidents. We didn't have bomb-racks either. [We simply] dropped them over the side. This was a particularly dangerous operation in a Voisin because everything was at the rear: the tail assembly and the booms of course, but also the propeller and the engine.'

With direct control of the bomber groups, GQG could deploy them tactically or strategically as required. In December 1914, for example, the men of GB1 – VB1 and VB2, plus the newly created VB3, commanded by the enthusiastic Major Louis de Goÿs – found themselves cooperating with the attacks of Second Army in Artois. On 20 December Barès gave them '[complete] freedom of action . . . to carry out special bombing missions' from their base at Herlin-le-Sec over a number of potential targets, including the villages of Souchez and Givenchy-en-Gohelle, and the railway stations at Hénin-Liétard and Lens. De Goÿs chose to cooperate with the planned ground attack against Givenchy-en-Gohelle 'as [the village] lay beyond the effective reach of our artillery and harboured many enemy reserves'. The raid was ordered at 9.45 am and within half an hour eleven machines were in the air. They dropped their bombs from 2,500 metres and two hours later were back at base.

But aircraft could also target strategic objectives far to the enemy rear. The development of the trench network from the Channel coast to Switzerland acted as an immediate spur to these ideas. Philippe Féquant (VB101), brother of the record-breaking Albert, and a bomber pilot before he was appointed to command N65 in 1916, later characterized this as a 'plan to systematically destroy German war production, first put together in late 1914 when it became clear the war was going to be an industrial struggle'. Free of artillery, machine guns and barbed wire, bombing raids could carry the war to the heart of enemy territory. 'If we can't break the German line,' wrote distinguished academic André Le Chatelier, 'let's use aircraft to turn it, cross it and undermine it from the rear'.

Plans for strategic interventions behind the German lines were also coloured by the desire for revenge. Barès was personally opposed to 'reprisal raids on centres of population' – judging them militarily worthless – but a powerful lobby of enthusiasts compelled him to envisage them from the start. When the Ottoman Empire entered the war in late October 1914,

Major de Goÿs called for a great aerial armada against Constantinople, confident that the threat of death and destruction raining down upon civilians would force the Turks to capitulate – and press, politicians and bomber manufacturers soon took up the cry. Destroying Germany's cities and demoralizing its civilian population would, they claimed, produce a victory seemingly unobtainable on the conventional battlefield. Pierre-Étienne Flandin, a qualified pilot and parliamentary deputy, suggested a fleet of 750 bombers could wipe out Essen and the Ruhr basin: 'I made it clear that [bombers] are just very long-range guns – 100, 200, 300 kilometres and more to come – that make it possible to strike at the heart of the enemy's military production. [The German] arms industry lies at the mercy of a well-organized bomber force.'

Enemy actions deemed contrary to the rules of war, such as the German gas attack at Ypres on 22 April 1915, were also mustered in justification. Five weeks later the first strategic raid was launched against Ludwigshafen and Oppau, home to the works of Badische-Anilin, manufacturer of explosives and poison gas. On the night of 27 May the crews were ready by 2.45 am, among them Adjudant Bernard, whose choice of equipment amused his commander: '[I was carrying] a little bag with a change of linen, my razor [and] toilet kit, a box of cola tablets etc. "Damn me," said de Goÿs cheerfully. "Are you planning on staying?"' Eighteen Voisins took off at 3.00 am, flying in a loose formation and each carrying several hundred kilos of explosives. Their plan was to rendezvous at 2,100 metres over the town of Baccarat, then de Goÿs would lead them in. Close to Wissembourg, well over German-occupied territory, Bernard began to feel hungry. 'I turned around,' he recalled. 'My observer was tinkering with his machine gun. Good Lord, this was hardly the moment! I asked him for a sandwich and took a bite but I was too tense to swallow. Then he passed me some cola tablets, which always slip down easily. He was munching chocolate.'

By the time his comrades arrived over the works, de Goÿs had already dropped his shells and was turning for home. 'On our right was the Rhine,' continued Bernard, 'with a fair few boats and the lovely city of Mannheim. Directly below us, the enormous factory site. We followed the main street and reached our designated target, the chlorine works. [Adjudant Marcel] Abran stood up and dropped our six shells in the blink of an eye. We were surrounded by gunfire but it didn't bother us much. Below us everything was ablaze, all turning yellow. Good news. I didn't hang about and headed straight for Nancy.'

A total of eighty-three modified 90mm shells and four 155mm shells rained down on the factories: 'three huge columns of smoke were visible at Ludwigshafen from 6.15 am onwards, and on their return the planes reported great clouds of smoke obscuring Ludwigshafen and Oppau from 6.30 am.' All the aircraft were home by 9.50 am, with the notable exception of de Goÿs, last seen going down over German territory. 'It happened right at the end, over the Rhine,' he wrote from captivity in the citadel at Würzburg to his comrade Captain Do Hûu Vi. 'Sudden engine failure. I can't tell you how disappointed we were. I'll send a detailed report to GQG giving the exact details if I'm allowed. . . . Send news of my comrades and get others to do so too. Not too many operational details though or they'll stop my mail.'

Further raids followed: against Karlsruhe in June, in reprisal for the German Zeppelin raids on Paris in March; against Dillingen in August, then against Saarbrücken, Trier and Mensdorf in September. The Germans condemned the raids as criminal, but the French remained unbowed. Deployment en masse was explicitly designed to demoralize as well as destroy: 'the more our planes operate together as a group, the greater will be the impact of our bombing raids – on morale and materiel,' Barès instructed his bomber groups in February 1915. Georges Kirsch (V29) was a reluctant supporter: 'There was no question of us trying to inflict physical damage on military targets,' he wrote of a raid on Saarbrücken. 'Our task was to sneak up on the major arteries and drop the lot at zero hour, midday German time, as people were leaving the factories. Four hundred and twenty dead. We thought it despicable, but that's war.'

Barès considered the results of these raids extremely promising. 'As our only means of operating over enemy-occupied territory, aviation must be expanded considerably,' he argued. The bomber force was increased, and the four existing bomber groups combined to form a larger provisional *groupement*. But this heightened offensive role demanded a sense of discipline and teamwork uncharacteristic of early aircrew: 'Air raids take a heavy toll of commanders, pilots, bomb-aimers and machine-gunners alike,' claimed Major Maurice Happe (MF29), the commander of GB4. 'They require qualities whose importance each must understand before assuming his role. The commander must have a clear appreciation of his responsibilities; he has to lead from the front in difficult situations and foster in his subordinates the qualities he deems vital. The pilot must forsake his independent ways and discipline himself to march in time with his comrades. The bomb-aimer needs a deeply ingrained sense of duty: a momentary loss of concentration during his few minutes of action and several hours of danger will have been run in vain.'

In the absence of de Goÿs, Happe – '*Le Corsaire de l'air*' ('the Pirate of the Air') to some sections of the French press – had become the leading French proponent and theoretician of bombing. Learning that the Germans had put a price of 25,000 marks on his head, he flew across the lines to drop a message: 'If that's your game, you'll find me in the plane with red wheels and a cross on its wings. Target me. Don't waste your time on my comrades.'

But the bombers, heavy and slow, were always at risk from enemy fighters, particularly after the Germans gained air superiority in the summer of 1915. 'The [enemy] fighters had definitely improved,' commented René Martel (VC110/V121), 'and the Voisin could no longer withstand the Aviatik and Fokker in daylight. The Nieuport [10] provided some sort of cover but its short operational range limited its effectiveness.' Attempts to arm some Voisins with a 37mm cannon were a failure, the weapon proving too unwieldy in aerial combat, and Major Happe began to experiment with close formation flying. After trying line abreast and line astern, with escorting aircraft at each end of the line, he eventually settled on a V-formation as the most effective. At Ludwigshafen in May the bombers had flown in a loose gaggle, but by August tactics were changing significantly. 'Close formation provides vital protection against enemy planes,' wrote one bomber CO after the Dillingen raid. 'During the mission . . . an Aviatik dogged us every inch of the way. It watched us drop our bombs and was poised to pick off any straggler, but it was reluctant to strike against the group. We clearly need to have our machines ready earlier so we can take off together and quickly adopt close formation. Met with the pilots to stress their crates must be lined up and ready half an hour in advance, take off in a tight group without worrying about collisions, and fly like that too.'

An alternative tactic was to move from day to night bombing. The French had launched their first night raid in February 1915, when aircraft from C17, based at Toul, attacked the barracks at Metz. Transferring day bombers to night-time operations also provided a role for the older pusher Voisin, Farman and Breguet-Michelin types that were fast becoming obsolete for daytime use. 'The pilots developed a real expertise with these much-reviled planes and drew a decent return from them,' claimed René Martel. 'Moreover, their lack of speed became an advantage at night because the pilot [needed time] to assess his position . . . He had to fly slowly to make accurate observations.'

Night flying certainly required great skill. 'We'd precious little training when you think about it,' recalled Major Paul Gignoux (VB101). 'I set off on my first night bombing raid with a total of just fifty-three hours' flying time. Needless to say, if I'd experienced any sort of technical problem . . . The first time you fly at night you can't see anything, just a black void beneath you. . . . After eight or nine raids I started navigating solo. I managed well enough but I still couldn't see anything to begin with. . . . You check your compass. You check the time. [So] you know, for example, that the target is 50 kilometres away and you've covered 15 kilometres in 8 minutes. Even when you can't see the ground, you still have a rough idea where you are, and that's when you start keeping your eyes peeled. The target is often illuminated and quite distinctive: a station, a railway, a factory. Ability to see the ground comes with experience. I could take comrades up with me and show them how to navigate. . . . The enemy could only use sound to identify us and very few planes were shot down. Engine failure was the biggest danger. The engine in the Voisin Peugeot 220hp had its hiccups. It broke down on me several times and that's when the risk was greatest.'

Sergeant Antoine Cordonnier (N57/SPA15) vividly described one night bombing raid: 'We took off by moonlight and were 1,500 metres over the lines an hour and a half before sunrise. We throttled back to reduce any noise and silently glided down to 1,000 metres. We located the target and carefully placed our bombs from [such a] low altitude that it was almost impossible to miss. Then we used our machine gun to finish off the job, firing on German convoys, railway lines and batteries on our way back to the lines. Although my raids didn't always produce the desired result, two were pretty successful: the first derailed a train, the second blew up a munitions dump. The latter was particularly memorable; my bomb produced a fantastic firework display that was ample reward for the risks I'd taken. An hour later I was 40 kilometres away, back over our lines. But I could still see enormous explosions coming from the seat of the fire and huge flames climbing up to 500 metres into the air.'

Lieutenant Étienne Brizard (VB133) explained more of the techniques involved: 'These are surprise attacks: the pilot throttles back well before arriving over the target and descends silently to a height of around 100 metres. The observer in effect places the bombs on the target. The aircraft climbs rapidly immediately thereafter. You derail trains using a very compact trail of bombs to cut the line about 100 metres ahead of the engine. Incendiary bombs are preferable for attacks on airfields. In every case, the observer turns his machine gun on the target while the aircraft is climbing after the release of the bombs. The gun can also be used to attack convoys and bivouacs.'

When heavy cloud disrupted the French formation en route to Saarbrücken on 6 September, some bombers carried on below it, while others turned back, leaving both groups vulnerable. Captain Paul Bousquet, commander of VB105, and the record-breaking Captain Albert Féquant (VB102) were both killed, and by mid-September strategic raids had been suspended, halted by the scale of French losses and by the forthcoming autumn offensive in Artois and Champagne. To support these attacks, GQG temporarily ceded control of the bomber groups to the army commanders. In Artois squadrons attached to Fifth Army were ordered to disrupt enemy troop movements by attacking stations at Cambrai, Morval, Busigny and Achiet-le-Grand. 'Heavy strafing between Bapaume and the lines,' reported a pilot from VB108 after a raid on Cambrai station on 23 September. 'Within sight of [the town] we came under attack from the Boches. They couldn't get too close, though. [That's] the advantage of group flying.' The French set off for home, leaving the station blanketed by a thick cloud of smoke: 'We fired at the Germans, but they didn't show much mettle. I was a little concerned for my comrades who had to follow as best they could. We crossed the lines near Arras and all got home safely. A couple suffered engine failure [but still] managed to put down inside our lines.'

But German air superiority was also exerting a heavy psychological, as well as a physical, toll. At 3.15 pm on 2 October 1915 sixty-two aircraft from GB1, GB2 and GB4 set off on a daylight raid over Vouziers, an important German command centre and railway hub on the Champagne front. GB1 put twenty-two planes into the air: seven turned back without dropping their bombs, one was forced down, while Lieutenant Robert (VB104) returned with a rear strut and a control cable severed, his observer's helmet pierced and his machine peppered with bullet-holes – twelve in the wings, ten in the fuselage and two in the propeller. Despite this bruising experience, just three planes were forced down in total: 'less than might have been feared given the superiority of the enemy machines,' claimed René Martel. 'The Germans had infinitely better planes than ours but still hadn't worked out how to use them. Their attacks were cautious and indecisive, and their Fokkers and Aviatiks had not yet mastered the techniques of aerial combat.' Yet the bomber crews described themselves as completely helpless before their German assailants.

Some pilots responded by aping Cesari and Prudhommeaux and launching unofficial raids – a practice winked at, if never formally approved, by senior officers. 'Around one in the morning, after Captain Coville and I had stood our comrades a fine dinner to celebrate his *Légion d'honneur* and my officer's braid, we decided to go and rouse the Germans with a few bombs,' confessed Sous-lieutenant André Quennehen (MF5) on 19 December 1915. 'I took off with Captain Coville as my passenger. You can imagine how fired up we were. After ever-so-carefully dropping eight bombs on X . . . we were delighted to see house after house light up – proof we'd done something to wake the sleeping Boches.' Returning in the dark, Quennehen still had to find his airfield. Fortunately, the mechanics had lit large bonfires to guide him home and he managed to land safely.

Captain Louis Robert de Beauchamp, CO of N23, had also undertaken two impromptu missions – at much longer range – earlier that autumn. On 24 September 1915 he and Lieutenant Pierre Daucourt dropped twelve bombs on the Krupp works at Essen, and two months later he bombed Munich, flying on over the Alps and landing in Venice. Jacques Mortane congratulated him on his initiative: 'We must make the enemy realize we're prepared to head deep into Germany to remind them of the horrors of war. The age of the Romantics is over: we now have a clearer idea of the Boche character. We must act to stop their barbarity . . . We must follow their example.' Yet he rejected the notion that Beauchamp's feat should encourage the resumption of large-scale strategic bombing. 'Is that really the role of our squadrons?' he asked his readers. 'I don't think so. Non-stop attacks on the enemy's front-line positions would be far more effective than a successful raid on Essen. That's where we must cripple the enemy, harassing him round the clock . . . dropping tons of explosives every day on stations, trains, convoys, batteries and troop movements will do much more to end the war than bombing Essen. . . . The game isn't worth the candle.'

Chapter 3

'Sweep the Skies Clean' – Verdun and the Somme

'An undeniable air superiority' – the air battle above Verdun

By late 1915 six months of German air superiority had left the French squadrons in crisis, their obsolescent Caudron, Farman and Voisin types increasingly vulnerable and unable to operate without escorts, and those escorts in turn outclassed by the Fokker Eindecker. Reconnaissance and spotting had been confirmed as the core duties of the army and army corps squadrons and would remain so until the armistice. Offensively, however, the picture was more nuanced. Early experiments in close air support had been disappointing, experience in Artois and Champagne showing that, however well planned in advance, liaison with ground attacks worked only as far as the first line of trenches; without two-way wireless communication it became impossible to maintain contact for any advance in depth, even when the French were gaining significant ground, as in late September 1915. Bombing had quickly become the main means of taking the battle to the enemy, both at the front and deeper behind the lines, but long-range strategic and reprisal raids were now in abeyance, halted by German air superiority and the scale of French losses. Meanwhile the fighter had yet to make its mark, with just a handful of reconnaissance/fighter units emulating de Rose's pioneering MS12. However, some senior commanders were beginning to appreciate its potential, among them General Foch, once so dismissive of aircraft and now commander of Northern Army Group: 'Air superiority seems at present the only way of guaranteeing the artillery superiority which is essential to safeguarding the infantry even after a successful ground attack,' he reported to Joffre after the autumn offensive in Artois. 'The aviation service must seek to secure it by every possible means.'

With the Nieuport Bébé slowly arriving on the front line, initially serving alongside the older Nieuport 10 two-seaters, France now had its first specialist fighter aircraft, superior to the rival Eindecker in speed, manoeuvrability and rate-of-climb. The early Bébés were still outgunned – but in February 1916 Sergeant Alkan successfully synchronized a belt-fed Vickers machine gun, at last redressing the balance in firepower and eliminating the need to change magazines in mid-combat. The Vickers made its debut on the front in May and soon became the standard weapon of the Bébé and its successors.

The first Bébés to arrive at the front 'defended the skies above Nancy [and] escorted the bomber groups, by then unable to operate without being engaged in tough, costly scraps by the enemy fighters', recalled Philippe Féquant (VB101/N65). 'The remaining [machines] were split between a number of army reconnaissance squadrons and allocated to pilots notable for their skill and enthusiasm.' However, fighter strategy remained undecided. Some senior officers wanted to distribute the new machines among the army, army corps and bomber squadrons to provide close protection. But others – like Barès, de Rose and Captain Paul du Peuty, aviation commander of Tenth Army – took the opposing view, advocating the concentration of fighter resources by combining a number of squadrons under a single command. They were also evolving ideas of 'indirect protection', creating a safety zone for the French cooperation squadrons on either side of the battlefront by sending fighters across the lines to destroy enemy machines. They accepted that operating over enemy territory would be a risky affair, forcing French pilots to nurse their planes home against the prevailing south-westerlies, all the time exposed to aerial attack and hostile ground fire. Yet they were confident that, though French losses might be heavy, those of the enemy would be heavier still.

But on 21 February 1916 a sudden German assault on the Verdun salient pre-empted all debate. With the collapse of the intelligence network in occupied France and Belgium, plus weeks of appalling weather that prevented any reconnaissance flights, the French were taken almost completely by surprise. Even when the squadrons finally gained the air immediately prior to the offensive they found little to report: nothing at all on the west bank of the Meuse; just a few new trenches and tracks around Damvillers and the Bois d'Ormont opposite XXX Corps, north and north-east of the city; and a single column of troops facing II Corps to the south-east. All the enemy supply dumps and troop concentrations had been missed.

To support their attack the Germans had assembled the largest aerial force to date – around 170 machines, including twenty or so of the latest

Fokker E.III fighters. In reply, the French could muster no more than seventy machines of all types – mainly out-dated Caudrons and Farmans – and on the opening day of the offensive the Germans simply swept them from the skies. The very active and aggressive enemy fighters overwhelmed the observation aircraft of C11, C18 and MF63, plus the balloons of 28th and 31st Companies, completely blinding the French artillery and greatly facilitating the German advance. 'German aircraft have been very active since daybreak,' complained Sergeant Edmond André (61st Artillery). 'They've spent long periods overflying our positions, quite undisturbed either by our own planes, of which we've seen not a single representative, or by the AA, whose battery on Cote 344 now lies in German hands.'

After their initial assault the Germans changed tactics: two-seater barrier patrols blocked access to their lines, with a supporting force of Fokker and Pfalz monoplanes ready to intercept any French machine that did get through. Meanwhile the guns, firing in pairs, targeted the remaining French balloons, one aiming at the balloon itself, the other at the winch.

The opening night of the attack did bring one small victory to boost French morale, after the Germans despatched three Zeppelins – LZ77, LZ88 and LZ95 – to bomb the railway junction at Revigny-sur-Ornain, south-east of Verdun. Some 30 kilometres away, at Dampierre-le-Château, lay 4th Corps Engineer Park, commanded by Lieutenant Haegelen. The park included a number of searchlights, which Haegelen wanted to show off. 'It was an incredible sight,' recalled Sous-lieutenant Jean Alloitteau. 'Quite spellbinding. Two, then three, beams of light swept the sky, picking out shrapnel. Suddenly: "Look! A Zeppelin!" It was coming from the east, still some distance away, hazy in the lights, quite high (perhaps 1,000 metres) and clearly heading west. The searchlights had locked on to it and weren't about to let go. We stood rooted to the spot. No one said a word. Inch by inch, the Zeppelin moved clear of the surrounding shrapnel. Then it turned sharply south, giving us a side-on view. The ship was brilliantly illuminated: magnificent certainly, but a very obvious target. The passengers must have been feeling pretty nervous. Not for long, though: the shells eased off and the Zeppelin moved out of range of the big searchlights. Relief for the Germans, a worry for us. The Zeppelin continued south. Where? Why? A searchlight seemed to pick it out for a moment. Hope flared, then nothing. The searchlights carried on sweeping the sky. Reluctantly and rather disappointedly, we were just about to take our leave, when they suddenly latched on to two faint shapes, more Zeppelins. They were still a long way off, far to the east. The guns stopped firing. Instinctively, we looked to the south and an enormous torch suddenly plunged towards the horizon, a vast ball of red topped by tendrils of flame. The six of us each let out a great whoop of joy: "That's it. We've got 'im!" The two searchlight operators were jubilant.'

The successful shot came from a gun belonging to a unit of self-propelled AA artillery, the 17th Section d'Auto-Canons, under Adjudant Gramling, who was awarded his commission for his part in the affair. None of the crew of LZ77 survived. Meanwhile the other two Zeppelins disappeared into the night, returning to their lines without dropping their bombs.

Aerial reinforcements were dispatched straight away, and first to arrive were N67 and MF72, plus 39th and 52nd Balloon Companies. MF72 was swiftly made available to VII Corps, C18 to XXX Corps, and C11 to II Corps, while barrier patrols were organized north of the city in an attempt to block the German spotting missions: N67 taking responsibility for the Cuisy to Ormont Farm sector; N23, Ormont Farm to Azannes; and MF63, Azannes to Morgemoulin. N67 and N23 were operating out of Ancemont, which alone received some 1,200 shells during the first two days of the attack, and concentrated German shelling soon forced the French from all the airfields immediately south of Verdun. A new airfield was hastily prepared at Vadelaincourt, and on 23 February five of the squadrons moved in, C11 shifting to Ancemont.

By 25 February another thirty-two squadrons had been assembled – twenty-six reconnaissance squadrons, five for artillery spotting and one for photo-reconnaissance – and General Philippe Pétain had been appointed to command all forces in the Verdun sector. He immediately took the innovative step of dividing his front into a number of 'army corps sectors', rotating individual regiments rather than whole corps into and out of the line, and creating a permanent corps-level command and support structure. Each corps now had its own aerial component: one army corps squadron, ten to fifteen machines strong, one or two smaller heavy artillery flights to spot for the big guns, two or three balloon companies, and one or two divisional squadrons – about fifty planes in all. The new system ensured greater continuity of command, improved internal communication and facilitated local intelligence gathering, and in general functioned so well that it was retained for the rest of the conflict.

While Pétain initially gave his planes a defensive remit, ordering them to 'reconnoitre enemy movements by road and rail, identify movements of enemy batteries, photograph new units and battery positions, establish a barrier, and attack any enemy aircraft operating over our lines', he also recognized the potential impact of aviation on front-line morale. 'If bad weather brings reconnaissance missions to a halt,' he continued, 'the planes can still wheel round and overfly the troops, even at low altitude.' Yet to stop and then repel the German offensive, much more was needed: he had to regain control of the air – a task handed on 28 February 1916 to Fifth Army's aviation commander, Charles de Rose.

At Pétain's Souilly HQ the general issued his instructions: 'Clear the skies for me, de Rose! I'm blind!'

The new aviation chief requested, and was granted, carte blanche.

'Everything is settled with GQG,' continued Pétain. 'Everyone is at your disposal – in the rear and at the front – so you can organize things how you like. Nothing will be denied you. But get a move on! You can see the situation with your own eyes. It's quite simple. If we're driven from the skies, we'll lose Verdun.'

De Rose had already devised a plan to wrest back air superiority. In early March he combined six all-fighter squadrons – N15, N37, N57, N65, N67 and N69 – in a provisional *groupement* under his own command, equipped them with the fast, manoeuvrable Nieuport 11, and based them at airfields south-west of Verdun like Issoncourt, Vadelaincourt and Souilly. Despite vehement protests from senior commanders, he then proceeded to assemble all the best pilots, including such notable fliers as Guynemer, Brocard, Le Révérend, Nungesser, Chainat, Chaput, Deullin, Boillot and Lufbery, in the process creating France's first independent fighter wing. His squadrons and half squadrons would cross the lines to a depth of 5 or 6 kilometres in formations three-, six- or even nine-aircraft strong: 'Regular offensive reconnaissance flights will be undertaken at times fixed by the commander,' he instructed. '"Reconnaissance" is defined as patrols made up of several aircraft flying in a group. . . . The [Germans] must be placed under threat of an attack in force from any quarter . . . Groups of several aircraft will cross the enemy lines at any time, quartering the skies to seek out and destroy their opponents.'

But in the meantime French reconnaissance planes remained all too vulnerable to enemy fighters. On 17 March Sergeant Marcel Garet (N23) and observer Lieutenant Jean Rimbaud were on reconnaissance in their Nieuport 12 two-seater north of Verdun. 'Attack by four aircraft, two downed around Montfaucon and Damvillers,' noted Garet in his diary. 'Surprised by a Fokker, escaped by manoeuvring at 2,100 metres. Fokker driven off by a Nieuport Bébé. We continued our reconnaissance while trying to regain height and rejoin our escort. North of Douaumont, a Fokker was lurking above us. Lieutenant Rimbaud let off half a magazine at close range. I lost sight of the Fokker while manoeuvring and it returned towards us firing from a few metres, seriously wounding Lieutenant Rimbaud and hitting me in both feet, very painful. Cable . . . on the port wing partly severed, lower leading edge of the starboard wing shattered. Engine hit, down to 1,050 revs and struggling. Plane completely unbalanced. Cables on port wing flapping. Descended, diving towards the line of observation balloons. Lieutenant Rimbaud tapped me repeatedly on the head. "Get her down," he murmured. Then he slumped against my shoulder and fell silent.'

Garet landed safely and later had two bullets removed from his feet. The unconscious Rimbaud also survived the incident but eventually lost a leg.

If a machine gun jammed, the peril was greater still. Fortunately, Maxime Lenoir (C18/N23) was a skilled bluffer. On 15 March 1916 he was escorting a reconnaissance machine over Verdun when he spotted a flight of Germans: 'We did our best. But after just a few rounds my machine gun jammed. What next? I couldn't fly off and leave my comrades . . . at the mercy of the enemy. Without a moment's hesitation, I bluffed. I used to pretend to be toying with my rivals. I'd stay in place and pull out all kinds of stunts, diving like a maniac to make it look like I was going to ram them. It was a dangerous game, but the result was always the same: though superior in number and weaponry, my opponents would soon scurry off.' This time the reconnaissance crew escaped unscathed, but Lenoir's own machine took a pasting: 'The undercarriage was broken, propeller pierced right through, wings too. Holed by bullets here and there, shattering one section of the frame, slicing through another.'

For the cooperation crews such aerobatics were out of the question. Observer Bernard Lafont (V220) was attacked by two Fokkers while flying in a Farman across the lines near Vaux. He coaxed just three rounds out of his machine gun before it jammed: 'Our situation was far from brilliant,' he recalled, with admirable understatement. But luck was on his side. Inexplicably, the Fokkers broke off their attack and Lafont and his pilot managed to stumble home – the damage confined to a dozen bullet-holes in the plane. 'What possessed me to climb into a Farman that day?' he wondered. 'It was a "chicken coop", a slow, decrepit old crock with no real means of defending itself. It offered no field of fire towards the rear, and the pilot hardly dare "manoeuvre" the lousy heap for fear of it breaking up. It was an absolute sitting duck.'

The cooperation aircraft were also coming under greater threat from the ground. German air superiority had put a halt to high-altitude reconnaissance missions taking vertical photographs deep in enemy territory, but improvements in equipment and interpretation techniques now made oblique shots viable from as low as 50 metres. Meanwhile the artillery spotters occupied a similarly perilous position. The French super-heavy artillery batteries – 305mm and 340mm calibre – could only manage one round every ten minutes, leaving the spotter dangerously exposed while the guns tried to zero in on their target. 'When I climbed into my plane, I never kidded myself about the potential outcome of my mission,' recalled Major Guy de Lavergne (C6). 'Time ticked by slowly above that shell-blasted terrain. Every pilot was nervous, manoeuvring in all three dimensions to avoid anti-aircraft fire. And you had to keep constant watch for lightning strikes by enemy fighters; the situation could change within seconds. You had to be able to identify the various denizens of the skies in a single glance – Is this one French? Is that one German? . . . and if necessary take immediate action to defend yourself. . . . On 1 July we folded our tents and touched down at Ancemont airfield . . . with orders to patrol the Les Éparges sector. It was a bit of a rest cure for us.'

Fresh from the Châteauroux flying school, Corporal Carroll Winslow (MF44/N112) 'felt a strong aversion to flying over batteries in action. You are bound to get in close proximity to the trajectory of the shells, and the constant sensation and sound of the passing projectiles is none too pleasant. You get them both coming and going, and, no matter which you are trying to avoid, you are always taking a chance with the other. It is a question of choosing between the devil and the deep sea, with the devil constantly stepping into your path.' Winslow endured two-seater work for just six weeks before requesting a transfer to a fighter squadron.

On 21 March de Rose's *groupement* was disbanded – the victim of backstage mutterings by army and group commanders. The squadrons were dispersed between the different sectors of the Verdun front, but within a week they had been reunited, this time under the command of Captain Auguste Le Révérend (MS23). 'Our fighter patrols couldn't ensure a permanent presence in force above our lines,' he later explained. 'They were operating over too narrow a sector of the front, which limited their effectiveness. It [also] became impossible to coordinate activity between sectors, so patrols often took place simultaneously in neighbouring sectors, while at other times the skies remained clear.' De Rose reluctantly accepted a promotion, replacing Barès as aviation commander at GQG, but never took up the post. He was killed while demonstrating the Nieuport Bébé on 11 May 1916.

During April 1916 – with experienced pilots, a good plane, resolutely aggressive tactics and resources concentrated under a single command – the fighter squadrons completely regained local air superiority: '[Our offensive] strategy forced the enemy to halt their own attacks to protect their planes, guaranteeing freedom of action for our cooperation aircraft,' noted Captain Jean Orthlieb, later aviation commander of Tenth Army. One enemy flight immediately turned tail on spotting four Nieuport Bébés from N23 – flown by the CO, Captain Louis Robert de Beauchamp, Sous-lieutenant Edwardes Pulpe, Adjudant Jean Baumont and Adjudant Maxime Lenoir – on patrol in German air space. 'I was on a Fokker which scuttled off like a [frightened] rabbit,' reported Lenoir. 'But my Nieuport Bébé was faster and I managed to catch up with him. I didn't want to spin it out, so I put myself a few metres away and let him have a full drum. Seconds later he was on fire and I had no need to return to the attack. He was finished!'

However, Paul du Peuty, then aviation commander of the Vaux–Douaumont sector, had a warning for his colleagues. Air superiority would never be permanent or absolute, and the French faced an ongoing struggle to maintain it. Technical, tactical or organizational innovation on one side would immediately provoke a response from the other, while even a weaker opponent could offer a threat by 'concentrating its aerial resources to achieve superiority in a specific area of the front; by performing the majority of its front-line reconnaissance, spotting and oblique photography missions at low altitude within its own lines; or by penetrating the lines with a surprise solo attack'.

On 22 May the enemy balloons were targeted in a concerted action that marked a new role for French planes, as well as the debut of the Le Prieur rocket, a weapon specifically designed for these missions. Attached to the inter-plane struts of an aircraft and fired electrically, the rocket had a range of some 200 metres and was named after its inventor, Lieutenant de Vaisseau Yves Le Prieur. Bernard Lafont (V220) had spotted him during one of the trials: 'a big, curt devil of a seaman, tall as a mast, weather-beaten . . . features, eyes bright as the distant sea, profile hooked like that of a bird of prey'.

'I got to spend several days with Captain Féquant's squadron [N65],' recalled Le Prieur, 'first equipping the eight designated planes, then making the [pilots] undertake target practice during their off-duty periods. . . . The pilots were Guiguet [N3], who staged a successful demonstration before President Poincaré [on 24 April], Nungesser [N65], Chaput [N31], de Beauchamp [N23], de Gennes [N57], Barault [N57], Boutiny [N23] and de Réservat [N65]. The German *drachen* [observation balloons] opposite hadn't moved . . . GQG was planning a big attack . . .

in an attempt to retake Fort Douaumont. The eight rocket-equipped fighters were to launch it at dawn by shooting down the German observation balloons to prevent the enemy from correcting its fire. The eight planes were ready at 4.00 am on 22 May . . . and executed the plan to the letter. At 4.50 am six of the eight balloons were downed in flames in less than a minute. Two misses were recorded: one by Barault and one by Boutiny. One pilot was reported missing: Réservat. He shot down his balloon but was hit by anti-aircraft fire. He escaped unhurt and managed to set fire to his plane on the ground . . . The Germans reacted almost immediately, rushing to bring down their observation balloons for 100 kilometres either side of Verdun and creating excellent conditions for the execution of our plan.'

The pilots had indeed pulled off a remarkable effort – the rocket soon became notorious for its inaccuracy – but this particular operation misfired. Targeting attention on a single, relatively narrow front gave the Germans sufficient warning of the French intentions to strengthen the defences around Fort Douaumont, and the counter-attack failed.

Newly recovered from his wounds, Marcel Garet also took part in operations on 22 May, flying two fighting patrols, each two hours long, on the right bank of the Meuse. The fighting patrol had been introduced by Le Révérend after it became clear that planes crossing the lines in groups were easily spotted, giving the enemy time to take cover and return when the coast was clear. One or two machines strong, its remit was to enter hostile airspace under cover of cloud and sun and catch the enemy by surprise. Two days later Garet was back in action again, but this time he almost bit off more than he could chew: '[I] pursued a plane north-east of Étain. Caught by a Fokker and four biplanes. Gave the Fokker a full drum at short range and it disappeared. A few spins and a descent to 1,200 metres took me away from the biplanes. My plane was hit: port wing longeron holed, tail longeron cut.' He spent much of the next six weeks in similar fashion, flying fighting patrols over Douaumont and Montfaucon: 'Continuous combat from 10.30 am to 12.30 pm,' he reported on 1 June. 'Attacked two fighters. Took a bullet in the port wing.' But eventually his luck ran out: on 2 July he was killed in a collision with a German aircraft, probably that flown by Leutnant Werner Neuhaus of FAA203.

High in the air, American volunteer Jim McConnell (N124) felt very remote from the struggle below: 'The battle passes in silence, the noise of one's motor deadening all other sounds. In the green patches behind the brown belt myriads of tiny flashes tell where the guns are hidden; and those flashes, and the smoke of bursting shells, are all we see of the fighting. It is a weird combination of stillness and havoc, the Verdun conflict viewed from the sky . . . Our knowledge about the military operations is scant. We haven't the remotest idea as to what has taken place on the battlefield – even though we've been flying over it during an attack – until we read the papers; and they don't tell us much.' However, Captain Antonin Brocard (N3) shared Pétain's conviction that fighter pilots could inspire those huddled in the trenches: 'Out of acute self-interest, our troops follow the planes that manoeuvre over their heads very closely indeed: offensive behaviour and attacking sorties over enemy lines boost morale. Particularly daring and reckless actions, even when of little apparent military value, can nevertheless serve to invigorate a unit and drive it forward. Aviators should remember this when their turn comes to set the example.'

One pilot who took this message to heart was the so-called *'Sentinelle de Verdun'*, Lieutenant Jean Navarre (MF8/MS12/N67). He had been unruly even as a boy, and many commanding officers found him hard to handle, but his flying skills made up for a lot. 'Navarre was a phenomenon in the air, a real prodigy,' recalled his CO in N67, Captain Henri de Saint Sauveur. 'He devised the range of manoeuvres known as "aerobatics" and spent hours developing them for use in aerial combat . . . I still have enormous admiration for him. I'm very grateful for the enthusiastic, dependable and cheerful way he tackled the missions entrusted to him. And I remain completely in awe of his artistry and skill.' De Rose was similarly charmed and exasperated in turn: 'Navarre always catches you on the hop,' he grumbled. 'Just when you want to put him on a charge, you end up mentioning him in despatches.'

Navarre had made his reputation with MS12 before requesting a transfer to join N67 at Verdun. Anxious to be as close to the front as possible, he moved with his mechanics to the suburb of Faubourg Pavé, well within range of the enemy artillery. He was soon driven back to Vadelaincourt, but as a visible presence in the sky during the darkest days of the German offensive he became a hero to pilots and ground troops alike. Private E. Louis, serving in the trenches with 25th Chasseurs, was one of his admirers: 'Lieutenant Navarre hated to waste a journey, so if there was no prey about he'd use the return trip to entertain the men crouched in the trenches. He absolutely worshipped the poilus. "Is that what they do in the trenches?" he replied, when asked why he didn't keep count of his victories. "No! Then why should I be any different?" Coming back from a sortie he liked to put on a bit of a show. He gave it everything, going through his full repertoire to show us poor sods that he hadn't forgotten us and was doing all he could to divert us.'

On 26 February Navarre shot down two Germans in one day, and exactly two months later he downed four, but on 17 June his career came to an abrupt halt. On patrol with Sous-lieutenant Georges ('Pivolo') Pelletier d'Oisy (HF19/MS12/N69) and Adjudant Urbain Guignand (HF13/N37/N67), he scored his twelfth victory, a two-seater, over Samogneux. Continuing over the Argonne, the three pilots then spotted a German observation machine on an artillery shoot. Navarre deferred to his comrades to open the attack: Pelletier d'Oisy made the first firing pass, but Guignand had disappeared and Navarre decided he would have to join in: 'The Boche focused all his attention on me, [seemingly] angered by the red fuselage I'd adopted to identify myself in the air. I dived into the attack without waiting for Guignand and just as I made another split-S I felt a terrible shock in my arm and chest.' Spitting blood, Navarre managed to land his plane using one arm only: 'I bumped down at Sainte-Ménehould with a bit of a flourish in case this was my last hurrah, bringing the nose into the wind with one of my special grass-cutter turns. The mechanics and the poilus were playing football on the far side of the camp and [I knew] they'd come running over to see what was up. I tried to leave the plane unaided, but my legs gave way as I stood up. I felt faint and shouted for help. The first face I recognized was that of bold Pivolo. Guessing what had happened, he'd stuck to my tail and touched down next to me.'

'Navarre is the leading ace in our service,' claimed Captain Auguste Pinsard (MS23/N26/N78/SPA23). 'He alone managed to give our cockades the better of the black crosses in the skies above Verdun.' Georges Madon (BL30/MF218/N/SPA38) agreed: '[Navarre] reigns supreme among pilots. He is the premier French aviator, the ace of aces in flying and combat. I admire him enormously as I showed . . . by pinching his tactics, methods and even his colours when I found out he wouldn't be returning to the front.' Claude Haegelen (F8/SPA89/100/103) went further still: 'along with the poilus of 304, Vaux and Douaumont, Navarre will remain the true hero of Verdun'.

By late June, when attention switched to Joffre's long-planned offensive on the Somme, the two armies had fought each other to a standstill. Verdun remained in French hands – but at huge cost to the nation's aviators. Around 100 pilots and observers were shot down between February and July 1916: fifty-one were posted as killed or missing, while the wounded included such famous names as Guynemer and Navarre. And on 18 August came a sad postscript to the list of the dead, when Lieutenant Marcel Brindejonc des Moulinais (DO22/N23) was killed in an accident after one of his wings broke up in mid-air.

'Nailed to the sky' – balloons
In 1903 captive and dirigible balloons had seemed to represent the future of military aeronautics, but just a decade later they were in complete eclipse. All production of captive balloons had ceased; the field companies had been disbanded and their balloons mothballed, and only the four fortress companies were still operational. However, the advent of trench warfare on the Western Front immediately changed the situation. Both sides now needed all possible means of observing the enemy, and Joffre acted at once to reinstate and expand the service. Existing balloons were removed from storage and new orders placed, but so great was the competition for resources that only forty were operational by the spring of 1915 – nowhere near enough to cover the Western Front. By January 1915 twenty new balloon companies had been created, with another sixteen to follow over the next year. Plans were then laid for a further seventy-five, thirty-one of which were formed between February and July 1916 during the battle of Verdun and prior to the Somme offensive.

Command of the revamped service went to Captain Jacques Saconney, a pre-war balloon specialist and a particular champion of the man-bearing kite, a flimsy affair consisting of a small one-man basket suspended beneath a chain of fabric-covered frames. Eleven companies were equipped with these kites but few of them ever saw action. In good weather they could provide a useful platform: 'The visibility was very good, bright sunshine, cloudless sky, so I could see over 50 kilometres,' reported Private J. Mathieu. 'The basket was perfectly stable. It didn't move at all. I felt as if I'd been nailed to the sky. It was marvellous.' However, high winds could compromise their effectiveness, as Marc Brillaud de Laujardière soon discovered: 'I had the opportunity to ascend to 600 metres in one of these contraptions on 9 May 1915 during the Artois offensive, but the wind was so gusty I spent all my time adjusting the cables. It made observation almost impossible as well as a complete waste of time.'

As a pre-war kite man, Félix Peaucou (46th Balloon Company) was singularly unimpressed by his experience of the balloon companies: 'The men . . . were nothing like the kite teams. A few old hands and the odd regular apart, they were a real mixed bunch. Only a handful had ever seen a balloon before or knew the first thing about them. And the same was true of the officers. Some were good, excellent even, but they were few and far between, so early in the war urgent action was needed. A call went out to all arms to find officers capable of taking command. Some of those who transferred to aeronautics were intelligent, dynamic and talented, but far too many were shirkers chasing a cushy billet who did a great deal of harm through their stupidity and endless mistakes. They also treated their men appallingly . . . [when] the poor chaps already had quite enough on their plates coping with the giant balloons, as well as the bad weather that complicated their lives even further. Mind you, anyone trying to shirk in the aeronautical service soon realized that we spent all our time dangling from mammoths that made an ideal target for the German gunners, who really let us have it whenever they got the chance.'

France's existing spherical Type E balloons dated back to 1880. They could operate at the relatively high ceiling of 800 metres, but their instability in any wind over 30km/h made their redesign an urgent priority. As a temporary measure the French initially copied the distinctive, elongated enemy *drachen*, and the first 'sausage' entered service as the Type H in early 1915. But when twenty-four French balloons were blown from their moorings during a storm on 5 May 1916, with five observers killed and nine more captured, GQG turned instead to an alternative design produced by a young structural engineer, Albert Caquot.

Newspaper reports suggested Caquot had thought up the idea in his dug-out, but he denied it. 'I didn't think much of the balloons I'd seen at the battle of the Marne, so I did a bit of research and made a series of small improvements to the existing equipment,' he replied modestly. 'I then decided I'd do better to go back to the laws of aerodynamics to see what worked best. I designed a balloon . . . that was tapered and finned so it would remain stable in flight. . . . If you weren't an insider, any suggestion you made was [normally] ignored on principle. The balloon service was full of technical types. It was the next thing to God. Colonel R[ichard, commander of the balloon workshops at Chalais-Meudon] knew virtually nothing about [tethered balloons], so when he received my report he passed it directly to Captain L[enoir], a high-flier in charge of dirigibles, who I later got to know well. "You've really burned the midnight oil here," said L[enoir]. He was the one who, when ordered to come up with a short-term fix, had simply copied the German balloon. It was a nonsense: he hadn't done any proper research, he had just assumed the balloon would work. Then imagine, a complete outsider turns up, blueprints in hand. It was all very irregular.'

With an operational ceiling double that of the *drachen,* and much greater wind resistance, Caquot's design swiftly overcame all the normal bureaucratic hurdles, and his new balloon, officially the Type M, went into immediate production. In January 1918 Caquot was appointed technical director of the aviation service's technical section, a reward for '[his] remarkable work, which over the past two years has led to tremendous advances in ballooning'. He later progressed to a stellar career in structural engineering, designing hundreds of bridges, tunnels and dams, as well as the internal structure of the statue of Christ the Redeemer in Rio de Janeiro.

Launching a captive balloon was a complicated business. Each balloon was inflated, then 'walked' to its launch point by the ground crew: 'Supported 3 or 4 metres off the ground by teams of old soldiers, the big yellow cylinder – 26 metres by 7 – makes slow progress, crumpled, bloated, held captive by its ten towing ropes. Beneath it hangs the rudder, limp and ridiculous. At the captain's chosen launch point, a long armoured vehicle, heavy, low-slung and full of machinery, waits to unspool the tough, thin cable attached to the balloon.

"'Halt!'"

'With much swaying, the "sausage" comes to a halt. The mooring gang hurry beneath its belly, as wrinkled as an old tortoise, and pull frantically on ropes, toggles and suspension gear. A minute later the basket is in place, the cable fixed and the telephone installed.

"'Ready!" says the sergeant-in-charge, elbow on the edge of the basket.

"'Ready!" says the sergeant-telephonist, clutching his headphones.

"'Ready!" says the sergeant-mechanic, three fingers on the drum of the winch.

'Then the observer makes his appearance. He jumps into the unsteady basket. If the weather stays fine he'll be up there for ten, twelve, even fifteen hours at a time. He's usually a sergeant or an adjudant and sports the winged anchor on his left arm. He stands in the willow basket, tests the telephone, sets down his big maps – as bulky as they are indispensable – and places his notebook close to hand. Three pairs of heavy prismatic binoculars hang from one of the toggles, each of a different focal length to be used according to the target. In the corner stands a powerful firearm should he come under direct attack from the air . . . Finally [in go] the knapsack and the thermos with the long-broken spare cup!

'The mooring team move off. The captain approaches the basket.

"'All set then? Possible troop movements behind C. And watch the crossroads. Start by looking for the battery that was in action yesterday. We thought it was to the right of that copse."

"'Ready!" calls the observer.

"'Let go the ballast! Cast off!" replies the leader of the ground crew.

'The "sausage", so formless at ground level, soars into the wide blue yonder and takes shape. At the end of its steel wire, it stretches out and disappears from view. Meanwhile the observer calmly buckles his parachute harness over his shoulders and between his legs as he's hauled up into the sky.'

Whatever the type of balloon, the task of the observer remained the same: 'As long as proper telephone protocol has been established, it's become quite usual for an observer to spot for two or three batteries at a time. Try, if you can, to imagine his daily routine. Each morning he climbs into the balloon, still tired and stiff from past ascents. Wearing his telephonist's helmet, strapped into his parachute, he sits in his willow basket and [tries to] ease the constant roiling of his stomach. Drunk with the wind and light, forced to remain stock still, numb with cold or burned by the sun, hands gripping the binoculars, he stays up there for hours at a time, scanning the sky for one fleeting glimpse, trying to identify a light that lasts under a second, lying in wait like a hunter for the distant flash that betrays an enemy gun, looking for the source of the sparks, scouring the ground between explosions, counting the seconds between the release of a shell and its arrival on target – artillery map unfolded on his knees, estimating, measuring, calculating. As evening falls, he descends to make his report, liaise with the artillery groups or staff and receive any further orders; the following day he checks and updates the target cards and the file on the enemy batteries; the day after that he climbs back into the balloon and starts all over again.'

In the air the observer was always on the alert: 'the wicker basket is his only means of protection, so if an unexpected squall snaps the cable . . . if lightning sets the balloon on fire, if it's bombed by a plane or strafed by incendiaries, if shrapnel shells explode close by, he knows he has only one option. Not a second to spare, unplug the telephone, straddle the edge of the basket, dangle his feet, check the parachute cord won't catch, hang from the basket with both hands, let go, say a Hail Mary and trust in a device that, God willing, will eventually open after ages in free fall.'

The earliest wartime observers received little or no formal instruction. The first batch consisted of volunteers thrown into action straight from the artillery school at Fontainebleau, and specialist schools set up early in 1915 at Châlons-sur-Marne and Saint-Pol were short-lived, closed down when all their staff and students were sent to the front to meet the need for observers during the spring offensive in Artois. Training was eventually formalized in December 1915, with a three-month course, the first month with a balloon company, the second at one of three schools established – one for each army group – at Cramont, Aubigny-sur-Aube and Toul, and the last on probation with a company at the front. 'The observer needs a particular mix of intellectual qualities, and artistic skills are more important than military ones,' claimed General de Langle de Cary, commander of Fourth Army during the 1915 offensives. Indeed, many early recruits were former artists, surveyors or architects – men who could reliably produce an accurate sketch – and even as late as 1918 the members of balloon companies tended to be older than average: long-service officers and conscripts drawn from the pre-war classes.

While the British used the 'clock' method of correcting artillery fire, the French preferred to estimate the actual distance to the target: 'The balloon climbs at an angle, its normal operational height halved by the wind. Up aloft, knees bent, both hands clutching his binoculars, the observer peers out. Although weary, he continues to seek his designated target . . .

'Suddenly the telephone squawks: the observer has spotted something and wants a "chinwag".

'"Target to my right, about 130 metres from the ruined bell tower."

'A few seconds later, "Boom! Boom!"

'The telephone rings again: "Fifty metres long, try another three millimetres right."

'"Boom! Boom!"

'"Thirty metres short."

'"Boom! Boom!"

'"That's it. Fire for effect."

'Immediately the guns begin to rage. An unholy din ensues for the next ten or fifteen minutes. Then the telephone breaks in: "Cease fire. Wait!"

'And that's another section cleared, trench wrecked or fortified farm destroyed.'

Joseph Branche was one of the old hands, a balloonist since his call-up in 1911. Taken prisoner shortly after the outbreak of war, three years later he escaped back to France and rejoined his former service. 'Attempts are sometimes made to compare the role of the balloon with that of the plane,' he remarked, 'but in fact their tasks are completely different. [Balloons] observe a fixed point from space, making it easier to monitor a sector. Planes move too fast. . . . An observer knows the landscape below him by heart. He can look down and stroll around as if he's in his garden at home. He can spot anything that seems out of place or a train unloading a division or heavy equipment.'

On one exceptionally clear day in July 1917 Lieutenant André Perrisin-Pirasset, serving with a balloon company in Flanders, was raised to a record altitude. In one direction his view extended to Dover and Ramsgate, in the other to the Scheldt estuary, Antwerp cathedral and even the dome of the Palais de Justice in Brussels: 'A few minutes later I was at 1,900 metres, 5 kilometres from the lines and 500 metres above the row of Belgian, French and English balloons that marked the front. The exceptionally clear and calm conditions lasted all day, sparing me the usual torture of airsickness. The first call came from the commander of a battery of long 155s, old Banges to be precise, who'd been trying for a while to get his fire corrected properly. Seeing a balloon climbing so high, he thought it might be able to help and called on the off chance. The target was a German battery already spotted several times before. Three 4-round salvoes were loosed towards it. They were extremely accurate thanks to the altitude and visibility, and the customer went away happy. Next came somebody else in a bit of bother, who was equally pleased with his three 4-round salvos. The news spread like wildfire among gunners in need of a bit of spotting. The trickle of calls turned into a flood, and the clerks on the ground were forced to hand out numbers. Everyone was calm and collected, methodical and orderly. Good will and good discipline ruled the day, so the different jobs dovetailed nicely and I completed them quickly. The hours sped by. No relief at midday. We fell so far behind [that] our only option was to call in the planes. They did what they could, but balloons can maintain a constant watch and continuous two-way communication via the telephone, while the aviators only had a rudimentary wireless.'

Close to Manre, Joseph Branche found himself the target of a 240mm naval railway gun firing from the mouth of a tunnel: 'Each time I saw [it] fire, I said "Go" to my telephonist-clerk. He noted the time and then counted the forty-two seconds the shell would take to reach me. Out of the goodness of his heart he warned me every time a shell was about to explode, counting down the seconds until, as he put it, I was blown to smithereens: five, four, three, two, one. Even from a distance of 100 metres, watching a shell of that size explode is an incredible experience. The envelope of the balloon expanded so much with the violence of each shock wave that I thought it was going to burst. You have to wait in the basket for a few seconds before you know whether the balloon has been ripped, or if it's stopped pulling on the cable.' Branche thought the whole day had been a waste of time. 'You can't do any proper spotting under those conditions,' he grumbled. Yet even after thirteen hours in the basket he was in no mood to admit defeat: 'As the light faded that evening, I wanted to stay aloft and stick it out so the Germans couldn't claim they'd downed a balloon. [But] having jettisoned my ballast, around 60 kilos of sand, I was forced to give in. My balloon was starting to descend.'

Branche made it safely back to ground level, where the riggers counted thirty-two holes in the envelope's fabric.

Personal parachutes were first introduced in 1916, and the following year some balloons were modified to allow the observer to detach the whole basket. These developments saved many lives, including that of Charles C., who received a call from his ground team while hovering 850 metres above the lines. An Albatros was heading his way: 'Long, slender fingers seemed to be reaching towards my balloon. The enemy's fire drew closer – and with it, danger. These tracer bullets are ignited by friction in the barrel of the gun. It only needs one to touch the balloon and it's curtains . . . Now two have pierced the "goatskin" and it's burst into flames. Another few seconds and things will be hopeless, a total inferno. No time to hesitate. I've got to dive . . . let's hope the parachute opens! My only memory of the first 35 to 40 metres in freefall is a dreadful feeling of suffocation. But almost immediately a violent jolt hinted that my saviour hadn't forsaken me. The parachute had opened. I'd escaped! . . . Then I descended calmly until my assailant gave me another fright. He'd turned around and was flying back towards me. Did the scoundrel intend to follow me down and see me off at his leisure? I was frightened to death . . . But his only concern was the materiel. As soon as he saw the "sausage" burning, he flew off for good.'

Even if the observer came down safely, he was still not out of the woods. 'One day a plane shot me down from around 1,000 to 1,100 metres,' recalled Joseph Branche. 'I jumped and landed 3 kilometres from the winch. I didn't as yet have one of the detachable parachutes, so the strong wind could have dragged me along the ground, but I was saved by the bushes.' Branche was now duty bound to make a swift return to the fray. 'Any observer who has made a parachute descent must go up again as soon as possible,' insisted balloonist Jean de Cagny. 'The honour of the corps demands it. Either in the neighbouring balloon or in his own if the incendiaries have only pierced it rather than set fire to it – and if, of course, he is unhurt.'

Captive balloons were highly vulnerable to enemy fighters. If the highly flammable hydrogen in the envelope caught fire, a balloon could be reduced to nothing within ten seconds and the observer sent plummeting to earth. '[Our] first balloon was set on fire on 1 October 1915, on the Champagne front, at Hill 204, at Perthes, east of the Somme–Suippes road,' recalled Max Verneuil (10th Company). 'The weather was pretty grim. It was a gloomy day, thick banks of cloud filling the sky with snowflakes. Around 9.30 am Maréchal des Logis Schmidt and his balloon went into a cloud. The balloon to his right descended rapidly. At the same time we could hear two machine guns rattling away behind the grey shroud, along with the sound of an aircraft engine. Down on the ground we conferred uneasily by the winch. We could find no plausible explanation, so we weren't too concerned at that stage. We comforted ourselves by concluding that it was one of our fighters testing his machine gun somewhere above the clouds before regaining our lines. But we wouldn't be left on tenterhooks for long. As the balloon emerged from the cloud, the men on the ground saw a flare sizzle towards it and hit its tail . . . We pushed the old steam-winch as hard as it would go but we could only bring [the balloon] down very slowly. At 600 metres it was a complete inferno. . . . Schmidt was standing in the basket, clinging to the ropes – flames, scraps of cloth and burning cables round his head . . . He landed on a heap of straw, burns to his hands and face, but miraculously unhurt. He said a German aircraft had passed 20 metres from the balloon. The observer was carrying a flare-pistol.'

Protection for the balloons and their observers was provided principally by the French machine guns and anti-aircraft artillery. Post-war statistics suggest that the 75mm field guns pressed into AA work managed to repel three out of every ten enemy attacks; the machine guns, two in every ten. Commanding a battery of 75s, Lieutenant Houel took a realistic view of his chances: 'Anti-aircraft fire is always unpredictable. There are so many variables and errors we can only partially correct for that it all becomes a bit of a lottery. If you consider the potential margin of error in speed, distance and drift, you soon realize you can never be mathematically certain of hitting the target. Bracketing fire is the only effective method against aircraft, bottling up the plane in a narrow box that's difficult to escape from without encountering, if not a direct hit, at least heavy shrapnel. . . . Unfortunately there's a but. This method presupposes a minimum of four guns – well coordinated and firing in unison – but, given the state of our anti-aircraft materiel, we can't often use it. Usually, [in fact] nearly always, you have to make do with a single gun, like me. It isn't impossible to get a result if you know what you're doing, but adjusting fire isn't a paper exercise, you have to act quickly and use a bit of nous. Ideally, you're trying to persuade the enemy that he has several guns firing at him. The important thing is to convince him there's no way through. Hitting him is a bonus. You always hope for a lucky strike, but it would be foolish to devote too much time to it. There's obviously something to my tactics. It's two months since the Boches last managed to target any battery, defensive work or cantonment in the wood that I'm guarding.'

With sufficient notice, French fighters could also be scrambled to defend the balloons. On 1 November 1917, on the Champagne front, the telephone rang in N155's squadron office. Corporal Jean Puistienne took the call: '"Hello! French 'sausage' burning. Tahure sector. Send cover." I left the office. I looked up. Another dazzling light on the horizon. The smoke dispersed . . . Then the telephone rang again. "Hello! Hello! Second sausage burning. Massiges sector. Send somebody now."' The two balloons, from 65th and 67th Balloon Companies respectively, had been flamed by Leutnant Fritz Pütter, a pilot from Jasta 9, who then made off while the going was good. N155 already had several aircraft in the air and Puistienne hurried to join them: 'Crack! A deafening noise, and a black snowflake blossomed just ahead of the Nieuport. A second crack sounded to the right, a third to the left, then another, and another . . . Dark balls appeared from every side, filled out, expanded and slowly unravelled . . . "Baaad!" as the Yankee Wright used to drawl in the mess. I flew into a handy cloud. Silence: the gun was dead. Then a sudden gust of wind brought a burst of machine-gun fire. The mist parted like a curtain. Down below, a cloud of black flies was zigzagging back and forth. My comrades had joined combat [and] I dived in too.'

The dogfight had pitted six planes from Jasta 9 against three Nieuport N24s – flown by Adjudant Georges Guiraut, the American Corporal Harold Wright, and the Argentinian Corporal Geronimo Wilmart – escorting a reconnaissance aircraft from AR16. 'Too late! One of the combatants was already spinning; [then] another plummeted down, a long trail of black smoke snaking out behind him.' Hit by flak, and the Albatri of Jasta 9, the A.R. was forced to land; Guiraut and Wilmart were credited with shooting down one German, but Wilmart fell in flames – probably the victim of Leutnant Otto von Breiten-Landenberg.

And, very occasionally, an observer managed to strike back. Around 3.00 pm on 14 April 1917 Corporal Henri Peltier (71st Balloon Company) was spotting for a French heavy artillery battery near Montenoy. Suddenly he spied a German Albatros D.III, reputedly piloted by Unteroffizier Hermann Jopp (Jasta 37): 'The machine guns had opened fire from below . . . Peltier fired four shots from his Winchester, the last when the plane was barely 25 metres away. Almost immediately he had the pleasure of watching a flame appear from the petrol tank. The Albatros was on fire and eventually hit the ground some 1,500 metres from the balloon.'

'There are fewer and fewer Germans' – the air battle over the Somme

The battle of Verdun was a turning point for military aviation – 'the crucible in which was forged the French aviation service,' according to

General Pétain. For the first time gaining air superiority was a key component of French and German strategy, and air power played a major, continuous part in the action. The battle also demonstrated the value of a specialist fighter formation, and in April Joffre created a new six-squadron *groupement* for his planned Somme offensive, basing it at Cachy, near Amiens, and placing it under the command of Antonin Brocard.

A vital part of the French preparations was the destruction of the enemy observation balloons. On 26 June Adjudant Henry de Guibert (N62) attacked a *drachen* near Chaulnes in his Nieuport 11, with his brother Charles in close attendance: 'I dived almost vertically at about 1,100 revs. The sausage grew very quickly in size and soon filled the windscreen. I waited a few extra milliseconds to be sure, then pressed the button and the rockets departed. So close did I come I thought I'd end up inside [the balloon]. I levelled out and turned my head to see a huge cloud of black smoke and the basket descending at apparently breakneck speed.'

Then the German fighter protecting the balloon joined in the fray: 'I didn't have long to enjoy the spectacle before I heard a machine gun rattling and bullets started whizzing past my ears. I looked all round and to my right spotted a big German twin-fuselage diving down from 300 to 400 metres above me, firing non-stop.' Henry was now 7 kilometres behind German lines, with his brother Charles equally beset and unable to offer any support. He went into a dive but failed to shake off his attacker: 'I fired a good 100 rounds without stopping the beast. We were now at point-blank range . . . I dived full throttle, then immediately pulled my poor old [plane] up so sharply that I seemed to be taking it beyond the perpendicular. My manoeuvre worked. Zooming had slowed me down and brought me out above my adversary. I'd allowed him to continue his descent, and his momentum had taken him past me. I dived [again]. Now it was my turn to give him a good hiding and do my utmost to prove myself the better shot. I used all my forty-seven rounds, and the tracers scored a direct hit on the fuselage. He gave it full throttle, dived at top speed and landed normally.'

Back on the ground there was more good news. Charles too had managed to escape the clutches of the Germans and the brothers were quickly reunited.

On 1 July 1916 Lieutenant Noel de Rochefort and Sergeant Frank Barra (N26) set off from Cachy on another balloon-busting expedition. They were due to escort their comrades Lieutenant Pierre Gaut and Lieutenant Charles Mallet, but the pair were nowhere to be found. 'No sign of the[m], not at the rendezvous, so set off to patrol the lines,' reported Rochefort. 'At

7.00 am I spotted a lone LVG below me. I was over Brie at the time. I swooped down, putting myself behind him and at the same height. He fired at me but as soon as I shot back he stopped and tried to manoeuvre. After thirty rounds he went into a vertical dive. I stuck to his tail for 1,000 metres, firing my last rounds. I levelled out at 2,500 metres and observed the LVG for a few seconds. I spotted no sign of movement. He dropped like a stone but I was able to watch him all the way down. A Fokker biplane and two LVGs swept down on me, then the Boches gave up the chase and I returned to our lines.'

Barra had also decided to make a solo patrol towards Péronne, spotting one enemy aircraft and one balloon in the process. Meanwhile the elusive Gaut, armed with the new Le Prieur rockets, had located the target: 'just as the *drachen* began to descend, my engine started missing. I couldn't attack into the wind so I fired the rockets from a height of 150 metres. Seven out of the eight released correctly. All missed. My engine caught again 50 metres from the ground. Recrossed the lines at 500 metres.' Mallet, too, was close enough to spot the action: '[I watched Gaut] swoop down to take on a *drachen* east of Brie and continue on below it. I followed him down to 1,100 metres and lost sight of him hedge-hopping across the marshland around the river.'

The casualties of Verdun had been replaced by some very raw recruits, causing a certain amount of apprehension among their more experienced comrades. On 14 June, with the build-up in full swing, one bomber officer (VB108) overheard a chance conversation: '[Someone] let slip a direct reference to a planned daylight raid 40 kilometres [behind enemy lines]. I'm rather worried since it's the equivalent of a ground attack. If it has to be, we'll gladly do our bit, but I would appreciate some confirmation so I can give my men extra training in close-formation flying, machine-gunnery, etc. A lot of our pilots are young chaps who won't have a clue.'

In the event these fears proved groundless. From the opening day on 1 July French fighters flying in powerful formations – at 3,000 to 5,000 metres against enemy fighters, and 1,500 to 2,000 metres against the cooperation aircraft – swept the enemy from the sky. The tactics so successfully deployed at Verdun proved equally effective on the Somme, while the arrival of planes like the Nieuport 11, the Nieuport 17 and a superior new type, the SPAD 7 – all fitted with a synchronized Vickers machine gun – meant the French could now match German firepower.

Caught unawares by the concentration of French aircraft, the Germans could summon little in response: just five army cooperation squadrons, three artillery squadrons and around thirty fighters. 'The superiority of the

French squadrons exceeded all our expectations . . . and gave them almost uncontested mastery of the air,' admitted General von Hoeppner, commander of the German Air Service. '[Our] squadrons were weak and quickly neutralized by the engagement en masse of their French counterparts, which could then reconnoitre, join in attacks and even undertake long-range reconnaissance missions unmolested.'

In early July, newly transferred from the Aisne, N15 was sending up patrols and reconnaissance missions over the villages of Chaulnes, Nesle and Ham. 'No sign of enemy aircraft,' stated its reports on 2, 5 and 6 July, and for most of the next month German aircraft were completely absent from the skies, or dived away when the French approached. 'The enemy squadrons were completely demoralized,' claimed Captain Albert Deullin, CO of SPA73. 'Their spotter and short-range reconnaissance machines tried to cross the lines as little as possible, limiting themselves to surprise attacks when the skies were clear. The attack of a lone Nieuport was enough to make their two or four two-seater barrier patrols shy away and disperse. Their single-seaters flew singly or in pairs, manoeuvred badly, systematically refused combat and were almost always easy prey.'

'My fifth victory was a long time coming,' confirmed Adjudant René Dorme (C94/CRP/N3). 'The Germans were fewer and fewer and any we did encounter were definitely growing more wary. It was a misty old day and I was trying to knock out an opponent ahead of me. Just as I was about to roll to avoid him, I hit another plane directly below me. I didn't see it at all. I thought that was it, especially since we were over Bapaume, around 10 kilometres inside Bocheland. All I can remember is the awful sound of the impact. I passed out for a few seconds but then found I'd throttled back and was opposite our lines. I must have manoeuvred instinctively to right myself. Thankfully my plane was sturdy and kept on going.'

Adjudant Gaston Vitalis was flying with C46, a squadron recently re-equipped with a new aircraft type, the Caudron R.4, a three-seater designed for reconnaissance and light bombing. 'We lost no time in leaving for the Somme to do our bit in the attack. It was a perilous mission for a young squadron commander [like] Captain [Didier] Lecour-Grandmaison. He'd worked on the R.4's armament, but few of his pilots shared his confidence in the plane and its abilities. He trained us by example and as soon as the weather permitted he took me over the lines every day on a Boche hunt. This was a perfectly reasonable use of our time as the precise role of the R.4 was still to be decided. We were lucky to begin with. On 15 July 1916, close to Bry [sic], we shot down the R.4's first Boche, part of an enemy group around 100 metres below us. Lieutenant Campion fired first, then I joined in, and the plane eventually crashed on the far side of the Somme. [But] that victory was a one-off. We met fewer and fewer Germans, eventually just one between 20 July and 20 August. We weren't idle, though. That's when we began the photo-reconnaissance missions that made our squadron famous, flying in a group of six to take photographs 15 kilometres beyond the front line.'

High above Sailly-Saillisel, 'or rather what used to be the village', was Sergeant Charles Delacommune (C66). 'The hail of shells was so intense that the smoke from the explosions merged to form one yellowish cloud!' he recalled. 'How could men survive such hell? The sky around us was full of moving dots, sometimes alone, sometimes recombining, like flocks of migrating birds! Above the battlefield was a whole host of aircraft – fighters, spotters, liaison – each performing its allotted task. Such a concentration of planes was completely new to us.'

In the French sector, mostly south of the Somme, the offensive seemed to be making good progress. 'The news is still good,' one pilot wrote home on 5 July. 'Our advance seems an excellent, well-coordinated effort.' But a fortnight later the initial assault was starting to get bogged down, and at least one bomber pilot (VB108) was uncertain of allied progress: 'In the south-east the attack doesn't seem to have produced the expected results. Whatever the case, few believe in a victory this summer. The British [squadrons] aren't yet good enough to give us the joint air superiority we require. [Victory] is more likely to follow this autumn or late next spring.'

Even for the best pilots, air superiority was no guarantee of an uneventful trip. Late July found Yves Le Prieur at Cachy, introducing his new anti-balloon rockets to the aces of N3, and on hand to celebrate Guynemer's eleventh victory. 'I ate with the pilots,' he recalled, 'fraternizing with the aces, idols like Heurteaux, Dorme, Deullin, de Latour and Guynemer – simple men mostly. Guynemer was physically unprepossessing but made up for it with his fighting spirit and an extraordinary capacity for hard work. He didn't waste a second. While his pals relaxed with a glass or two in the mess, he often headed off to the butts for machine-gun practice. Over dinner in the mess one day we heard news of a German plane in the vicinity. Guynemer took off without delay [but] unusually for him was back within half an hour. He landed with difficulty – his propeller was bust. It was immediately obvious the canvas had parted from the frame. He'd located his German [an LVG C] and shot him down, but the synchronizer gear [of his Nieuport 17] had malfunctioned on the final burst, shearing off a propeller blade and causing a lot of vibration. He only just had time to cut his engine. His instruments had been shaken from their mountings. He'd enjoyed a very lucky escape.'

On 18 August Guynemer was back in the air in a new SPAD 7. 'Did you see that I baptized the SPAD?' he wrote to the plane's designer, Louis Béchereau. 'It was all a bit of a lark because there were six of them: an Aviatik at 2,800 metres, an LVG at 2,900 metres, and a group of four Rumplers flying 25 metres apart at 3,000 metres. I dived like a meteor on the Rumpler at 1,800 revs and gave them all a fright. By the time they'd got hold of themselves and their machine guns (what a din!), it was too late.' One of the Rumplers, probably that flown by Unteroffizier Johannes Schröter and Leutnant Paul Wagner (FA108), provided Guynemer with his fourteenth victory.

More were to follow: an Aviatik on 14 September, a Rumpler on 15 September, and two Fokker Eindeckers on 23 September. But as Guynemer returned to his lines, the unfamiliar silhouette of his new aircraft provoked a reaction from the French anti-aircraft batteries and a shell hit the upper wing, sending the SPAD into a near-fatal spin. 'I ended up crash-landing a few metres from the battery,' the ace later told Jacques Mortane. 'They were very cut up about it. It was me who had to buck them up a bit. They were sure they'd killed me. But it shows the handiness of our anti-aircraft guns. If hitting a SPAD at 3,000 metres isn't a bull's eye, I don't know what is.'

The Germans had by now recovered air parity, thanks to precisely the kind of technical, tactical and organizational response predicted by Paul du Peuty. Enemy squadrons had been transferred from Verdun and new aircraft types despatched to the front, just as the French SPAD 7 was beset by teething troubles. 'Our fighters were hampered by the problems that inevitably follow any change of equipment,' explained Captain Philippe Féquant (N65). 'The new enemy planes [the Albatros D.I and D.II] outclassed our Nieuports, but the SPAD represented a considerable advance. Its speed, approaching 200km/h, manoeuvrability and the firepower of its synchronized Vickers machine gun made it king among aircraft, but a whole host of minor difficulties with its armament and Hispano engine remained unresolved. In addition, the pilots and mechanics were still unfamiliar with the new plane and hadn't worked out how to get the best from it. In short, with all the mechanical problems and hold-ups, the aces had stopped downing any Boches.'

Resuming the ground offensive on 3 September 1916, the French had met with immediate success, taking large sections of the German front line just north of the Somme and around Chaulnes at the southern end of the battlefield. Some of the newly captured ground was quickly relost, but elsewhere the French infantry continued edging forward until the attacks petered out in early November. Straining every sinew to keep pace, N15 spent most of the autumn in regular combat, losing two pilots on a contact patrol on 6 September, including its CO, Captain René Turin, killed over the German lines at Vermandovillers. 'He volunteered for a particularly important and dangerous infantry observation mission,' read his posthumous mention in despatches. 'He descended to a handful of metres above the enemy. They rushed to attack him and he fell gloriously in their midst.'

To accompany their powerful new Albatros, the Germans had also introduced a new fighter formation, the elite Jasta, each five to ten machines strong. For Jasta 2, the German ace Captain Oswald Boelcke had followed the example of de Rose and assembled some of the best pilots in the service, among them Erwin Boehme, Hans Reimann and Manfred von Richthofen, the future 'Red Baron'. 'The squadrons had suffered several days of heavy losses during their photographic and reconnaissance missions,' recalled Adjudant Paul Tarascon (N3/N31/SPA62). '"Downed by a red Albatros," stated the reports, so I volunteered to protect them. On day two, the patrol set off to photograph the lines while I climbed higher to assess the situation. As I expected, the famous red Albatros came hurtling towards me and a stirring encounter ensued. After three or four passes and a fierce exchange of machine-gun fire, [von Richthofen] quite literally flew straight at me . . . He passed just a couple of metres beneath my wing, and as he did so raised his arm in greeting! . . . It took my breath away. I can still see him now waving to me in his black balaclava. We were both out of ammunition . . . and I wanted to withdraw without seeming to run away. I banked and pointed my Lewis gun up in the air so he could see it. Then we both flew off, each to his own side. It was a pleasure to meet this knight of the air.'

'We can draw two conclusions from the period since the Verdun campaign,' reckoned Major Paul Armengaud, aviation commander of Central Army Group. 'Operating in groups confers an advantage and so too does taking the offensive. We must match numbers with numbers.' For Captain Henri Langevin (N65/312/12/313), the time had come to give fighters their independence. 'Fighter squadrons already have specialized aircraft, dedicated armaments and a particular role in battle,' he wrote on 21 September 1916. 'What they need now are their own pilots, tactics and doctrine. They form a separate arm of service, no less than the cavalry which reconnoitres and attacks, the artillery which makes the breakthrough, and the infantry which occupies. The common doctrine which defines any autonomous trade, profession or arm of service will follow once they have freed themselves from other branches of aviation.'

Langevin's appeal was ignored. However, General Joffre was prepared to make his provisional fighter *groupements* a permanent feature of the order of battle, and in October and November 1916 he created three permanent fighter groups (variously known as Groupes de Chasse or Groupes de Combat) under the direct control of GQG: GC11 (commanded by Le Révérend); GC12, the former Groupement de Cachy (Brocard); and GC13 (Féquant). 'It was clear that fighting enemy aviation on favourable terms in active sectors [of the front line] demanded squadrons specifically trained in aerial combat, grouped together and acting under the orders of a single commander,' he later remarked.

'Air superiority is our main priority,' stated GQG. 'It is vital to operational success and must be sought throughout the battle. [It is based upon] numerical advantage, the quality of our personnel and materiel, the effective deployment of these resources, and effective liaison with other arms of service (particularly the artillery and the machine guns).' Operating through de Rose's system of permanent patrols – 'essential if our fighter squadrons are to intervene rapidly against enemy aircraft' – the new fighter groups would try to secure control of the air by combating German fighters, attacking the enemy balloons and conducting long-range reconnaissance missions. They were also authorized to respond immediately to targets of opportunity on the ground: 'A group commander may order enemy troops to be bombed or strafed as soon as their presence is reported, whether in concentration, on the march, embussing or debussing.'

The fighter groups were explicitly offensive in purpose, providing cover for cooperation squadrons, bombers and ground troops by indirect means. Barrier patrols and escort duties were the least important of their designated tasks, to be undertaken only in exceptional circumstances. 'So-called barrier patrols are always a waste of time,' explained Captain Étienne Cheutin, aviation commander of Tenth Army. 'The protection they provide is purely illusory. The crux of offensive action is to bring numbers to bear against a given point, and it is impossible to be everywhere at once.'

However, army and corps commanders were hard to convince: they found the specialist fighter squadrons remote and unresponsive – particularly after command of the Groupement de Cachy was transferred upwards from Sixth Army to General Foch's Northern Army Group in September 1916. What they wanted was an immediate, visible presence in the skies, not a self-proclaimed elite more interested in glory hunting across the German lines, and by late October Foch was forced to accede to their demands. The pressure exerted by resurgent German air power had become irresistible and two permanent barrier patrols were introduced on Sixth Army's front.

Regaining air superiority would also require new tactics. Boelcke had spent the summer devising sophisticated collective manoeuvring techniques for the new German Jastas, and the French needed to respond in kind. '[Early in] the [Somme] offensive, the lone single-seater was king,' explained Albert Deullin (MF62/N3/SPA73). '[Our] patrols served only to drive off the enemy. Everything fled when they approached, only to return when they departed, so they could hardly shoot down any Boches. In contrast, a lone single-seater could use cunning, hide more easily in sun, mist or cloud, take advantage of his opponent's blind spots and launch lightning strikes impossible for a big patrol. But gradually the situation changed. Learning from experience, the enemy coordinated his efforts and formed flawlessly disciplined two-seater and single-seater patrols. Their cohesion enabled them first to resist any solo attacks, then to take the offensive and quite easily bring down any Frenchman venturing across the lines. After a number of fruitless and sometimes painful experiences, our fighters had to accept that the era of the lone wolf was over. We had to find an alternative.'

While de Rose had always believed that a fighter pilot '[should] be humble enough to set aside short-lived personal triumph and fight alongside [his] comrades', actual combat had thus far remained an individual joust. 'Every pilot fights as he pleases, greatly reducing the combat potential of the group as a whole,' complained Pétain on 2 July. 'We need to devise a doctrine.' On the Somme Sixth Army ordered a basic combat unit of two fighters and a patrol strength of three pairs of two, but actions continued to break down into individual dogfights and fighter tactics remained primitive. The French then considered using a full ten-strong squadron. And with good reason, thought Captain Marcel Jauneaud, commander of MF71: 'The squadron is a company, and like all companies it fights in a group under a single command. Its main strengths are its discipline, teamwork and experience of collective manoeuvring.' But ten planes soon proved impractical: 'Forming up was a long and laborious business,' countered Deullin. 'It was just about possible to fly together in a straight line, but the group dissolved into complete chaos at the slightest hint of a manoeuvre. And that's without mentioning combat, when every man did as he pleased, with no agreement on tactics, no discipline, the leader powerless to rein them all in, angrily stamping on his rudder bar and cursing darkly into the wind. We had to simplify things. We came up with the three-man patrol and after a few false starts it produced good results.'

The French also needed more and better aircraft. 'The operations on the Somme have provided a startling demonstration of the absolute necessity of achieving air superiority,' warned Foch. 'It gave our observation squadrons and balloons the opportunity to work in favourable conditions, while condemning their enemy counterparts to remain at low altitude behind their own lines. The Germans suffered considerably as a result and are now doing all they can to snatch it back, building more planes, concentrating squadrons in the active sectors [of the front], deploying them in a more attacking role [and] appointing one of their leading generals to head the aviation service. If we are to achieve air superiority in future battles, our squadrons need immediate and substantial reinforcement. We should concentrate our efforts on two areas in particular: increasing the number of fighter squadrons and replacing our current reconnaissance aircraft with a better type. The [Farman and Caudron] reconnaissance aircraft now in service no longer meet current needs. They are too slow and their field of fire is restricted by large blind spots. They cannot take off in high winds nor combat the routine reconnaissance aircraft and barrier patrols inevitably encountered in the course of their missions. They are "easy meat" for German pilots. Replacing them with faster types (150km/h), better suited to combat, is our main priority.'

'But still we got through' – the bombing war falters
From the autumn of 1915 the lack of effective bomber types and adequate fighter cover had led to the temporary demise of strategic and reprisal raids, particularly in daylight. A plan to revitalize the bombing effort via the Escadre Michelin, bringing together a hundred BM machines under the command of Lieutenant de Vaisseau Charles Dutertre, was first scaled back and then abandoned in January 1916, although an eventual resumption of strategic and reprisal activity was not discounted: 'While some targets may lie beyond our current capabilities, we must start planning now,' instructed General Joffre. 'Very long-range raids are extremely important for morale, and better aircraft types will gradually bring them within reach, first for individual planes, then for groups.' But in the short term the bomber groups were diverted to tactical and short-range targets: Joffre permanently transferred command from GQG to the individual armies, and each army group was ordered to produce a bombing plan, covering ongoing targets 'such as major stations, rail hubs [and] known factories and airfields', as

well as 'liaison missions conducted in conjunction with operations planned on [its] front, especially those directed against enemy lines of communication and installations, [whether] immediately behind the front line or further to the rear'.

At Verdun the bombers attempted to strike back against the invader: MF25, C66, V101 and V110 all undertook daylight raids against railway lines, munitions dumps and bivouacs during March and April 1916, but the losses were deemed unacceptable and the raids were discontinued. Tactical missions intensified once again during the battle of the Somme in July, when troop concentrations, camps and assembly areas were targeted and enemy airfields were also sought out and hit. However, the concentration of fighter resources demanded by these two major offensives left French bombers in other sectors of the front struggling with inadequate fighter cover. Around Belfort and Luxeuil at the eastern end of the line the losses sustained by GB4 during a 100-kilometre round trip to bomb Habsheim airfield and Mulhouse station in March 1916 demonstrated all the dangers of the daylight raid. All twenty bombers – thirteen Farman MF.11s, four Farman F.42s [sic] and three Breguet-Michelins, one armed with a 37mm cannon – were pushers unable to defend themselves against attacks from the rear; the three Caudron G.4 escorts supplied by C34 and C61 were ineffective; and the Nieuports lacked the range to accompany them beyond the German lines.

Led by Major Maurice Happe, GB4 left Belfort at 3.00 pm on 18 March 1916. The planes crossed the front line and '[that was when] the fun started,' reported Caporal Jean de Gaillard. 'We were met by a swarm of Boches.' Sergeant Édouard Leroy and Captain Victor Bacon were attacked from the rear by a Fokker: 'Leroy tried to resist: a few shots and the Farman came down in flames. Beside the aircraft, a small dark shape fell fast, burning like a torch and trailing smoke. Captain Bacon had realized he was finished and jumped.'

With one blast of his 37mm cannon, Lieutenant Michel Marinkovitch, a Serb, 'brought down a huge German, armed with several machine guns. The shell went clean through the fuselage and tore the monster to shreds. You could see the debris tumbling through the air.' On his first operational mission, Sergeant Henri Rins rammed a German and took his opponent down with him. So too did Lieutenant Robert Floch. Lieutenant Léon Mouraud (MF123) was wounded by anti-aircraft fire as soon as he crossed the front line but flew on regardless, just making it back to the French side before dying from his injuries. Adjudant Robillot and his observer Lieutenant Patriarche were also wounded: Robillot blacked out at the controls but was revived by Patriarche, and the pair survived. Maréchal des Logis René Weisé managed to coax his aircraft home, his propeller shattered by a shell-burst.

In total, four of the two-man crews failed to return, four men were wounded, one fatally, and nearly every plane was damaged to some extent: 'Still we got through,' concluded de Gaillard, 'the captain at our head. We bombed Habsheim and returned to our lines. The Boches accompanied us as far as the front line but declined to venture further since our Nieuport fighters were on guard.'

On 1 April 1916 GB4 moved 50 kilometres north-west to Luxeuil, where they were joined on attachment by the fighters of N124, the Lafayette Escadrille, in that squadron's first operational posting. On arrival, Captain Georges Thenault took his eight pilots to meet their new group commander: 'As [we] walked into the office, [Major Happe] was addressing eight small boxes, sealed with red wax, set out on the table before him. I asked him what he was doing. With great composure, he replied, "Each box contains a Croix de guerre. I'm sending them to the families of the eight pilots [and observers] shot down by the Boches during the recent raid on Habsheim."

'This was a less than reassuring start. My men looked at each other in silence. Happe continued: "During the mission, one of the pilots, Lieutenant Floch, his machine in flames, rammed his opponent, a big three-seater, and took it down with him. The Germans have informed us that the two Frenchmen and three Germans have been buried in Habsheim cemetery."

'The losses sustained by this group were too heavy for the meagre results produced. That's why we'd been sent to Luxeuil to act as escorts. "Get yourselves settled in quickly so we can start working together," concluded Happe.

'I assured him that my pilots and I wanted exactly the same thing. We couldn't wait for our planes to arrive. I promised him we'd take good care of the "flock" entrusted to us.'

On 1 June 1916, a glorious summer's day, the Germans were attacking Fort Vaux, north-east of Verdun. At 12.45 pm two waves of enemy bombers raided Bar-le-Duc, the southern terminus of the Voie Sacrée, the lifeline carrying vital supplies and reinforcements to the front. The townsfolk had just finished their midday meal when the roar of engines sounded in the skies above. They left their houses to watch 'as if it were an air display' and casualties were high: sixty-four people died and many more were injured. On 3 June the victims were given elaborate funerals, the mourners led by the wife of President Raymond Poincaré, and the following day the local newspaper, *Le Réveil de la Meuse*, reminded its readers of the need to seek shelter: 'When the birds of ill-omen are sighted, caution must outweigh curiosity. This is no time for sabre-rattling, and a judicious retreat to the cellars is not a mark of cowardice.' Nevertheless a second raid on the evening of 16 June brought another seven deaths.

Although GQG was conscious that a 400-kilometre round trip over enemy territory without fighter escorts was a perilous undertaking, the calls for retaliation were irresistible. The town of Karlsruhe was selected as the target, and C66, based at Malzéville, was chosen to undertake the mission. At noon on 22 June nine aircraft took off together under the command of Captain Henri de Kérillis. Sergeant Jacques Rapin had to drop out with engine trouble even before the squadron had crossed the lines, but 20 kilometres into German-held territory he rejoined the formation, having swapped his crippled plane for the squadron hack. The flight seemed endless, recalled pilot Charles Delacommune, until around 3.00 pm Karlsruhe came into view, 'apparently sleeping on a bed of mist from which rose steeples, roofs and domes'. But Delacommune could also see people: 'I recoiled for a moment before this awful realization. Are we no less cruel than our enemies? But then another image loomed before me: the eighty-eight [sic] dead of Bar-le-Duc, women, children too, horribly mutilated by lethal shells. The [Germans] had killed, and so would we!'

The French believed they were targeting the railway station, but a new one had opened in 1913 and the old building was now home to Hagenbeck's Circus, its matinee performance in full swing. In what became known locally as the 'Massacre of the Innocents', 117 people were killed and 152 injured. 'Justice done!' reckoned Delacommune. Corporal Fournet and his observer were forced down by engine trouble over the town and taken prisoner, while his comrades turned around into a strong headwind. They flew high enough to remain beyond the reach of the German fighters, but when Sergeant Bousquet and his observer began to fall behind and lose height, they were shot down and killed. The remaining seven aircraft split into two groups and flew on, but 40 kilometres from the lines they began to run short of fuel. Suddenly Sergeant Seitz dived, one engine dead. He tried – and failed – to regain lost height. No alternative: observer Lieutenant Mirabail waved farewell to his comrades and started dumping surplus weight overboard. The pair landed safely, but they too were captured. After safely negotiating anti-aircraft fire over Lunéville, the six survivors eventually staggered home. Two pilots – including de Kérillis – were forced to make an emergency landing near Toul, while a third ran out of fuel and glided into the French lines peppered with bullet-holes.

By late June the Germans were bombing the airfield at Luxeuil with impunity. Tired of requesting support from a separate squadron, Happe demanded urgently – but in vain – that fighters be integrated into his bomber squadrons. 'GB4 cannot defend itself adequately and is doomed to perish without the fighters I have repeatedly requested,' he wrote angrily on 25 June 1916. 'Each squadron needs five machines: two 110hp Rhône Nieuport 11s and three 110hp Rhône Nieuport 12s per squadron if I restrict myself to the types currently available or, if we really have requested 200 Sopwiths [from the British], five Sopwiths per squadron. All I have left are five [Farman] F.43s and three Nieuport two-seaters. As this is "Suicide Corner", perhaps GB4 might be moved to a sector that can make better use of its excellent personnel.'

On 14 July 1916 Adjudant Henri Baron (F123) decided to celebrate Bastille Day with some impromptu action: 'he went to pay a call on the enemy, drop a few bombs and put on a bit of a firework display. Precise and methodical, slow but sure in word and deed, Baron never left anything to chance. Once over the target, he could have released his load and scarpered. But no. He was there to bomb Mulhouse so that's what he was going to do – without any chance of a mistake. He descended to 500 metres to be sure of hitting the target [and] dropped two 200mm shells plumb on the station. . . . He decided to hang about until he could see some proof of his passage, but he wanted to keep busy. Another dive took him below 200 metres while his gunner fired 110 rounds at the barracks, then he diverted his attention to the Mulhouse–Basel train.'

The following day Baron set off again, only to be thwarted by engine trouble. Two days later he was back over Mulhouse, and on 2 September he set out for the powder works at Rottweil: 'Unable to see the works, he descended, then descended again to 300 metres, but he still couldn't spot the target. . . . He spent forty-five minutes at 200 to 300 metres, dodging the shells.' Eventually, even the dogged Baron had to admit defeat. He turned reluctantly for home and dropped his bombs instead over the station at nearby Villingen-Schwenningen.

By the autumn of 1916 the French were once again contemplating strategic missions in support of the Somme offensive. When GB4 took part in an eighty-strong raid with the Royal Naval Air Service on the Mauser works at Oberndorf am Neckar on 12 October, Nieuports from N68, N75 and N124 were positioned on the right of the bomber formation in an attempt to mask the German airfields at Habsheim, Ensheim and Freiburg – a tactic described as 'most useful' in GB4's war diary. A diversionary raid south of Mulhouse was also successful 'in holding five enemy aircraft 50 kilometres south of the route followed by the bomber squadrons'. GB4 claimed five enemy aircraft shot down during the raid, all behind the German lines, including two over Germany itself. However, these successes came at great cost. Combining slow Breguet-Michelins and Farmans with the faster Sopwith caused difficulties in maintaining formation; the Nieuports could only travel part of the way; the pushers remained unsuitable for daylight raids; and ten of GB4's forty-one machines were lost with their pilots – among them the unfortunate Henri Baron.

According to GB4's war diary, the losses sustained – one of the fifteen Sopwith 1½ Strutters, two of the twelve Farman F.42, three of the seven Breguet-Michelin BM.5, and four of the seven Breguet-Michelin BM.4 – accurately reflected 'the relative worth of [these] different types in terms of their ability to defend themselves and maintain formation. The number of aircraft that returned without dropping their bombs [five F.42 and five Sopwiths] reflects the poor quality of the Farman F.42 series and its 130hp Renault engine and the difficulties experienced by the Sopwiths in formating properly in the mist. We may be able to resume very long-range raids without significant losses, once [M]F29, [M]F123 and BM120 have been converted to Sopwiths and can operate missions with the British.'

The Oberndorf raid was a disaster for the French. In the short term Happe was forced to make do with more Farmans, and his squadrons were restricted to night bombing. MF29 and MF123 were fully re-equipped with Sopwith 1½ Strutters in November and December 1916 – though by then the Sopwith too was virtually obsolete as a bomber – and long-range actions during 1917 were limited to a handful of reprisal raids and a few under-resourced attempts late in the year to blockade the important iron-and-steel producing areas of Lorraine and Luxembourg by cutting their rail links with Germany. Meanwhile BM120 had to soldier on with the under-powered, under-armed Breguet-Michelin BM.4 until it was replaced by the fast, modern Breguet 14 in September 1917.

Enemy fire remained just one of the hazards faced by bomber crews. Working out of Salonika, Captain M. was flying as observer on a night raid over Serbia when he noticed that one of his two bombs had failed to release properly: 'It was caught among the wires of the undercarriage with the risk it would explode on landing. Making light of the darkness, he stood up, climbed out of the plane, squeezed between the cables, worked his way under the cockpit with some terrifying acrobatics, unhooked the projectile and dropped it on the enemy . . . After this vertiginous manoeuvre 800 metres in the air, he then clambered back in and resumed his seat.'

However, such bravery went largely unrewarded. 'A fighter pilot notching up five victories can have his name broadcast to the world. But a pilot completing 100 bombing raids, 200 spotting missions or 300 reconnaissance flights can only be identified by his initials,' complained Jacques Mortane. 'Our pilots are all part of the same service and they cannot understand why some are entitled to publicity while others have to remain anonymous. There is simply no justification for it. . . . By any yardstick the bomber pilot is a hero. . . . He carries tons of explosives in a plane most likely to be heavy, inadequately armed, difficult to manoeuvre and incapable of defending itself. He never deviates for a second from the direct route to the target, scorning guns and planes alike, aware of the terrible death awaiting him if he falls victim to a successful attack. Yet still he carries on because it is his duty to do so.'

'More like a family' – squadron life

'The [squadrons in late 1914] were nothing like as organized or disciplined as they are today,' commented 'R.S.' in 1917. 'There was a certain spirit of anything goes. It may sometimes have harmed the service, but it was accompanied by an enormous good fellowship that is now increasingly less apparent. It was more like a family than a squadron. . . . From the humblest of deeds to the most heroic, mutual reliance plus a strong desire to do the right thing were much more important than discipline. Each pilot had his favourite observer and they formed a team. They worked closely together and developed an unwavering trust and camaraderie. We felt our losses much more keenly then. When a comrade fell, you really were mourning a brother.'

The accommodation provided for the squadrons varied enormously in type and quality, from chateaux to village houses, Adrian huts and tents. 'Pol' was one of the lucky ones, billeted in a small village, in a 'chateau' with a view of Reims on a clear day. 'The pilots travelled to their planes in low-slung racing cars, while a variety of improbable vehicles, all petrol-driven, shuttled the mechanics between the hangar and the workshop . . . Everyone showed the cheerfulness characteristic of the squadron. No one ever appeared without a smile on his face. It was de rigueur, part of the uniform, worn by everyone from captain to cook – any time, anywhere . . . There were no "aces" among them, even if some deserved that title. Few were fighter pilots. They were the breed that handled all the tough jobs unheralded by the communiqués – reconnaissance, spotting, even bombing raids. Eight such men, in four aircraft, flew sixteen missions in one night over the same target, releasing a deluge of bombs. . . . Their billet was the "chateau" . . . a vulgar, pretentious edifice. With a little ingenuity they had managed to make it, if not elegant, then at least habitable. They could do nothing to alter the exterior and remove the bits of "renaissance" sculpture decorating the roof of the place, but they did contrive to introduce some hitherto unknown warmth to the interior. They . . . hung jolly cartoons next to the "ancestral" portraits, and put recent photographs – nothing too racy, mind – beside the old-fashioned bric-a-brac on the side tables. They took down the heavy, dusty curtains hanging over the beds. The aroma of cigarettes replaced a general air of mustiness, and technical books, maps and cheap novels ousted the fine bindings in the unread library. At first-floor windows more familiar with stylish peignoirs and immaculate skirt suits, rough hands now shake out, brush and clean flying-suits torn and stained in the cockpit . . . On the ground floor, the captain has cleared the drawing room of furniture and set up his office. Shorn of their lace curtains, the windows now look straight out on to the countryside. The antique clock no longer mumbles away, but the telephone still rings brightly. Everything has been given a new lease of life, including the rusty old bell that . . . calls them for meals. . . . The chateau – the squadron's den – is bedlam.'

When Sergeant Emile Jannekyn joined the newly formed N155 near Châlons-sur-Marne in July 1917 he was equally delighted with his more modest accommodation: 'Not half bad, this Camp de Melette. Top-quality Adrian huts with revolving doors, and glazed windows rather than oiled canvas. Sandy paths wind between them through the pines. Everything is well maintained and it rather resembles an English bungalow village.' R.S. was also satisfied with his situation: 'Our squadron was in Artois, nicely encamped in a field next door to a railway line. We were on the outskirts of B[ruay-la-Buissière], a little village in the Pas-de-Calais, where everyday life carried on cheerfully enough despite the occasional, sometimes fairly heavy, bombing raid. Pilots, mechanics, observers and drivers left the camp each day at dawn – by road or air – for a little airfield close to the lines where we awaited our orders from the army commander. We were very close to Vermelles, scene of many glorious dogfights, and the slightly elevated position of our airfield gave us a perfect view of the bombing raids round and about.'

However, Armand Viguier (VB107), a Tarnais from the balmy south-west, found northern France much less to his liking. '[We're billeted in] a very small village west of Saint-Pol-sur-Ternoise,' he reported on joining his squadron at Humières in October 1915. 'Damp single-storey houses in the middle of the huge, flat beetroot fields of the north. Every Sunday, the peasants head to the local estaminet to down their "*bistouille*", an evil mixture of [chicoried] coffee and local rotgut!'

Many aircrew lived a nomadic existence, and the Adrian huts, tents and Bessonneau hangars were all designed to be easily dismantled and re-erected as squadrons moved around the front. 'Since 1916 the squadron has encamped . . . on fields of all kinds, at the edge of a wood, or in the shelter of an orchard if the fruit trees survive,' said Captain Z. 'We're far from a village so the day-to-day life of the squadron unwinds between the Bessonneau hangars and the Adrian huts. Airfields this close to the line are often subject to enemy artillery fire [and] whenever the night is clear enough the German bombers come and plaster the field and huts.'

'My tent is in a field next to some farm buildings,' related Charles Biddle, stationed close to Bergues with SPA73, 'and the pasture is full of horses, cows and three or four big fat sows. The latter are very inquisitive and every now and then try to come in and pay us a visit, but a heavy army shoe, well placed in the spare ribs, generally results in indignant grunts and a hasty withdrawal. We came in one day to find them all asleep in our tent.' Carroll Winslow (MF44/N112) also slept in a tent – albeit one with added amenities. 'Our cots were raised on wooden platforms,' he remembered. 'At one end we fitted a shower bath, for which purpose a gasolene tank punctured with holes proved ideal.' But there was no such luxury for André Duvau (BR29). 'I'm very nicely billeted in the back of beyond, 7 or 8 kilometres from [the nearest] town,' he told his family. 'The only thing missing is water.'

The basic requirements for an airfield were very simple: 'Whether landing, or picking up speed to take off against the wind, an aircraft needs a piece of hard, even ground, open in all directions'. 'Pol' described a typical field and its hazards: 'Any trees, telegraph lines or nearby houses force [the pilot] to climb or descend too quickly, risking a stupid accident. The smallest clod of earth or furrow can make the plane nose over or break the propeller, endangering the crew. In winter a frozen molehill can scythe the undercarriage clean off. An old hand who senses an unexpected bump will guess what has happened and land immediately. If nothing arouses the pilot's suspicions, both he and his plane will meet their maker on their return.' Good road access was also vital. When a squadron moved, the aircraft could fly to the new base, but everything else had to go by road. At least thirty lorries were needed – eighteen to move equipment, petrol and spares, and another twelve for the two Bessonneau hangars – plus a fleet of other vehicles for the huts, tents, mechanics, clerks, armourers, cooks and hangar erectors.

In 1917 the journalist René Chavagnes visited the base occupied by GC12, the famous Cigognes or 'Storks': 'The airfield is surrounded by Bessonneau hangars and SFA [Société des Fabrications de l'Aviation] tents. The hangars house between eight and twelve SPADs and can be erected by specialists in forty-eight hours. One has a windsock, rather like a butterfly net, to show the pilots which way the wind is blowing. Some squadrons fly their flags above their tents – unit and individual. When the pilots are off-duty, the big tobacco-coloured hangars are closed and resemble a herd of mammoths frozen on the plain. . . . On hot summer days nothing moves. Flying is hard work, so the pilots find a patch of shade and take their siesta lying in a circle. Occasionally you can hear the hum of a phonograph some obstinate music-lover has failed to return to the mess. A while later come a few sharp retorts from the carbines, the rattle of machine-gun exercises, the sudden revving and backfiring of engines under test. The small grey tents and the big hangars stand half open . . . [Then] led by the mechanics, the SPADs slowly emerge and roll across the airfield. They look rather like penguins. But come patrol time, no force can contain their tremendous power. The engines vroom, the air trembles, then suddenly they hurtle over the ground, their propellers dazzling [in the sun]. You watch as they climb together and muster in the air. The fighters are off on their rounds.

'For serious matters, the life of the group revolves entirely around the Intelligence Office; for the more frivolous, the bar. Each is equally important in its own way. The former is housed in an SFA tent with tiny, rectangular portholes for windows – wood framed and tape latticed. The only furniture, and only decoration, is provided by some whitewood trestle tables, chairs – some of them canvas – two telephones and a few chests filled with maps and reports. When the communiqués come in, the sector artillery map provides a guide to operations. Photos of enemy fighters adorn the opposite wall . . . A chart with photographs of British types reminds younger pilots of the need to distinguish one plane from another. On the wall facing the door hangs a huge map of the French front from the sea to Alsace, marked out with the inevitable string. Yet more maps decorate the temporary partitions. Among the most important is that showing enemy airfields photographed from the air or identified via intelligence sources. The order from GC12 designating the squadron of the day is pinned up next to the weather forecast, along with a list of duty officers, another of reports due, and a tally of the 11mm Desvignes incendiary rounds fired by the Vickers guns. At the table in the centre of the room where the pilots sit to write their reports, intelligence bulletins on French and German aircraft, GQG's air operations summary, copies of *La*

Guerre aérienne illustrée, patrol reports and an album of aerial photographs are passed around. Since all our fighter pilots are blessed with a sense of humour as well as fighting spirit, one notice, attributed by evil rumour to the adjutant, Captain de Billy, is addressed to them. "Pilots are requested to treat the contents of the Intelligence Office with respect. Even when compelled to do so by the force of your tactical or strategic ideas, please don't tear or otherwise damage the maps. And as you so expertly manoeuvre your armies, or explain the law of gravity and its effect on bomber tactics, please don't break the pencils and penholders or upset the inkwells."'

Off-duty pilots headed to the bar: '[GC12's] bar is an oblong table with pilots in front of it and bottles behind. A barman dashes between the two, trying to reconcile the natural thirst of his chums, his desire to please, and the need to go to Paris to restock. The barman has the advantage of his fellows in one respect: he's acquiring a profession for after the war. Of course, since bars are an American innovation, the real gamblers will only play poker. The bar is home to the *Club des Cigognes* ('Storks Club'), whose furniture is no less basic than that in the Information Office: just two long trestle tables and some folding garden chairs. Here the young "assassins" gather to play draughts and ludo or flick through the magazines. Photographs of Auger, Dorme, Brocard, Guynemer and de la Tour, still among the great names of GC12, provide the only decoration in the club, where the Storks can practise the fine art of issuing invitations to comrades from other arms of service. In the mess tent next door a woollen stork presides over the feasts of the "musketeers". With its black and white wings, pink legs and beak, adorned with the lanyard [of the *Croix de guerre*], it's a copy of the stork presented to the group by Mme Herriot [wife of the minister of transport]. Above the table hangs the satin *fanion* of SPA3 – a stork within a diamond embroidered on a background of [red, white and blue] – decorated with the *Croix de guerre* and lanyard.'

'What a magnificent way of waging war,' mused observer Paul Hatin (N3). 'Hygienic, comfortable, senses constantly engaged, the feeling of doing something useful. There's really nothing like it.' Jean Beraud-Villars (MF44/N102/N85) agreed: 'We're the privileged members of a privileged service, a bourgeoisie among the other arms of service. Pay, accommodation, interesting white-collar work, chivalrous individual combat, praise, the prospect of a mention in despatches: privileges every one of them.'

The young men of the aviation service certainly had money to burn. By 1918 an officer pilot received an extra 10 francs per day flying pay; an officer observer, half that amount. Adjudants, sergeants and corporals received 5, 4, and 2 francs respectively when flying as pilots, and half rate when flying as observers. Mechanics and craftsmen received an extra 75 centimes to 1 franc 50 centimes in skill pay. In addition, all aircrew received a year's seniority on gaining their wings, and a further six months' seniority for every year spent as aircrew.

Some of this bounty was evidently spent on uniform. 'General X was inspecting a group of pilots one day when he realized that no two were dressed alike,' reported Jacques Mortane. 'When he eventually came across an NCO in the regulation uniform, he reportedly sentenced him to "fifteen days' punishment for failure to conform". A pilot in the regulation uniform was evidently a rare bird. Why? . . . Since we're among friends, I can tell you. The aviation service contains legions of men more modish than the most fashionable woman. All it takes is one pilot to return from Paris in a jacket with a step collar, plus a civilian shirt with detachable collar and tie, and most of the squadron immediately follow like sheep. Another wears trousers with turn-ups and immediately they're all the rage. The pilots wear the most daring of colours in huge variety, up to and including black, which – irony of ironies – makes them look like an undertaker's assistants. You even expect to hear the customary "Are you gentlemen part of the family?"'

Paul Waddington (SPA154) found that his fellow pilots came from a wide range of backgrounds: 'We had men from every arm of service, infantry, artillery . . . It was no bad thing. Fighter pilots aren't cast from a single mould. They're all individuals and each man fights and behaves differently.' Pilots who transferred from other arms customarily retained their original uniform, simply adding new distinctions – pilot's badge, aviation collar badges (a single winged star on each collar point) and in 1914/15, though rarely thereafter, winged-propeller sleeve badges. Adjudant Henri Baron (MF123), an ex-Chasseur d'Afrique, even managed to hang on to his regimental red fez. Previously with 9th Cuirassiers, Sous-lieutenant Henri Decoin (SPA77) wanted to display his former regimental distinctions while on leave in Paris, but the provosts quickly got the upper hand: 'The encounter only lasted a few seconds. After a few classic passes I managed to break off the duel, but it ended to the advantage of my opponent. I rejoined my squadron peppered with threats of close arrest.'

'Damn me, you're still wearing your boots . . . I thought they'd been banned,' comments a pilot in a wartime cartoon. 'Not for the SPAD squadrons, old chap,' replies his companion. 'In aviation, more than 200hp under the bonnet and you're counted as cavalry.'

Colonel Paul du Peuty disapproved of such showiness, and as aviation commander of GQG in 1917 he tried to give his objections the force of orders: 'I have noticed that dress regulations are not being observed, in particular the ban on open tunics. Aviation commanders should be alert to this and take immediate action as required. It would also be desirable for young pilots fresh out of flying school to stop making fools of themselves, donning extraordinary overcoats like the pilots in the pages of *Vie parisienne*, or appearing on the airfield in long trousers when they should be in working gear, ready to jump into their plane or adjust an oily, grease-covered engine or machine gun.' Jacques Mortane was another puritan: 'Where are the old winged propellers?' he wondered. 'The austere, but elegant, garments of the years before the war? Why don't we copy the British? Their uniform is sober, proper and restrained. Everyone wears it and they look much more serious and martial than the caricatures seen here on a daily basis.'

But Mortane also recognized that airmen were a breed apart, typically unsuited to regimental discipline: 'The aviator is a special kind of soldier. He is allowed greater licence than the poilu and serves under a less strict discipline. He is regarded as more of an artist than a worker. His officers give him orders and he obeys, but they know that a pilot needs inspiration to do great things. His life may well be more agreeable than that of the front-line soldier, but it is also much more eventful. For the Fifth Arm, danger lurks round every corner, not only when facing the enemy. It's just as easy to be killed behind the lines! . . . I know some readers will be quick to object: "It's all well and good to celebrate the pilot, but what about the infantryman?" Of course, we never neglect the poilu. Like the aviator, we bow to no one in our admiration for him. But the courage of the infantryman is that of the group. The pilot is a solitary hero. He has no one beside him. He cannot share the contagion of battle fever. He could turn around, fly home and dream up all sorts of excuses. In the sky, he can do what he likes; no one is making him fight. Simple devotion to duty is all that compels him to seek out danger and so often emerge triumphant.'

Addressing the new pilots of MS12 at Jonchery-sur-Vesle in 1915, Major de Rose listed the characteristics he expected of his men: 'Most of you are new to me. Nevertheless, I feel that I know you. You are all cavalrymen like me. I love the cavalry spirit. It underlies all my achievements in the aviation service. I know most of you took part in races before the war. That's just what I require. I don't say it will be the only quality needed, just that it's essential to our purpose. In time we will identify others. You are sportsmen and risk-takers – that's a good start.

I hope you are also single-minded, confident and determined, for without these qualities we can do nothing. When I say "I hope", I mean "I am certain". You are all volunteers, after all.'

'The fighting spirit of our service stems from our independence and imagination,' thought Jean Beraud-Villars (MF44/N102/N85), 'from our young COs and our pilots, younger still, who love to fight and enjoy life in equal measure. We provide a refuge for anyone unhappy with the strict discipline of other units, who loathes all the boredom and hanging around, but loves danger and adventure and wishes to serve. These individualists come to us.' Jacques Boulenger (F223) agreed: 'In the aviation service the only ones who don't get on are those who don't want to. Consequently, everything is done by volunteers whose good work is always carried out with cheerfulness and enthusiasm.'

Pilots like Bernard Lafont (V220) certainly chafed at enforced inaction. Over the winter of 1916/17 he and his comrades were suffering through a spell of prolonged bad weather: 'They've put up some huts for us – comfortable and warm but still pretty rough and ready. We've nothing to do and we're bored, killing time around our smoke-belching stoves. Reading and bridge, bridge and reading – these are our pastimes for winter days and long evenings! But we're fed up with bridge. And as for books, we're not intellectuals, or not any more, and we've lost the habit of studying and thinking. Action is the only thing that interests us.' Not that pilots were above relishing a break during a particularly tough offensive: 'So far . . . we have had perfectly ideal aviators' weather,' reported Stuart Walcott (SPA84) in 1917, 'nice low misty clouds about 300 or 400 feet up, which quite prevent aerial activity, and yet one is not bothered by mud or depressed by rain. In the morning, one awakes, pokes his head out the window, says "What lo! More luck, a nice light *brouillard*," and closes the window for a few hours more of sleep.'

Many of the sportsmen praised by de Rose saw nothing wrong in a little stunt flying, but senior commanders took a different view. 'The minister has received reports that some military pilots are trying to rival the professionals with their lunatic stunts,' complained General Bernard in 1914. 'In so doing, they are neglecting the most elementary of military duties, that a soldier puts himself in harm's way only in pursuit of a worthwhile objective. The aerial exercises required of our aviators are quite dangerous enough without increasing the likelihood of an accident by adding extra complications whose execution does nothing to make the aviator a better military pilot. On the contrary it constitutes an act of deliberate disobedience which simply will not be tolerated.'

To Maurice Chevillard (CRP), a pre-war pioneer of aerobatics, this was nonsense: 'In other words, "Fly like a twerp! Get yourself killed! But do it by the book!" . . . It's no longer the gifted pilot who gets himself noticed. Nowadays it's the man who flies "like a flat iron" who is top dog. For him, the stripes and medals: for the maestro, punishment and perhaps a court martial.' And Charles Nungesser (V106/V116/N/SPA65) simply carried on regardless. After transferring from bombers to a fighter squadron in 1915, he flew back to his old airfield at Malzéville determined to show off his new Nieuport: 'Adjudant Nungesser, Squadron 65, ignored two official warnings and performed a number of stunts over the plateau,' read the charge sheet.

The sober Mortane wanted audacity in the air tempered by restraint on the ground: 'Aviation attracts a very mixed bunch, so not every flyer will know how to behave. The great majority of pilots are young men of good breeding and good manners. However, there are many who have learned how to die but not how to conduct themselves away from the front. Those who are, or hope to become, famous must disabuse themselves of the idea that their braid, palms and crosses justify all sorts of shenanigans once they've quit their steeds. The public admires, loves, nay idolizes pilots. [But] this veneration must be earned in the air and on the ground. Pilots should realize that the more modest and decent their behaviour, the greater will be their popularity. Heroes do not act with coarseness and impropriety. These would-be masters of the air should model themselves on Garros and try to emulate his humility and good manners. By doing the opposite, some pilots tarnish not just their own reputation but that of the entire service.'

Gamekeeper's wife Madame Conaut certainly found the pilots of MS3 a disagreeable bunch. In September 1915, only a month after the squadron arrived at Breuil-le-Sec, she wrote to the CO, Captain Antonin Brocard: 'The pilots of Squadron No. 3 are indulging in all kinds of poaching. They are deliberately throwing their planes at the game and have been spotted on several occasions landing three or four times in a row on flocks of partridge, particularly near the wood at Breuil-le-Sec. They have been seen getting out and picking up the dead birds.' Madame Conaut confronted a lieutenant but found him unabashed. 'Soldiers are entitled to take whatever they like at the moment!' came the scornful reply.

Yet by 1917 the squadron, now N3, had taken on a very different character. Captain Alfred Heurteaux, CO from November 1916 to May 1917, described the mess as a quiet, sober place: 'The [only] real chatterbox was [Lieutenant Mathieu] de la Tour. [Lieutenant Albert] Deullin and Father [Adjudant René] Dorme were both dumb as carp.

Guynemer and I were good friends. We talked tactics together, but the rest of the squadron were never particularly voluble. And we never wore the ridiculous outfits you saw elsewhere. That didn't appeal to us at all. . . . Games were banned, so too aperitifs and drinking, except for a glass of port before dinner. But we really weren't all that bothered.'

'Like squadron commander, like squadron,' observed Major Xavier de Sevin (N12/SPA26). According to René de Chavagnes, Heurteaux '[had] an iron will [and was] cultivated, highly intelligent, a musician, an outstanding shot and an ace fighter pilot, whose daring in combat displayed unparalleled nerve. Still, [he was] rather uncommunicative. His guarded replies and distracted air soon deterred the yappers.' For Louis Lelandais (SOP104/BR287), the different types of squadron had little in common: 'I served on airfields where, for example, there might be an observation squadron and a bomber squadron. With few exceptions, they didn't have much to do with each other.' But even within a single fighter group the squadrons might keep their distance. 'We didn't have much contact with the other squadrons in the group,' said Captain Heurteaux. 'We just kept in touch with a handful of friends. There was never any friction between us . . . just the kind of rivalry you'd expect between classmates at school.'

Mess life in C11 was markedly different to Heurteaux's N3. 'At mealtimes the room was full of conversation and general merriment,' recalled René de Lavaissière de Lavergne. 'Apart from a few sad days when a comrade was killed or injured and the banter and the laughter fell silent, we were all happy and carefree. An impressive phonograph, plus the latest records, made our mealtimes and evenings boisterous, cheerful affairs.' N152 also liked its music. 'I've taken up the flute again,' ex-seminarist Sous-lieutenant Léon Bourjade told his parents shortly after transferring from the artillery. 'The squadron has a little orchestra – piano, violins, flutes etc. – that I'm planning to join. I also intend to study a bit of philosophy and theology. It can't be any worse than mudlarking in the trenches. So you can see I've no reason to grumble.'

The American volunteers of N124, the Escadrille Lafayette, were another musical bunch. 'I don't know what would have become of us without the gramophone,' ventured Captain Georges Thenault. 'We had two very good ones and Hill had brought back from America a whole series of excellent records, so that the strains of fox-trot and rag-time alternated with airs from French or Italian operas according to the taste of the individual. Lufbery preferred strange melodies, often melancholy in character, which are, it appears, very popular in America. It was Hawaiian music, tunes played by a sort of banjo called a Ukelele.'

N124 developed a particular reputation as a bibulous unit. 'If one goes into town any day with any of the fellows it's impossible to keep from going in and drinking without absolutely being discourteous and incompatible,' noted Edmond Genet in his diary for 25 February 1917. 'They were a pretty hard drinking kind, some of them,' confirmed Edwin Parsons. 'It was a mighty difficult and quite improbable proposition to keep entirely away from drink with the Escadrille.' Indeed, when Lawrence Rumsey transferred from Luxeuil to Cachy with his squadron, he took off while still drunk and landed at the wrong airfield, mistakenly assumed it was German and astonished the watching French aviators by promptly setting fire to his plane. He was asked to leave the squadron with immediate effect.

'There was a tremendous camaraderie to squadron life,' recalled Paul Waddington (SPA154). 'You knew your chums would never bail out on you. The fellowship was absolutely extraordinary. It permeated everything we did. Of course, there was plenty of personal "friction" between certain pilots, particularly the youngest, who sometimes lacked a sense of proportion. But from an operational point of view the members of a fighter squadron would do anything for each other.'

During a 'very important and dangerous espionage mission' behind the German lines, two pilots demonstrated just this paradox. 'The pair loathed each other and never spoke – woman trouble,' recalled Auguste Heiligenstein (MF5/MF44/C106/229). 'One day they received orders to fly a joint operation. They each had to carry a passenger and ensure that one of them at least arrived safely. The idea was for the two planes to land side by side close to a wood to provide cover and enable the spies to hide and rendezvous quickly. It was a very tricky manoeuvre on unfamiliar ground: throttling back on the descent without stalling the engine, landing, giving each passenger time to get out, then taking off again. Passing over the spot where the first plane had landed, the second pilot saw his comrade signalling to him. Obviously engine trouble. He realized something serious had happened, turned round and touched down nearby. After landing amid the barbed wire and breaking his propeller, the first pilot had lit a windproof match and thrown it into the tank, immediately setting fire to the plane. Those were our orders if we broke down behind enemy lines. The second pilot picked up his comrade and returned to the airfield without further mishap, but as they approached the airfield, he rejected the hand of the man he'd just saved. "I've just been doing my duty," he said. "Nothing between us has changed."'

The aces could certainly antagonize their fellow pilots. 'Guynemer wasn't all that likeable,' remembered Maurice Delporte, who flew with N23, another squadron in GC12. 'He wasn't very pleasant, even towards his comrades in the flight. Of course, he was bit of a toff, from a very good family, but that's no excuse. Not that it detracts from his qualities as a pilot, though.' René Fisch also served with N23. 'Not everyone liked Guynemer,' Fisch later observed. 'He was very remote and self-centred. If he went into combat alongside other pilots, he always claimed any kill.' Nor was René Fonck (C47/SPA103) particularly amiable. 'The ace is very shy,' reported Jacques Mortane. 'He blushes when asked a question, hesitates before answering, and does nothing to hide his discomfort when people cast him admiring glances. He seems ill at ease on the ground. He's out of his element.' Pierre André Tournaire (GB8) claimed that Fonck stuttered, perhaps explaining his reluctance to make conversation. Joseph Batlle, his CO in SPA103, thought him 'a bit rough around the edges. He worked for a locksmith in a godforsaken hole in the Vosges. . . . A sound enough fellow but no social graces. Very sharp, though. You wanted to push him forward . . .'

Mortane considered the qualities required of officers like Batlle and his ilk. 'What is a squadron commander?' he mused. 'His pilots must be made in his image. They must have complete confidence in him and obey his orders to the letter. His manner must show that their actions are worthwhile and that any advice he offers is based on experience. . . . He must have earned his stripes and command respect through his deeds. He must have started out in the ranks or as an active pilot, flying different types of mission, discovering what is feasible and what is not, getting results, obtaining his rank on merit, not through force of circumstance. He must be an extraordinary personality as well as an inspiring leader. Through his advice, experience or good judgement, he must be capable of creating an atmosphere conducive to gallantry. . . . His pilots must regard him as a brother-in-arms in every sense of the word.'

Louis Lelandais (SOP104/BR287) confirmed that the squadrons were relatively egalitarian, shared exposure to danger nullifying distinctions of rank: 'Although the captain was conscious of his rank and we respected him for it, there was no great difference between us. We flew the same missions, so he was aware of their dangers and potential hazards.' As the CO was normally the most experienced pilot in the squadron, he often took part in missions over enemy lines, and his loss in action was a particular blow. Captain Albert Moris, CO of MF8, was shot down while leading a raid on the railway at Saint-Quentin on 25 May 1915: 'on arrival over the target, the highest aircraft were at 1,500 metres and preparing to descend further to ensure greater accuracy. Meanwhile Captain Moris was at a mere 600 metres. The target was defended by machine guns rather than lorry-mounted artillery, and the ominous sound of their regular rat-tat-tat started up as soon as the squadron appeared. Suddenly the captain's plane took a hit. A control cable had been completely severed. The biplane lost speed, went over on one wing and dropped like a stone.' Moris survived, although badly injured; but not so his successor, Captain Jean Sallier, who fell victim to an Aviatik while on reconnaissance over Champagne in September 1915. A bullet set fire to his petrol tank and he plunged to earth behind German lines.

When Captain de Beauchamp (N23), the hero of Munich and Essen, was killed over Verdun in December 1916, Jacques Mortane felt compelled to speak out. 'Any officer worthy of the name should hold himself back for the sake of his men. The officer commands the unit. He is responsible. He should not behave recklessly. De Beauchamp was a very great hero and his loss creates a gap that cannot be filled. He had a duty to his men. A captain with the honour of commanding a squadron will make a greater contribution by getting the best from his men than by distinguishing himself in individual action. How would you have responded if Marshal Joffre had got himself killed at the battle of the Marne by taking risks and putting himself in harm's way, or later General Nivelle or General Pétain. The arms are powerless without the head.'

Ground crew too played a vital role in any squadron. Each pilot had two mechanics: a first mechanic responsible for the engine, and a second mechanic who cleaned the aircraft and changed the tyres. Marcel Jeanjean (MF/AR/SAL33) paints a vivid picture of this 'irreplaceable elite': 'Dented kepi or cap pulled down over his ears, fag dangling from the corner of his mouth, a street urchin in uniform, the mechanic only had eyes for his pilot.' 'Our mechanics followed us whenever we changed squadron, and the first mechanic stayed with us all the time,' explained Paul Waddington (SPA154). 'I had the same mechanic for two years, throughout the war. We got to know each other well. I trusted him, it was vital.' Indeed, when Lieutenant Robert de Brun (DO22) requested a move to distant Salonika as squadron commander of MF85 in 1915, his mechanic Sergeant Bernard Fromentin (DO22) asked to accompany him.

'The armourer replaced the ammunition drums and checked the machine gun after every mission,' continued Waddington. 'You had to have confidence in your gun and especially your engine; as long as your engine didn't fail, you were fine. . . . Anything technical was left completely to the mechanic, so they had to be extremely dedicated individuals. After two years with a pilot, a mechanic became very attached to him, I can tell you.

You could rely on him checking the engine and all its working parts with absolute thoroughness. . . . I never heard one of my comrades complain about his mechanic, or anyone say "this happened to me because of my mechanic", not once in two years.'

'Our mechanics were wonderful chaps,' confirmed Alfred Heurteaux (MS38/N/SPA3). 'Once my mechanic called "Ready for take-off", I didn't look at my plane again.' Louis Lelandais (SOP104/BR287) agreed: 'The mechanic was devoted to the pilot and plane whose maintenance and smooth running were his responsibility. Plane, mechanic and pilot formed a single unit. Day and night the mechanics were covered in oil and grease, often forced to improvise with whatever lay to hand to ensure the bus was ready for its next mission.' Captain Z. also applauded their wizardry: 'Behind the cheeky slang, the slouching gait of a Parisian kid off on the razzle, the mechanic hid a complete mastery of anything technical and any problem liable to occur in an aircraft engine. And God only knows, they were legion!' Marcel Jeanjean was another admirer: 'Gracious healer of asthmatic machinery, the mechanic plunges gleefully into the convoluted tangle of the engine, listening intently for any kind of grating, juddering, banging, hiccough, cough or sneeze. With the quick, sure glance of an experienced surgeon rummaging expertly through the entrails, he puts everything right in no time at all.'

The more talented mechanics often tinkered with the aircraft to improve its performance. For example, Léon Bourjade's mechanic, Charles Maheu, invented a device that allowed his pilot to jettison fuel quickly in case of emergency, so reducing the risk of fire. The squadron CO, Lieutenant Louis Delrieu, demanded to see it in action while the plane was on the ground: the tank was full, but Delrieu insisted and to Bourjade's disgust 220 litres of precious fuel disappeared into the grass. To add insult to injury, Delrieu then tried to poach Maheu. 'You know full well you've no right to steal my mechanic,' railed the normally mild-mannered pilot. 'Maheu has been assigned to me and I intend to keep him. If you carry on like this I'll put in a report.'

Mechanics could also be pressed into service as gunners, running all the risks of aircrew, but receiving precious few of the rewards: 'We're soldiers, not officers. And [our badges] embody this distinction. The observer, the officer in the passenger seat, receives a golden wing on a silver wheel. All we get is silver on white metal.'

Pilots, observers, mechanics – what did the other arms of service make of this motley crew? 'They think we're in it for fun,' complained Jean Beraud-Villars (MF44/N102/N85). 'They chide us for our independence, our youth, our style of dress, our flippancy, our camaraderie between ranks. They criticize us in particular for not being [proper] soldiers.' But Beraud-Villars was defiant: 'What good will it do the aviation service when [our] crates are dressed to the right in fours, pilots line up on parade in uniforms drawn from the quartermaster, and mechanics are told to "present arms", King-Dick pocket-knife in one hand and petrol can in the other?' he mused. '[Our critics] must accept that we're a bunch of individuals, not an organized unit.'

Chapter 4

'Kill or Be Killed' – 1917

'Search out the enemy and destroy him' – the Chemin des Dames
For the men of C64, 1 January 1917 brought an unexpected call to action.
'It was one of those dreary grey days we spend hanging around because
flying is a wash-out,' reported 'Jim'. 'The NCOs' mess was eagerly
anticipating the chance to celebrate New Year's Day together, when in
walked the CO: "Airfield in an hour, gentlemen. We're going in as low as
we can to strafe the Navarin [Farm] trenches and the German cantonments
at Dontrien." Sensational news that raised few objections apart from a
couple of chaps reluctant to interrupt their delicious lunch. We headed out
to the airfield and hangars, gathering our teams as we went, excited by this
sudden opportunity for action. . . . The lieutenant lifted his arm to signal our
departure – like a charge of old – and the planes of C64 took off in perfect
unison. . . . The weather was nasty, windy and wet and our progress
painfully slow. The heavy, fleecy clouds were down to no more than 80
metres and stopped us climbing at all.'

The French reached their target and dived, strafing the enemy and
spreading confusion. But then came 'a terrible explosion under Lieutenant
le Coz's left wing . . . his red-winged Caudron went into a nosedive and an
ominous blue flame shot from its left tank. [He'd been] hit! His dive grew
steeper but it still looked as if he might land. H. and Sergeant C. followed
him down, but he couldn't level out in time and hit the ground hard, full
throttle. An explosion, a huge black and red flame. Fire!'

Sergeant C. nursed his own aircraft 6 kilometres back to the French
lines. Meanwhile Sergeant [Émile] G[rès] had also been hit: 'petrol
streamed from the holes in his tanks. Would the plane catch fire? The
needle on the rev counter was falling. A bullet had knocked everything out.

'"We can't land here," [Grès told his observer.] "We're over their lines!"'

'"But we'll be done to a crisp!"

'"Can you see the barbed wire? That's what we're aiming for."

'The petrol was still leaking, vaporizing in the draught from the propeller and soaking the tail fins. One spark and it would send up the lot.'

Mercifully, Grès managed to limp across the wire and make it home. 'And that,' concluded 'Jim', 'was how a French front-line squadron saw in the year 1917.'

Pilots normally used machine guns or bombs for this kind of ground attack, but Pierre Violet (MF55/N57) turned to his Le Prieur rockets during a mission in the Woëvre on 15 December 1916. 'Dived on an enemy battery of 105s east of the Jumelles d'Ornes,' he reported. 'Fired my eight rockets from 150 metres.' Two days later Violet was back in action, landing safely after his plane caught fire in the air. 'Everything fine here,' he ended his next letter. 'Life is dull.'

'The war affected our attitudes so profoundly that we came to accept these vile missions as normal,' observed future film director Lieutenant Jean Renoir (C64). 'The memory of these monstrous acts turns my stomach today. It's perhaps because I was there that I hate them so much. . . . We loathed the pen-pushers [at HQ] whose life was so cushy compared with that of the actual combatants. We retained some affection for the German soldiers, who were having an equally hard time of it. They were our brothers-in-arms. The pen-pushers were shirkers.'

Meanwhile the bitter winter was creating problems of its own. 'None of the squadron's eight available planes would start,' recalled Jacques Boulenger (F223), 'but the mechanics refused to give in. Two of the radiators burst with the cold. The rest imbibed some water-and-glycerine but still the engines wouldn't budge. A combination of alcohol and hot water – plus warm petrol poured, or rather forced, into the cylinders – eventually persuaded one of them to turn over. As its silent comrades looked on reproachfully, this false friend thrummed away and the plane took off. But 50 metres off the ground the little tinker began to play up – first pretending to be a revolver, then increasing the number of explosions as though eager to tell the tale of The Engine That Wanted To Be As Noisy As The Machine-Gun – and the pilot had to rush back to the airfield. And that was the start of the engine strike, which lasted precisely as long as the fierce cold. It wasn't a proper strike in trade union terms, more of a go-slow. With endless cosseting and sweet talk – heaters in the fuselage, card over the radiator grilles, tots of hot water and alcohol – we occasionally got the engines ticking over, but they soon revealed it was all for show . . . All you could hear was [their] defiant backfiring and running off key, while pilots rained down from the sky. Might the infantry at last appreciate that, contrary to popular belief, most of the planes flying over their heads are friends and not enemies? Not a bit of it! They still reckoned every crate above them was a Boche. That's been their custom since August 1914 and I can't see any sign of it changing.'

After the sacking of General Joffre in December 1916, the French had a new commander-in-chief, General Robert Nivelle, who confidently promised to end the stalemate with a decisive battle aimed at 'nothing less than the destruction of most of the enemy forces on the Western Front'. Nivelle had succeeded Pétain at Verdun, where in a series of limited attacks he had quickly forged a reputation as a bold and successful commander by copying the German tactics of offence in depth. He now planned to use the same 'formula' to put his strategy into effect: a preliminary barrage would enable the French to break through the German front line on the ground and roll it up left and right, while a parallel aerial assault destroyed the enemy squadrons to an unprecedented depth – up to 40 or 50 kilometres behind the lines instead of the usual 5 or 6 – clearing the way for French planes to harass the retreating Germans without let or hindrance.

Nivelle's planned objective was the salient around Noyon, but in March the Germans abruptly withdrew from the sector. Braving frequent hailstorms, Adjudant Charles Larrouil (MF20) and his observer were flying a contact patrol towards Ham and Saint-Quentin: 'I made a few turns at 25 metres above the village [of Nesle] to confirm no enemy troops remained. Seconds later we spotted a man brandishing a tricolour from the roof of a house. Then a crowd of villagers waving flags and handkerchiefs appeared in the streets and main square.' Larrouil decided it was safe to land and his plane was immediately surrounded by hundreds of incredulous civilians. Then, four horsemen appeared on the horizon: '"Uhlans!" shouted the villagers, and immediately made themselves scarce. Some walked backwards, others with heads bowed almost to the ground, leaving the two of us alone.' The observer trained his binoculars on the new arrivals. Good news: not German at all, but British!

The German withdrawal from Noyon did nothing to change the overall plan: Nivelle simply shifted the point of attack 40 kilometres south-east to the Aisne – and the much tougher terrain of the Chemin des Dames ridge. A massive aerial force, nearly a thousand machines of all types, was assembled in preparation for the assault, and reconnaissance crews took to the air non-stop. Among them was Corporal Clément Massier (R213). Scarcely had he and his Caudron R.4 crossed the front line near La Fère than two German fighters appeared: 'I had twin machine guns. No time to

Clément Ader: 'Aviation is the arm-of-service capable of defeating the enemy with the fewest number of casualties! . . . Whosoever is Master of the Air will be Master of the World.'

'The established methods of intelligence-gathering remain important but will be even more useful if employed in tandem with aerial reconnaissance.' A troop of hussars clatter past on pre-war manoeuvres while the dirigible *Dupuy-de-Lôme* hovers above.

'We took off armed to the teeth, full of enthusiasm. Just think, our first real taste of action.' Pierre Perrin de Brichambaut.

'Overjoyed to be at war.' Marcel Brindejonc des Moulinais after a medals ceremony early in the conflict.

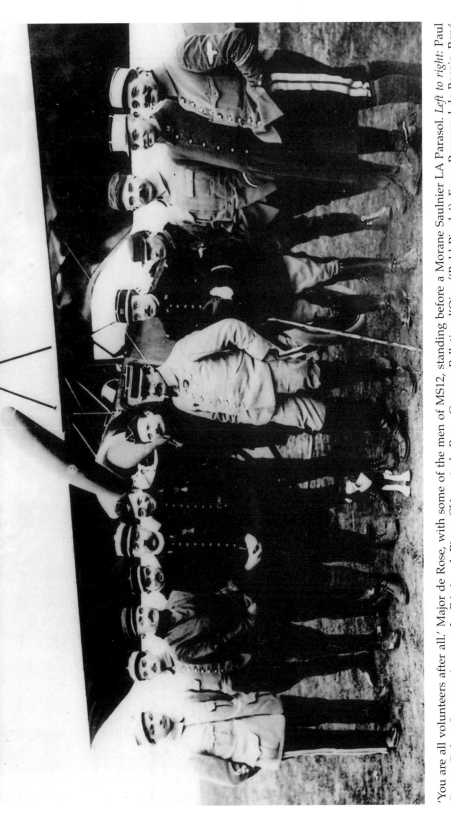

'You are all volunteers after all.' Major de Rose, with some of the men of MS12, standing before a Morane Saulnier LA Parasol. *Left to right:* Paul Gastin, Robert Jacottet, Auguste Le Révérend, Pierre Clément, de Rose, Georges Pelletier d'Oisy ('Bold Pivolo'), Fenn, Raymond de Bernis, René Chambe, Jean Navarre, René Mesguich, Paul Moinier, Gabriel Pelège.

Édouard Barès, aviation commander at GQG. 'He dragged aviation from the abyss. He created it, he gave it life.' But that failed to prevent his sacking in 1917.

'I do not consider that I am fighting for France alone, but for the cause of humanity, the most noble of all causes.' Captain Georges Thenault demonstrates a portable moving map display to a group of pilots from N124, the Lafayette Escadrille. *Left to right*: Kiffin Rockwell, Thenault, Norman Prince, Alfred de Lâage de Meux, Elliott Cowdin, Bert Hall, Jim McConnell, Victor Chapman.

'No doubt about it, that's how to tackle German aviators.' Joseph Frantz (*left*) and Louis Quenault, the first men to obtain a confirmed air-to-air victory.

'Sheer determination was all that was needed.' Jules Védrines in his cockpit, ready for take-off. Garros-style deflector plates have been fitted to the propeller of his Morane. Note also the tray of bullets extending from the side of his machine gun.

Roland Garros. 'If only they'd listened to us and consulted us in peacetime we'd be completely *au fait* with military aviation by now.'

Jean Navarre and his Morane-Saulnier monoplane. 'He always catches you on the hop. Just when you want to put him on a charge, you end up mentioning him in despatches.'

'If he hasn't made the grade in a fortnight, I'll show him the door.' Georges Guynemer (*left*) and his squadron CO, Antonin Brocard. Guynemer made an uncertain start to operational flying.

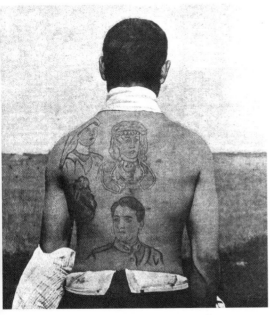

'Guynemer was the hero personified.' Here, a soldier of the African Light Infantry – a regiment of enthusiastic tattooers – has had the ace's likeness inscribed on his back.

Alfred Heurteaux had 'an iron will and was cultivated, highly intelligent, an outstanding shot and an ace fighter pilot, whose daring in combat displayed unparalleled nerve. Still, he was rather uncommunicative. His guarded replies and distracted air soon deterred the yappers.'

'We came up with the three-man patrol and after a few false starts it produced good results.' Fighter tactician Albert Deullin (*centre*).

'With his blond hair, battered face, china-blue eyes, mocking smile and scarred chin, he had the bearing, the self-confidence and the voice' – Charles Nungesser also broke most of the major bones in his body during the war.

Pilots of SPA37 check the loading of their ammunition belts. Aligning each round correctly was important to reduce the chance of jamming.

René Fonck and his SPAD fighter. 'He seems ill at ease on the ground. He's out of his element.'

'The pilots travelled to their planes in low-slung racing cars . . .' and who would dare deny the privilege to champion boxer Georges Carpentier of MF55.

'We lumbered about like deep-sea divers.' The pilot of a two-seater dressed to combat the cold.

'Pilots all want a belted mac or boots with complicated laces.' Artillery spotter supreme René Roeckel demonstrates a masterpiece of the bootmaker's art.

Maurice Happe, commander of GB4. To the French press, '*Le Corsaire de l'air*'; to the Germans, a man with a price on his head. Happe remained undaunted: 'You'll find me in the plane with red wheels and a cross on the wings. Target me. Don't waste your time on my comrades.'

Loading bombs into a Farman. 'The things always scared me to death. It was a clumsy business and there were several serious accidents. We didn't have bomb-racks either. We simply dropped them over the side.'

'Drunk with the wind and light, forced to remain stock still, numb with the cold or burned by the sun, hands gripping the binoculars, he stays up there for hours at a time . . .' A balloon observer in his basket.

Lorry-borne anti-aircraft guns. 'Hitting the enemy is a bonus. You always hope for a lucky strike, but it would be foolish to devote too much time to it.'

'A squadron without aviation is a squadron lost.' A Caudron J floatplane is hoisted aboard the seaplane carrier *La Foudre*.

'I never heard one of my comrades complain about his mechanic, or anyone say "this happened to me because of my mechanic", not once in two years.' Mechanics at work outside a mobile workshop lorry.

Politician René Besnard, under-secretary of state for aeronautics, surrounded by student pilots at a flying school. 'Young, dedicated and affable, he had all the qualities required to succeed in his difficult task, particularly that of reconciling those two warring brothers, the front and the rear.'

'My programme is the maximum.' Women (in daring modern trousers) and Indo-Chinese workers on a production line, part of the massive industrial mobilization that transformed aircraft construction.

'Aviators were something special. They displayed qualities that were particularly attractive to a young man: love of danger, because the risks then were considerable . . . plus a taste for adventure.' Charles Godefroy flies a Nieuport through the Arc de Triomphe in 1919.

stop and aim. I fired tracer bullets with one and used the other to correct in short three-round bursts until I had one of the Boches in my sights. I gave him a good burst with both guns and he turned away immediately. Meanwhile a second Boche had arrived and was really letting us have it. I saw his bullets hit our bus. Several of my rounds had struck home, but still he charged on. I thought he was going to ram us and split the plane from nose to tail. Just then my gun jammed and in clearing the blockage I spotted the photographer at the gun mount firing over the upper wing. I managed to reload and just when the Fritz was dead centre and beginning his turn I gave him both barrels from 60 metres. . . . It didn't take long. He climbed vertically, side-slipped and dropped like a stone in an enormous trail of smoke. Three minutes later the second Boche also fell in flames.'

Nivelle also created two more fighter groups, GC14 (de Marancour) and GC15 (Ménard), bringing the total up to five. On the Chemin des Dames GC11, GC12 and GC14, plus three fighter squadrons, were combined in a single provisional groupement under the command of Reserve Army Group (Fifth, Sixth and Tenth Armies) – its primary mission, 'outweighing all others potentially detrimental to its completion', to claim air superiority by destroying the enemy fighters. Meanwhile in Champagne bomber group GB1 was with Fourth Army, ready to intervene in either sector. 'Victory in the air is the prerequisite of victory on the ground,' urged GQG's newly appointed aviation commander Colonel Paul du Peuty. 'It will not only play its part in that victory, it will guarantee it. . . . We must seek out the enemy and destroy him. From 15 April the fighter groups will resume their offensive tactics without restriction: their aim to destroy the German squadrons. From that date, no fighter should be found behind French lines.'

But in their enthusiasm Nivelle and du Peuty had ignored all the lessons of 1916: large-scale sweeps were easily spotted and avoided by the enemy, air superiority never absolute, and cooperation crews constantly vulnerable to surprise concentrations and attacks by enemy fighters. Having committed all their fighters so far behind German lines, they had provided no back-up if their strategy failed. Fifth and Sixth Armies had just one organic reconnaissance/fighter squadron each – 'scarcely enough to carry out their normal reconnaissance duties, let alone combat missions' – and thus no means of protecting their cooperation machines over a front some 60 kilometres long.

Throughout the artillery preparation phase, the fighter groups penetrated deep into enemy-held territory, but lax security had betrayed French intentions and their enemy counterparts simply avoided confrontation. On 5 April a patrol of twenty SPADs flew Laffaux–Laon–Camp de Sissonne–Aubérive, over 90 kilometres behind the German lines, without engaging the enemy, and two days later a similar formation flew the route in reverse with identical results. Instead, the German fighters concentrated their attentions on the army cooperation squadrons – to considerable effect. C47, SM106, F211 and C220, the four squadrons attached to II Colonial Corps, lost fourteen of their thirty-three aircraft during the build-up between 10 and 16 April.

The morning of the attack found the CO of C6, Captain Guy de Lavergne, monitoring the action at 10th Colonial Division HQ. Alongside him were divisional commander General Jean-Baptiste Marchand and corps commander General Ernest Blondlat. 'Red-faced, big-nosed, bright-eyed, coarse-featured, Blondlat had never quite grasped the difference between twin-seater, twin-winged and twin-engined,' claimed de Lavergne. 'He thought these terms were synonymous. So when the first of C6's planes appeared he couldn't believe it was all three at once. And he was completely amazed by the wireless messages it was transmitting. Aircraft had come into his life too late for him to understand the first thing about them or make proper use of them.'

Mist, sleet and snow were hampering the crews and restricting the flow of information. Then slowly the news began to trickle in: 'Three Brothers Trench taken,' continued de Lavergne, 'front lines wiped out on the Vauclerc plateau. Halted north of Craonne. The wide circles described by the plane from my squadron had brought it almost directly above our heads. I could see it struggling on in the cloud.'

Planes from C47 were flying contact patrols for 10th Colonial Division towards the key position of Hurtebise. 'Not much to report,' they admitted. 'All we know is the first wave is holding the northern edge of the Plateau des Dames.' Meanwhile C220 was performing similar duties for the neighbouring 15th Colonial Division: 'Cornelius, Salzburg and Kaendec [sic] trenches taken. Fifth Army has made discernible progress. [But] three of our planes have been lost in the fog, delaying completion of their mission.' By 3.00 pm C220 claimed to have spotted 10th Division, but not its extreme right flank: 'It should be noted that 15th Division, which marked out its route, has been identified very precisely from the start of the attack. The confusion over 10th [Division] is caused by lack of signals and problems in making out the colour of the greatcoats in the trenches.' But even the progress suggested by these fragmentary bulletins was illusory. As early as 9.00 am 10th Division had lost just over 5,000 men for precious little gain, while so great were the losses sustained by 15th Division that its attacks had been called off. 'That's how the day went,' concluded de Lavergne, 'simultaneously very long, frustrating and depressing. Towards evening they let me go. I don't remember exactly when. I got back to base at midnight.'

The rain, sleet and snow persisted throughout the opening days of the offensive, rendering the cooperation squadrons powerless to assess accurately the effectiveness of Nivelle's massive preliminary barrage. On 17 April II Colonial Corps could put no more than four planes into the air, and its balloons were completely grounded: 'Dreadful weather most of the day,' it reported. 'We could neither complete our missions nor identify our line.' Nor did the following day bring any respite. Hampered by snow, the observation and anti-artillery aircraft again returned without accomplishing their missions and the balloons remained earthbound. French fighter patrols eight, ten or twenty strong swept the skies of Champagne and the Aisne whenever the weather allowed. N15 despatched an eight-strong patrol several times a day during that period. 'In general,' recorded the war diary, 'the patrol saw plenty of aerial activity but always at a distance, deep within the [enemy's] lines.' En route to Sissonne four days later ten SPADs detailed to escort the bombers from GB1 met only one enemy aircraft (and were unable to shoot it down), while a similar expedition on 1 May encountered no Germans at all. Meanwhile any plane that ventured towards the German balloon line quickly attracted the attention of the enemy fighters. On 25 April one half of an eight-strong patrol from N15 clashed repeatedly with a group of twelve Germans over Laval-en-Laonnois, while their comrades launched 'several attacks on spotter aircraft near the Reservoir [close to Laon]'.

As the offensive wore on, Lucien Laby (294th Infantry) watched as a French observation balloon came down in flames: 'As night fell, an Aviatik bore down full speed on a "sausage" almost directly above our heads. Before we could winch it down, the Aviatik circled it, firing explosive bullets. The balloon caught fire and descended abruptly. You'd pay a fair price to see a repeat performance. One after the other, the two observers jumped from the basket and dropped like stones until their parachutes opened . . . Then the "sausage" got hold of them and the poor sods started kicking out wildly to try to speed up their descent. If the column of flame reached them, they were done for. We really feared for one, so close did he come to the flames. Fortunately he didn't catch fire, but the wind was blowing them towards the enemy. They jettisoned their papers, photographs, etc., and managed to come down close to the lines. A few days later the same thing happened again. This time the Aviatik returned, swung its machine gun on the two defenceless observers and killed them both.'

Although part of a nominally Farman squadron, 20-year-old Sergeant Jean Argaud (F215) was actually flying a Sopwith 1½ Strutter. 'It was great,' he wrote to his parents. 'The cloud ceiling was at 800 metres. We were flying at 700 metres, with the assault waves below us, and in between a distinct spider's web pattern created by our shells hammering the Boches. It's half past nine so I'll say goodnight. I'm nodding off and I'm first away at five in the morning. I've been flying seven hours a day since the offensive began, although for the past couple of days it's been no more than four or so.'

Throughout all the hard fighting, fortune smiled on René de Lavaissière de Lavergne (C11) and his pilot, Sergeant René Lafouillade. On 29 April, while spotting for a heavy artillery battery in their Caudron G.4, engine problems and a subsequent crash-landing had left the pair hanging upside down in their seat-belts. Five days later, during a contact patrol near the Fort du Brimont, north of Reims, the same thing happened again: 'An hour into the flight the engine's rocker arms jumped out and ripped the casing. The debris broke one of the struts so the pilot couldn't steer. We had to land immediately. Lafouillade spotted a field but it was heavily cratered and we nosed over into a shell hole on landing. So there I was once more, stuck upside down under the plane. Both of us escaped with just a few grazes.'

The following week two six-strong enemy patrols pounced upon the pair: 'We engaged one of the[m]. A bullet shattered one of our propellers, forcing us to break off and return to the airfield. Perhaps affected by the combat, Lafouillade rolled the plane on landing and put us on our backs again. This really had been a month for accidents. But once more luck was on my side and I escaped uninjured. When I realized we were going to roll, I curled into a ball, pulled my head in and waited. Honestly, I was never afraid. I trusted in my lucky star.'

C46 was flying a mixture of the Caudron R.4, first received the previous summer, and a new type, the Letord. 'We're not on the Somme now,' their CO, Captain Didier Lecour-Grandmaison, reminded his crews. 'Our opponents outnumber us; they're faster and better armed. We will definitely take our share of losses here [but] we must fight on. Our job is to kill or be killed.' Lecour-Grandmaison's gunner, Adjudant Gaston Vitalis, shared his captain's fears, but he was confident that C46 could make the most of the R.4's limited capabilities: 'Our aircraft was neither very fast nor particularly manoeuvrable, so our tactics were always to make ourselves the target. If we ran into a group – their fighter patrols always contained at least five or six single-seaters – we approached them quite openly, then suddenly turned our backs as if flying away. That usually brought them on to us. Then we formed a circle to make best use of our firepower while simultaneously limiting theirs. We did this every time, always at 3,500 metres, our usual combat height. We penetrated 4 or 5 kilometres behind their lines, always unescorted. Captain Lecour-Grandmaison didn't want SPADs for company. He thought they just got in the way.'

On 10 May Lecour-Grandmaison was returning from a mission over Juvincourt when three enemy aircraft suddenly appeared. Three quickly became five, five became nine, and Lecour-Grandmaison's Letord was still 2 kilometres from the French lines. 'The first plane charged towards us,' recalled Sergeant Alfred Boyé, one of the two gunners on board. 'I recognized them immediately. It was the ace Boche squadron [Jasta 15], the famous Tangos.' The first German plane attacked, then dived away steeply. 'The others were upon us,' continued Boyé. 'Corporal Crozet, the forward gunner, suddenly stopped firing. I looked up [but] couldn't see him. He'd been hit by the first rounds and slumped down in the fuselage. Just then a second Boche dived straight at us, targeting the exposed pilot. Armour plate protected him against an attack from below. I fired, but two rounds struck me while I was bending to change the drum on the machine gun – one of them grazed my scalp, the other hit me in the head. I rolled into the bottom of the fuselage. I rallied, managed not to pass out and fired on our Boche, who was now pulling away and trying to fly beneath our tail. He made off under control, but with a dead propeller. Now another enemy dived above the upper wing. I could see the flapping canvas. Scraps of white floated all around us. Suddenly I felt the plane judder. There was no one in control. I turned round. Captain Lecour-Grandmaison was sprawled to his left, no sign of life. I knew he was dead . . . [and] that I was done for. I carried on firing at the Germans. Suddenly there was smoke everywhere. I could hardly breathe. . . . I tried to throw myself out, but the 'bus' went into a spin that extinguished the flames and put paid to any threat of suffocation.'

The aircraft carried on spinning and Boyé kept on firing. 'The dual controls were right in front of my eyes. I gave them a try and the plane levelled out. . . . I dived towards [the French trenches], crossing the German lines at 80 metres. A jerky manoeuvre spilled petrol towards the rear of the plane and fire broke out again . . . [At least] I'd fall behind our lines. I cut my speed and put the plane on its tail and wing . . . I knew we were falling. I knew I'd done all I could and with that I blacked out.' Boyé came round to find Lecour-Grandmaison and Crozet both dead. He

clambered out of the wreck, headed for the safety of the French trenches –
and as soon as he recovered he applied for pilot training.

A measure of French impotence on the Chemin des Dames was the
German ace nicknamed '*Fantôm-As*' ('The Phantom Ace') who, regular
as clockwork, appeared at mealtimes to strafe the trenches, unhindered by
French fighters. Named after Fantômas, a criminal anti-hero of pre-war
novels and films, his real identity (if indeed he was one man and not a
succession of enemy aviators) was never established. Jacques Arnoux and
his comrades were sure that they'd seen him as they headed into the line
near La Malmaison: 'Fantôme-As! It's Fantôme-As! I saw him. He glided
down, opened fire, spun round and launched his rockets. He skims so low
that, apart from the tilt of his wings as he banks, you'd think he was
running across the ground. We opened fire on him as he turned to attack
. . . He shied away at the first bullets, speeding north in a flurry of wings.'

Nivelle's strategy had failed completely – in the air and on the ground –
and in mid-May he was sacked and replaced as commander-in-chief by
General Pétain. The fighter groups were dismissed as 'an aristocracy of the
air', mere glory hunters who had failed utterly in their primary task of
protecting the cooperation crews. '[They] repeated the tactics of the Somme
and tried to clear the skies by intervening in force with high-altitude
missions behind the German lines,' reported Fifth Army after the battle. 'The
enemy refused combat with our fighters, and our sweeps met empty air. The
large German fighter force, composed mainly of single-seaters, prowled
along the lines at low altitudes in small groups, each two or three planes
strong, and launched lightning strikes on our cooperation aircraft, pursuing
some as low as 600 metres, posing a constant threat to the French observers,
and distracting them from the task in hand. Our losses were severe.'

'Enemy aviation activity and dense barrier patrols made it very difficult
to carry out [our photo-reconnaissance missions],' commented the aviation
commander of II Colonial Corps, Étienne Cheutin. 'Even after the
somewhat belated arrival of the fighter group, whose contribution soon
made itself felt, we were forced to commit planes to provide extra
protection for any mission behind the German lines. Our experience also
showed the difficulty of providing close protection with planes drawn from
different units. It is very hard to create an understanding between crews
unused to working together, flying a variety of different aircraft types.
However able and willing the individuals involved, these missions lack
teamwork and formation flying skills.'

Cheutin believed the solution was clear: 'The answer lies in providing
each army corps sector with fast, well-armed machines and three-seater

fighters, enabling cooperation squadrons to mount their own missions using crews who are familiar with each other, well trained in collaborating towards a defined objective, and accustomed to manoeuvring under the command of a single leader. The fighter groups should carry on clearing the skies of enemy barrier patrols, a task they are currently performing very well.' Cheutin's suggestion was never pursued, but the new commander-in-chief immediately made improved liaison between fighters and cooperation aircraft a cornerstone of his aviation strategy. Major Auguste Le Révérend, commander of GC11, summed it up as follows: 'On the battlefield, aviation has to cooperate closely with the other arms of service. The decisive factor is always the infantry, which in turn is supported by the artillery, so the squadrons that cooperate with these two arms must take precedence. The fighter's role is to clear the way for these squadrons, protect them and provide them with the largest safety zone possible.'

During the summer of 1917 army group commanders like Franchet d'Espèrey (Northern) and Fayolle (Central) allocated one fighter group to each of their armies, enabling the fighters and the cooperation squadrons to develop a closer relationship, while still allowing for the potential concentration of resources when required for an offensive. The patrol zone was returned to its original depth of 5 or 6 kilometres behind the German lines, and high- and low-level barrier patrols flown at fixed times to a set itinerary were combined with offensive patrols designed to surprise the enemy. The French also continued to work on their tactics. The three-man unit, flying in a V, with the two wingmen some 200 metres above and behind the leader, was finally increased to a 'quadrille' of four, flying and attacking in diamond formation with the leader in the point. Barrier work, suggested Albert Deullin (MF62/N3/SPA73), was best undertaken by two quadrilles, the second following 800 metres behind and 150 metres above the first to act as a reserve and commit itself only after all the Germans had joined the fray.

'The V formation was simple to maintain but also gave the pilot great freedom of manoeuvre,' continued Deullin. 'Each pilot already knew what action to take in any given situation. He couldn't be influenced by the mistakes of his comrades since all he had to do was follow his leader; and with only two comrades to keep an eye on, the leader was easy to follow and recognize in combat. The leader could also maintain the formation, control his men, attack or break off an encounter as necessary, without fear of being shackled indefinitely to an idiot. In practice, particularly after the 180hp SPAD [an improved model of the SPAD 7] was introduced [in April 1917], a three-man formation proved quite sufficient for a successful attack on the normal five- or six-man German patrol. It was clear that big patrols were fine for barrier work over our own lines, but not as an offensive formation in enemy airspace, whose main requirements are speed, manoeuvrability, teamwork and complete obedience to the leader. But nothing is ever perfect. Planes, and especially engines, often break down. Not every patrol set out with a full complement, pilots often had to abandon their comrades after an incident en route, and the resulting two-man patrol was too weak. We thus settled on the four-man patrol, now almost universally adopted . . . except for a handful of real aces who prefer the freedom and flexibility of a smaller group.'

'The veterans want to hunt individually through overconfidence and a preference for working alone,' complained Jean Beraud-Villars. 'The novices imitate them through vanity and ignorance. And both end up by getting themselves killed.' Jacques Mortane agreed. 'The era of the champion is over,' he pronounced in March 1917. 'The Germans operate with at least four aircraft. We have the numbers. We must do likewise. They're hoping for a quadrille. We'll make them dance. Any man who plunges into the middle of a group is a hero, but more often than not he falls victim to his own courage. And we can't afford to lose any pilots just now. We'd rather they didn't go courting death.'

If proof were needed, it came with the death of Georges Guynemer (MS/N/SPA3). With fifty-three victories to his credit, the ace left on patrol from the airfield at Saint-Pol-sur-Mer at 8.25 am on 11 September 1917. He was nervous and impatient. The previous day had been a frustrating one: he had spent five and a half hours in the air, taking off three times, in three different aircraft, only to be forced down each time by engine trouble. With just Sous-lieutenant Jean Bozon-Verduraz as his wingman, Guynemer took off into the misty morning. Turning south-east over Bixschoote and Langemarck, he pounced on a German two-seater and in turn was attacked by a flight of enemy fighters. Bozon-Verduraz briefly spotted Guynemer on the tail of the spinning two-seater. He dived into the attack to assist but, by the time he emerged, the ace had disappeared.

Guynemer came down near the village of Poelkapelle but no trace of man or machine was ever found, undoubtedly both obliterated in a subsequent artillery barrage. Guynemer's probable nemesis was Leutnant Kurt Wissemann (Jasta 3). Desperate for a propaganda victory to counter the loss of their champion, the French claimed Wisseman had been downed in his turn on 30 September over Poperinghe by René Fonck (C47/SPA103). However, the German had been killed two days earlier; Fonck's victim that day was simply an enemy pilot with a similar name.

'A state of permanent crisis' – aircraft manufacture

The disaster on the Chemin des Dames was the result of more than just tactical failure. By the early summer of 1917 the aviation service, like the wider army, was suffering from a triple crisis: of tactics, morale and materiel. The service was hamstrung by a large number of obsolete machines, many dating from 1915. But their replacement was blocked by administrative and industrial failings, disputes over doctrine and strategy – and thus the number and type of aircraft required – and a command divided between front (GQG and its aviation commander) and rear (the aviation directorate and the ministry of war).

The procurement process was a complex one. An initial estimate of front-line requirements was formulated by GQG in consultation with army and corps commanders, passed to the minister of war for approval or amendment, then handed down to the director of aviation for fulfilment. The director decided whether to reorder an existing type, move to something new, or commission a design from scratch; then finally the in-house Service des Fabrications de l'Aviation (SFA) took over, placing the necessary contracts and supervising production. Even if everything went smoothly, it took around twelve months to bring a new aircraft type to the front in any numbers, but the involvement of the minister introduced an extra element of confusion and delay, opening up the system to pressure from airmen, soldiers, politicians, press and manufacturers, all agitating publicly to influence the coalition government of the day.

In August 1914 the French aircraft industry was the largest in the world and the government its biggest customer, but the early months of the war saw both parties struggle to supply the front-line units. The aviation directorate was dealing with nineteen different aircraft types from a dozen different manufacturers, all badly disrupted by the outbreak of war: skilled craftsmen had been called up; most of France's key iron-, steel- and textile-producing regions along the Belgian frontier were under enemy occupation; and factories had been evacuated from Paris to the provinces – Caudron, Farman, REP and Voisin all heading to Lyon. To stimulate production and simplify maintenance and training, director of aviation Édouard Hirschauer soon decided to concentrate on a limited number of types ordered in quantity, increasing monthly output by almost 50 per cent between January and August 1915, from 262 to 383 airframes. Nevertheless the politicians – and particularly those of the National Assembly's influential army committee – were quick to attack. 'The initial [procurement] programmes were too modest,' later opined its president, retired general Jean Pedoya. 'The committee eventually began to wonder if GQG had any faith in aviation, whether it believed in it at all.' In the lower house the directorate was targeted by a deputy who deplored 'its ignorance until recently of the production capacity of our manufacturers, of the current potential for growth, and of the support and guarantees required for this new military industry to expand fast enough to meet the rapidly increasing needs of the armies. . . . What is required,' he continued, 'is a competent directorate concentrating less on issuing press communiqués that fool no one but the layman and more on setting up a diligent, organized and methodical rear capable of supplying the army with skilled mechanics, well-trained pilots and shrewd observers, and the valiant aviators now risking their lives in aerial combat with the . . . fast machines, powerful engines and top-quality weapons crucial to victory.'

In September 1915 the critics reaped their reward: the government abolished the staff post of director of aviation, sacking Hirschauer and appointing a politician, Senator René Besnard, to the new position of under-secretary of state for aeronautics. Georges Huisman, who worked within the aviation directorate, rated the newcomer highly: 'Young, dedicated and affable, he had all the qualities required to succeed in his difficult task, particularly that of reconciling those two warring brothers, the front and the rear.' The energetic Besnard threw himself into his work, returning specialist craftsmen to their former employers, militarizing the flying schools, and supplementing the existing SFA with a new research and development section, the Service Technique de l'Aéronautique (STAé).

While Besnard knew that gaining and retaining air superiority required modern production practices and continuous technical innovation, he found it impossible to implement an effective industrial strategy. Ignoring patriotic sentiment, manufacturers were prompted primarily by profit. In creating the Breguet-Michelin BM series and the Escadre Michelin, claimed GQG aviation commander Édouard Barès, Michelin had sought 'a bomber which was *its* bomber and a bomber group which was *its* group', a nakedly commercial desire to advertise its wares that GQG found unacceptable in wartime. Manufacturers planted false 'news' stories to denigrate their rivals and did their best to influence politicians, airmen and soldiers alike: Gabriel Voisin gave off-duty pilots free use of his Paris house, engine manufacturers presented them with cars, and every company had its parliamentary mouthpiece. The ministry lacked any power of coercion, and contracted suppliers – protected by large deals for a fixed number of aircraft – were reluctant to invest, preferring to keep costs down by making incremental changes to existing types rather than develop new designs, and tying the air service to essentially obsolete machines long after their competitors – and the enemy – had moved on.

By the autumn of 1915 outdated cooperation machines like the Caudron G.4, Farman MF.11 and newer Farman F.40, all under-powered pushers completely unprotected against attack from the rear, were in desperate need of replacement. Yet for the politicians – with the vociferous support of bomber specialists like Breguet, Michelin and Voisin – heavy bombers were the first priority: 'The most urgent task', the army committee had insisted in July, 'is to create a bomber force capable of long-range group operation, with the aim of striking at the lifeblood of enemy manufacturing.' Besnard, however, ignored these pleas. Instead, he allied himself with front-line opinion, soon becoming 'the target of a lobby that prevented him from completing his work'. When he placed orders for the Caudron R.4 three-seater and the powerful new Hispano-Suiza 150hp engine, rival manufacturers orchestrated a vituperative parliamentary and press campaign against him, and on 8 February 1916 he was forced to resign.

The post of under-secretary was abolished and replaced once more by a director of aviation, Colonel Henry Régnier, an artilleryman with a very limited view of the service. Planes, he believed, were little more than adjuncts to the guns. Barès and Besnard had worked well together, but relations with Régnier quickly deteriorated and an attempt to remove Barès from his post was thwarted only by the untimely death of Charles de Rose in May 1916. Emboldened by the success of the fighters at Verdun, Barès immediately repeated his earlier attempt to gain control of all front-line aeronautical units: 'Recent operations have shown the value of ensuring the closest possible coordination of all elements of the aeronautical service: balloons, army corps and heavy artillery squadrons, fighters, day bombers and night bombers. The only solution is a single command. It is the only way to make best use of all our resources.' But his proposal fell on deaf ears: in the highly politicized atmosphere of GQG, some senior officers accused him of simple empire-building, and Régnier rejected the idea outright. 'An aviation commander reporting directly to the commander-in-chief, with rights of inspection over army corps and armies, will create nothing less than a state within a state,' he replied. 'The Third Bureau [GQG's operations branch] will simply not allow it.'

With deputies and senators sniping relentlessly from the sidelines, the crisis of materiel gathered pace over the next few months. The existing Breguet-Michelin, REP-built Caproni 2, Farman F.40 and Voisin 5 bombers all lacked the power and armament required for long-range, large-scale daylight raids, and competitions run in 1915 and 1916 failed to produce any viable new designs. The cooperation squadrons were still littered with antiquated Caudron G.4, Farman MF.11 and Farman F.40 machines; the new Nieuport 12 was judged difficult to fly (and even harder to land); and Caudron's G.6 and R.4 three-seaters were only just beginning to reach the front. Despairing of French industry, the ministry decided to act, instructing the STAé to start producing its own designs, while also purchasing a number of Sopwith 1½ Strutters from the British and then manufacturing them under licence.

The fighters so successful at Verdun and the Somme in the spring and summer of 1916 had soon been leapfrogged by new enemy types. The Nieuport 17 was already outclassed by the German Albatros D.II and D.III on its introduction late in the year, and its more powerful stablemates, the 24, 24bis and 27, were still under development. Meanwhile the superior SPAD 7 was yet to reach the squadrons in any meaningful numbers, its delivery delayed by problems with the Hispano engine and a lack of manufacturing capacity. Barès had championed the SPAD 7 from the start – '[Its] entry into service was entirely his doing,' affirmed STAé engineer Albert Etévé in 1970 – and to speed up production he had asked the Michelin brothers to stop turning out their much despised Breguet-Michelin bombers and start building SPADs instead. But his appeal was in vain. André Michelin went straight to the prime minister and received permission to build another 100 examples of a type damned by Barès as 'indubitably one of the worst machines ever acquired by the service'. By February 1917 only 268 SPADs had been received, of which just 70 had reached the front.

Twelve months of intense unrest culminated in a report drawn up in December 1916 by Radical senator Daniel Vincent, a former observer with V116, who underlined the huge number of now-obsolete machines, bemoaned the division of command between front and rear, and highlighted the weakness of the industrial infrastructure, with manufacturers incapable of streamlining production or making the necessary investment in new types. As coalition governments came and went during the spring of 1917, a new minister of war, General Hubert Lyautey, reorganized the whole aeronautical establishment and, in February 1917, it was Barès who paid the price.

'Barès was confronted by a coalition of powerful industrialists whose aircraft he quite rightly rejected, politicians who demanded control of the aviation service . . . a complete failure of a minister . . . anxious to divert the gathering storm and find a scapegoat for his own mistakes, [and] embittered and unhappy pilots whose incompetence . . . had been spotted by a good judge of men who deliberately refused to promote them,' claimed one supporter on 28 February 1917. 'All of them whispered against [him]. Completely ignorant of the issues involved but aware that [the war] wasn't going well, the general public joined in the clamour to dismiss a man who resolutely kept his own counsel.'

Barès was exiled to command the fighter and bomber groups of Eastern Army Group, and later a front-line infantry regiment, thus depriving the air service of his knowledge and experience for the rest of the war. 'Barès dragged aviation from the abyss,' continued the same anonymous voice. 'He created it, he gave it life. . . . He had an unparalleled knowledge of every member of the service. He travelled continually all over the front and made things happen wherever he went.' Jean de Pierrefeu, author of GQG's daily communiqués, also admired the man: '[He] was one of those [officers] with a real understanding of the psychology of the troops under his command. It was his idea to mention pilots in despatches, first Guynemer, then everyone. Within the ministry, he was loved and loathed in equal measure. This kind of division permeated the aviation service, whoever was in command. Those with real influence seemed to be civilians working for heaven knew what interest. . . . His successor Major du Peuty later aroused equally violent opposition. Naturally impatient, he couldn't endure the Paris cabal. He returned to active service as soon as he could and sadly was killed shortly afterwards. Major du Peuty was a man of absolute rectitude and loyalty, completely unsuited to intrigue.'

The collapse of the government on 20 March 1917 ushered in a new minister, Paul Painlevé, and a new under-secretary, Daniel Vincent, whose appointment coincided with the belated arrival of some new bomber and cooperation types. 'At last,' commented an optimistic Major Antonin Brocard (GC13), 'we have squadrons with aircraft capable of looking after themselves.' True enough in theory, but in practice most of these new types proved less than satisfactory. The Voisin 8 bomber was no match for the German fighters; the Paul Schmitt 7 – designed in 1915 but delayed in production – was a complete and costly failure; and by the time the Sopwith 1½ Strutter entered service, it too was obsolete, so much so that GQG eventually pleaded with the minister to stop sending them out and supply the superior new Breguet 14 instead. But, with long contracts, the minister's hands were tied: 'I have to,' he replied. 'I don't have anything else. With the best will in the world, I can't turn out Breguets from a factory currently producing Sopwiths.' The army committee was unimpressed: better to cancel the contract, it suggested, than supply squadrons with an obsolescent type. Meanwhile, the STAé-produced designs were little better: the A.R.2 was little improvement on the Farman it replaced, while the Letord was so big it caused overcrowding problems on the airfields. Vincent, whose tenure lasted just six months, immediately ordered the STAé to stop designing aircraft and return to its original function of offering research and technical support to existing manufacturers.

Accusations of profiteering muddied the waters throughout: Caudron's receipts grew thirtyfold in 1914–15 alone; Nieuport's, fortyfold. In his bitter 1917 polemic *Les Profiteurs de la guerre*, the pseudonymous 'Mauricius' railed at 'the degree of incompetence or complicity required of officials when the army was charged 42 francs for an altimeter worth 3½ francs and was still paying 14 francs even after the renegotiation of prices in 1917'. Manufacturer Henry Potez became a leading supplier of the French Air Force in the 1930s: '[Manufacturers] clearly had fairly substantial costs,' he observed. '[Nevertheless] constructors like Blériot, Caudron etc. [were] very nicely placed. It was certainly . . . a very happy period for them.'

On his appointment as commander-in-chief in May 1917, Pétain introduced new operational ideas based around limited offensives launched only after achieving sudden, overwhelming local superiority in firepower – and aviation was key to his plans: 'To achieve tactical surprise we must attack without warning,' he explained, 'using either our artillery and bomber squadrons in as short and intense a period of preparation as possible or tanks to make the breakthrough and clear the way for the artillery and infantry without any preliminary bombardment. Aviation is now vital to overall victory. We must acquire air superiority.'

To implement these ideas two key appointments were made: Colonel Charles Duval replaced Paul du Peuty as GQG's aviation commander, and Deputy Jacques-Louis Dumesnil, a former observer with C13, succeeded Daniel Vincent as under-secretary for aeronautics. The pair quickly established a good working relationship, soon threatened when incoming prime minister Georges Clemenceau moved the SFA from the ministry of war to the ministry of munitions, distancing aircraft procurement still further from front-line operations and divorcing it from the STAé's research and development function. Duval and Pétain were incensed: 'All rear area services should be combined under a single firm hand,' Pétain complained to the minister of war. 'The recent reorganization . . . has fragmented responsibility and destroyed any effective chain of command. . . . The decree of 19 November 1917 completely failed to specify how the new command structure will operate. It is vital that we develop a close working relationship between front and rear and this will only serve to make it more difficult.'

Dumesnil became deputy to the minister of munitions, Louis Loucheur. 'The job before me is undoubtedly the hardest I have ever faced,' Loucheur warned the parliamentary munitions sub-committee on 6 December 1917. 'I am not sure whether I'll be equal to it. You can rest assured I will do my best, but I wouldn't wish it on anyone to sit in my place and assume such a terrible responsibility.' The current expansion plan called for a force of 4,000 aircraft by March 1918, but Loucheur remained deliberately vague: 'I am reluctant to make predictions, to promise you this or that number of aircraft,' he continued. 'My programme is the maximum.'

Despite Pétain's forebodings, the personalities involved managed to make the system work. By the spring of 1918 Loucheur, Dumesnil, Duval and new director of aviation Colonel Paul-François Dhé had overseen a substantial increase in production, using a large number of sub-contractors to manufacture just half a dozen types, among them a number of significant new aircraft. The fighter squadrons were equipped with the new SPAD 13, a powerful, manoeuvrable type armed with twin Vickers machine guns and superior to any of its opponents. The day bomber squadrons received the Breguet 14B2, a stable but agile platform, armed with three machine guns and capable of carrying over 250 kilos, while the night bomber squadrons were first given the Voisin 10 – with a payload of 300 kilos and a Renault engine to replace the under-powered Peugeot – and eventually the Farman F.50. The Caudron R.11 long-range fighter replaced the Letord as a bomber escort, while the reconnaissance squadrons received either the Breguet 14 or the new Salmson 2 A.2. Paul Waddington (SPA154) certainly appreciated these new types. 'By mid-1918 our planes were more powerful than their German counterparts. It gave us a considerable advantage and conferred a certain peace of mind on anyone capable of using his aircraft's rate of climb.'

In a time of rapid technological change, producing the right planes in the right numbers at the right time was no easy task. 'The aviation service made steady progress throughout the war while apparently in a state of perpetual crisis,' recalled Dumesnil. 'After each advance some new requirement forced itself upon us, and obviously there was always enough of a gap between the appearance in prototype of a wonderful new aircraft and its subsequent testing and entry into production for the appearance of an improved design that superseded its predecessor.' Yet by November 1918 a massive state-sponsored mobilization had transformed the embryonic aviation industry. The sector was now worth some 5 million francs, equivalent to almost 13 per cent of pre-war national output, and employed 183,000 people – almost a quarter of them women. During the conflict French manufacturers turned out over 52,000 aircraft in 365 different types, annual production of airframes rising from 541 in 1914 to 24,652 in 1918, and output of engines from 860 in the last five months of 1914 to 3,502 in November 1918 alone. The French aircraft industry was also vital to the wider allied effort, supplying some 10,000 airframes and 25,000 engines to the United States, Britain, Russia, Italy, Belgium and Romania.

Sixty-two different companies operated just over a hundred factories, with the early inventor-constructors like Blériot, Caudron, Esnault-Pelterie [REP], Farman, Nieuport and Voisin gradually eclipsed by newcomers initially employed as subcontractors. Among them were firms which later came to dominate the inter-war aviation industry, such as Latécoère and SECM (Amiot) for airframes, and Hispano-Suiza and Lorraine for engines, as well as the Michelin tyre company, which pioneered 'American mass production techniques in the aeronautical industry, as well as working from templates, undoubtedly becoming the leading French constructor in terms of daily output'.

However, Dumesnil's plans favoured companies with ready access to capital and production capacity, disadvantaging smaller, potentially innovative, competitors. 'In 1917 the inventors lost out to constructors who hadn't produced a single new aircraft or engine type since mobilization,' complained Georges Huisman. One of those inventors was SFA engineer Marcel Bloch, who in 1917 'realized [. . .] there was no decent two-seater fighter and decided to build one'. His designs did not even reach the prototype stage, and the armistice temporarily put an end to his dreams. 'Everyone thought the war we'd just won, and at such cost in human lives, was the last – hence the expression the "war to end all wars". The SFA told us we could make doors, windows or wheelbarrows if we liked, but it would be a while before any more aircraft orders came along and any that were placed would go to the larger concerns like Voisin, Breguet and Farman, with a bigger workforce and more resources.' Bloch rejected a move into civil aviation: 'I had too much to lose. It would have been easier to sell ties in the metro than long-distance aircraft.' Returning to the industry in 1929, he changed his name to Dassault and went on to found a firm that remains one of the world's leading aerospace companies.

Every model that rolled off the production line was tested, as were the prototypes for new and updated types, either by the STAé or the manufacturer's own in-house test pilots. 'It was vital that no plane entered front-line service without first being thoroughly tested,' insisted Auguste Heiligenstein (MF5/MF44/C106/229), who became an STAé inspector after crashing at the front. 'The missions themselves were quite dangerous enough without the risk of an aircraft unfit for service breaking up in mid-air.' The Swiss aviation pioneer François Durafour – who, like all foreign volunteers, had entered the aviation service via the Foreign Legion – was a *réceptionneur* stationed at Buc, where his main role was testing two-seaters destined for the front. A mechanic – often Marcel Bloch – accompanied him in the observer's seat, taking notes on the aircraft's performance. Durafour tested 816 aircraft, including some 500 Nieuports, but his career came to an abrupt end on 18 July 1918 when he nosed over on landing: 'I went sailing over the upper wing with my head between my knees and before ending up amid some apples I had just enough time to see Ricaux following the same trajectory . . . We were reunited in hospital, knees and ankles dislocated, covered in cuts and bruises.' Durafour was demobilized on discharge, returned to Geneva and in 1921 became the first man to touch down on Mont Blanc.

Testing prototypes was even more dangerous, as Durafour discovered when he took the controls of the Vendôme A.3, a three-seater army cooperation aircraft that proved too complicated for front-line service and was never chosen for production: 'The Vendôme was . . . specially designed to leave the observer a clear field of forward fire, so its two engines were buried crosswise in the fuselage between the passenger and the pilot. Although a magnificent plane, it was still an unknown quantity, and my job was to test it. My instructions were simply to taxi in a straight line a few times. Fine in theory, less so in practice . . . As soon as I started her up, I realized I couldn't move in a straight line because the engines weren't synchronized. Fine, a bit more juice and they started ticking over properly . . . I picked up speed . . . and there I was on Villacoublay airfield. I prepared to stop. Then suddenly my height was 10 metres; a little hop and a skip and I was off the ground. I was in the air in a new, previously untested plane . . . Now what? Every pilot knows cutting the engines and returning to the ground means crashing. Full throttle and ease back on the controls then. But now I'd something else to worry about. How would the plane react when I turned? The centrifugal force exerted by two rotary engines each a metre wide could certainly do some damage. I suddenly lost airspeed and landed nose first, wheels in the air – quite an unusual sight. I was trapped in the fuselage, head buried 30 centimetres in the ground. "Don't light up, lads!" I shouted from the depths of my prison. "Fetch help! I'm suffocating in here!" Luckily they were back within minutes to rescue me from my unhappy predicament.'

Louis Breguet's test pilot was André de Bailliencourt: 'I saw the pilot of a SPAD 17 killed testing a 300hp engine fitted in a frame intended for a 180hp,' he later recalled. 'He was conducting speed trials. We saw that his plane had lost its wings. It continued its trajectory like a shell and hit the ground, the propeller still turning full speed and the fuselage spinning in the opposite direction.' On another occasion, a Caudron test pilot and an STAé representative had joined de Bailliencourt to inspect a four-engined Blériot: '"What do you reckon?" one of them asked. All three of us pointed to a spot on the tail: "It's definitely going to break there." All we could do was advise [the pilot] to fly in a straight line and not to attempt a turn.'

The pilot ignored their advice and tried to complete a circuit: 'The tail began trembling ominously. Suddenly it broke exactly where we had feared. The plane went straight down and immediately burst into flames. It had 4,000 litres of petrol on board. Poor devil!'

Specialist knowledge was absolutely vital, yet in March 1918 Louis Breguet chose a complete unknown, Maréchal des Logis Jean Sauclière (N79), to test the experimental Laboratoire Eiffel fighter. (De Baillencourt, a bomber specialist, had refused to do so without extra training, and other test pilots had all demanded a substantial bonus.) '[Sauclière] behaved very oddly,' wrote de Bailliencourt. 'Settling before the controls, he started up the engine, shouted "chocks away" and taxied on to the airfield. Once beyond the hangars, he opened the throttle and pulled right back on the joystick. The plane climbed a few feet and then fell to the ground, causing some damage particularly to the undercarriage. But the pilot was undeterred. "Wonderful," he said as he walked off. "I'll get my bonus." We [later] discovered he'd been offered a bonus "for the first flight". Who was this individual so ignorant about testing? We [later] learned he was a front-line pilot recently discharged from hospital after coming down in flames in a SPAD. His mother was a famous actress [Jeanne Saulier] who had asked Louis Breguet if her son could do some testing to keep him in the rear.'

The plane was repaired and the following morning Sauclière returned, this time 'accompanied by a bevy of girls'. In vain de Bailliencourt tried to dissuade him from flying: 'I told him it was the wrong time of day. I'd just been up and the heat was causing a lot of turbulence. Better to come back early tomorrow. . . . "I'll be fine," he said. I told him to ease open the throttle so he could test the plane's reactions. "I'll be fine," he repeated, starting up the engine. . . . The chocks were removed and he taxied clear of the hangars. But instead of continuing to the end of the airfield he opened up the throttle immediately. The plane took off perfectly and passed in front of us in impeccably level flight. But after 300 or 400 metres it dived full throttle and burst into flames as soon as it hit the ground. A dreadful sight to behold!'

In the end the accident was attributed to human error, but de Bailliencourt knew better: Breguet and Gustave Eiffel should never have employed 'a pilot with no experience of testing, and I suspect no knowledge of the role'. The L.E. never went into full production: pilots questioned the plane's structural integrity, while Breguet himself was preoccupied with building the Breguet 14.

'A supreme joy' – aerial combat
In September 1916 Captain Henri de Kérillis (C66) was waiting by the roadside with Georges Guynemer (MS/N/SPA3), near Villers-Bretonneux, when an infantry column marched past. 'Guynemer stepped aside and clambered up the bank,' recalled de Kérillis. 'The soldiers were returning from the trenches. We always stopped when soldiers were passing. Crowned by a forest of rifles, these men looked wretched, weary and drawn, but they were trailing clouds of glory. Guynemer looked on. Suddenly someone shouted, "Guynemer! It's Guynemer!" The troops all rushed to join in. "Guynemer . . . Guynemer," they bellowed. A great hubbub broke out in the ranks. Men who had been staring at the ground, consumed by unknown torments, looked up and recognized him. The sentimental songs and the murmuring ceased. Something incredible happened. "Guynemer . . . Guynemer . . .". Infantrymen who ran across aviators normally chaffed them about their fancy lace-up boots and grey runabouts. But Guynemer was immune from all that. He was no mere pilot . . . he was a man apart. He was the hero personified. He was Guynemer.'

Although Guynemer was lauded as the apotheosis of French fighter pilots, the deeds of his comrades also received plenty of publicity. As a small boy, future general and Free French fighter pilot Raymond Brohon had been caught up in all the hero worship. 'I was born in 1911,' he remembered, 'and we happened to live . . . close to the front line in the Toul sector, not far from Bois-le-Prêtre, famous in the annals of 1914–18. As a youngster in 1916 I used to watch the planes chasing each other across the sky. I wouldn't go down into the shelters. I used to give my mother the slip and watch it all. I was spellbound. It was so exciting! And even as a child I always tried to snap up all the literature. They used to sell short biographies of Navarre, Guynemer, etc. I had quite a collection.'

Aviators, and fighter pilots in particular, were lionized from the start of the conflict, particularly after February 1915 when Alphonse Pégoud (MF25/MS37/49) shot down three enemy aircraft in one day. In an increasingly industrialized war with its enormous toll of anonymous casualties, the successes of pilots from MS12, in their single-seater MS Parasols, could be presented as 'victories' in an otherwise sterile year and served a useful role in moulding public opinion. Newspapers and magazines, particularly Jacques Mortane's *La Guerre aérienne illustrée*, borrowed the sporting term 'ace', and the usage was officially adopted for any pilot who had obtained five or more victories – defining a victory as a plane seen by two independent witnesses 'to have broken up in the air, come down in flames or crashed into the ground'. By 1918 the official qualification had been doubled to ten, although unofficially the older usage remained current. Over the course of the conflict just 182 men – 3 per cent of all trained pilots – achieved five victories or more, together accounting for almost half the final tally of 3,950 confirmed victories. The forty leading aces, all with a minimum of twelve victories, were alone responsible for a fifth of the overall total; of these forty, ten were killed during the conflict, three more were invalided out of combat flying, and a further ten died in flying accidents during the decade after the armistice.

'It's easier to down a German than it is to get a victory confirmed,' grumbled leading French ace René Fonck (C47/SPA103), who reckoned he could have added another sixty-four victims downed behind enemy lines to his final tally of seventy-five. Sous-lieutenant Arnaud de P. was equally frustrated by the rules. 'I attacked and downed a Boche,' he reported at Verdun. 'Unfortunately, he managed to get home and land about 100 metres inside his own lines. I'm hoping someone on our side . . . saw him. Two kilometres less and it would have been the *Croix de guerre* for me. I might get a mention in despatches if one of our balloons spotted him. But did they, though? I'm off to find out. You must have two witnesses.'

Arnaud presumably looked in vain – no claim was ever registered in his name – but when Georges Guynemer needed to track down a victim on 5 December 1915, he had help from an unexpected quarter. Flying close to the family home in Compiègne, Guynemer shot down an Aviatik and saw it fall in the forest. He landed and immediately contacted his father, who promptly telephoned every commune in the vicinity to ask the mayor to organize a thorough search. The wreck was located and Guynemer duly notched up his second victory (and first in a single-seater). The rules hit naval pilots hardest of all: they seldom recorded a confirmed victory, most of their actions taking place at sea, out of sight of any observer.

Pre-war star Marc Pourpre (MS23) was particularly celebrated for his long-distance flights in France's Asian colonies and expected the appropriate recognition for his military deeds. 'I'm really down in the dumps,' he wrote to Jacques Mortane in the autumn of 1914. 'For reasons that remain a mystery to me, I'm still just a private. Our captain came to apologize. Apparently it's an oversight. My wound in September and mention in despatches deserved the *Médaille militaire*. The officer flying as passenger on the day I brought my plane back peppered with shrapnel has been awarded the *Croix* [*de guerre*]. It's very demoralizing. My comrades don't understand it at all. I've been terribly unlucky. I'd been put forward for the *Croix* before mobilization; now it seems to be eluding me because of the war. I've put in seventy-eight hours' flying time over the enemy since the conflict began and not a single stripe. I'm the only man in the squadron who's been hit and wounded by the Boches. It's dreadful. I'm only telling you this because I'm feeling so low and want to get it off my chest. I still love fighting the Teutons and shooting them down, but this sort of favouritism really does rankle.'

Pourpre died in a crash-landing in December 1914, still undecorated and still a simple private. During 1915, however, privates gaining their wings began to receive an automatic promotion to corporal, and ten hours of accumulated combat flying usually guaranteed a promotion to sergeant. Further advancement, first to adjudant and then to commissioned status, depended largely on a combination of experience and deeds.

If a plane came down behind French lines, pilots might be tempted to land beside their victim – to make certain of their victory, capture the crew or perhaps pick up a souvenir. In 1917 Major Brocard, the CO of GC12, issued orders forbidding such 'glory hunting': 'Pilots are expressly instructed not to land beside a plane shot down behind our lines. At most, they are permitted to land at the nearest airfield. Unjust as it may seem, the CO will not confirm the victory of any pilot who lands next to a Boche, risking a crash and showing an excessive mistrust of his comrades. This kind of behaviour also displays a total ignorance of our real objective, which is to shoot down and kill the Boches, not claim more or less personal success.' René Fonck would have scoffed at this idea. Like Georges Guynemer, he was intensely ambitious: 'I hit a man square in the chest and his plane broke up as it fell,' he wrote. 'I was still excited when I landed. I told myself I'd done a good day's work. If every day went similarly, the other [aces] would find it hard to stay ahead of me in the table.' But journalist René Chavagnes suggested that many aces shared Brocard's view: 'The whole idea of competition or a league table is anathema to them.

'There is no first! There is no second. We're all just pilots,' replied Nungesser, when a chap went up to him in the Ambassadeurs and congratulated him on holding second place.'

One ace who cared little for numbers was Jean Navarre (N67). 'Navarre was greatly loved, particularly by the younger men,' commented Adjudant Jean Casale (N23). 'If he fought alongside a comrade . . . he gave him the victory, unless the aircraft came down behind our lines, which didn't happen often.' According to René Fisch, Casale had personal experience of this generosity: '"I almost downed my first aircraft this morning," [Casale told us]. "It was an Albatros. He couldn't see me because he was blinded by the sun [and] I crept up behind him. I had my finger on the trigger, just about to fire, but before I had time to let off a shot, a red plane swooped down like a bird of prey. Bang, bang, bang . . . he passed straight between us, and the German fell in flames." Just as he finished speaking, the captain walked into the mess. He solemnly approached [Casale] and embraced him: "Ah, Casale! Congratulations. You've downed your first victim. That's your first mention in despatches. Navarre has just been on the telephone. You fought like a lion . . ." Well, we could hardly contain our laughter. And with some justification, don't you think, when [Casale] had just told us he hadn't even pressed the trigger? Still . . . it didn't stop him from eventually shooting down twenty planes.'

According to Jacques Mortane, the adulation accorded the fighter aces extended to the aviation service in general. 'I've interviewed a lot of poilus and asked them what they think of pilots,' he reported. '"They're wonderful," they tell me. "We don't know where we'd be without them."' Maréchal des Logis Pierre Cazenove de Pradines (N81) certainly received a warm reception when he scrambled for safety into the French trenches after being shot down over no man's land: 'I'll never forget the way the poilus of 213th Infantry welcomed their brother from the sky, nor the supreme honour for a pilot and ex-cavalryman [de Pradines had previously served in 19th Hussars] of a mention from the colonel in regimental despatches.' Even the pilots of a cooperation squadron like C51 had their admirers. 'We infantrymen follow you from our holes,' Private A. Glaure wrote to the CO. 'Nothing you do escapes our attention. You are our gods. In fact, I'd even say our guardian angels. If a day goes by without us seeing you, we're like children sent to bed without pudding.'

In return, many flyers felt a sense of obligation towards the men in the trenches. 'How can we possibly be compared to the infantryman who goes over the top?' responded one group of pilots quizzed by Mortane. Some, like Navarre at Verdun, would overfly the troops just to raise their spirits.

'[I flew] at a height of 50 metres, just 250 metres from the Boche front line,' reported André Quennehen (MF5) on 22 October 1915. 'Heavy gunfire obviously [but] not a single round hit my plane. The poilus were thrilled. These stunts were great for morale.' Auguste Heiligenstein (MF5/MF44/C106/C229) agreed: 'Our very presence showed the [poilus] that they hadn't been forgotten. Each time I visited the colonel of a regiment resting in the rear, he told me how much we helped the poilus by flying low over their heads. The fact that we were sharing the same risks was also very important.' And, he continued, aviators could also have a more practical impact: 'We could stop an advance by determining whether or not a machine-gun post had been destroyed and that more than anything boosted the morale of the ground troops.'

Yet, as the war dragged on, contrary opinions began to be heard. Fighter pilots were accused of arrogance, particularly by their comrades in the two-seater squadrons. 'The gentlemen of the fighter squadrons were inclined to think themselves our superiors,' claimed reconnaissance pilot Louis Lelandais (SOP104/BR287), ' . . . as ex-cavalrymen, they rather looked down on us.' *La Guerre aérienne illustrée* admitted this was so. 'Some fighter pilots treat the [reconnaissance crews] with the same disdain as the cavalryman for the infantryman, the aristocrat for the commoner, the spoiled brat for the working man,' wrote Jacques Mortane. 'The pride of the fighter pilot stems from his plane,' added H.–C. in November 1917. 'He thumbs his nose at his fellow aviators, slaves to their heavy, sluggish machines. They [in turn] are irritated by his scorn. They feel like the poor relations of the great family of the air.'

Mortane reminded his readers that there was good reason for this hauteur: 'The fighter squadrons are the basis of our aerial superiority. They are the reason the skies are clear. They are the ones who have seen off all the unwelcome visitors [and] allow the other specialists to carry out their duties.' But Lelandais was annoyed by the publicity accorded the fighter aces. 'A pilot who shot down one or two aircraft didn't attract much attention,' he complained. 'But after four or five he received a mention in despatches and got his name in the papers. And after downing twenty-five, thirty or forty, he wasn't just an ace, he was a super ace. We reconnaissance pilots spent all day over the lines. We followed the infantry into the attack, sometimes flying very low over the lines at risk from guns and bullets, not to mention our own artillery, and German planes.'

La Guerre aérienne illustrée was sympathetic to the two-seater crews, arguing that they needed their own list of 'aces' and suggesting a minimum qualification of 100 missions over the lines. Just over fifty men met the standard, but the newspapers found nothing glamorous in their work and the scheme came to nought. Meanwhile *La Mitraille*, the trench newspaper of 64th Division, pressed the claims of the humble infantryman: 'There are plenty of aces in the aviation service. The newspapers celebrate their victories every day and we pay sincere tribute to the heroism of our brother soldiers. We admire them greatly. But why do our so-called "newspapers of record" continue to overlook the infantry aces who are no less their equal? Many ordinary infantrymen hold five, six, seven or even eight citations. Thirteen have received the *Légion d'honneur*. Why do the press never mention them? Is the infantry perhaps the "poor relation" of the French army in some eyes?'

For many infantrymen, volunteering for aviation was simply another form of shirking. 'While our fearless officers are nicely tucked up in the bottom of the sap, we have to stay here and be slaughtered,' grumbled one member of 241st Infantry in 1917. 'All three were patriots before they left for the front, [but] one has gone into aviation, one has headed for the depot and the other has stayed in hospital.' Another cynic served with 101st Infantry: 'While our pilots woo and bed the wives of the mugs at the front, along come the Boches and bomb the rear.'

Criticism intensified during some of the big set-piece offensives, ground troops complaining bitterly that friendly aircraft were unable to protect them from enemy spotters and strafers. At Verdun Colonel Rohan (358th Infantry) took a sceptical view of the offensive deployment of the fighters: '[The] shortcomings [of the aviation service] . . . weighed very heavily on the spirits of our men,' he fumed. 'There was a complete lack of organization and discipline. The aces were allowed to do pretty much as they pleased and naturally chose the dashing, dangerous missions in preference to th[os]e thankless tasks that are nevertheless so vital. And no one had yet organized continuous cover over our lines, if only to give our infantry, who felt completely abandoned, the sense that their winged brothers were fighting alongside them.' Sous-lieutenant Prevot and the men of 87th Infantry were more forthright still in their opinions: 'An enemy aircraft flies very low over our position and turns his machine gun on us. We all agree that the enemy aviators in this sector show a lot more pluck than our own.'

On the Chemin des Dames the complaints were identical. 'German planes come strafing our lines all day, while our own are invisible,' grumbled a member of 112th Heavy Artillery. 'You aviation types all looked the part,' snarled a lieutenant colonel of zouaves, 'but enemy aircraft were out spotting our positions every morning. That's why I lost half my men on 17 April.' Even Jacques Mortane was forced to admit the fiasco had damaged the reputation of the service: 'Don't be surprised after this if you see a mud-spattered soldier with a month's worth of beard give an old-fashioned look to the elegant maréchal des logis wearing a tunic with the famous [pilot's] badge.' Mortane pinned the blame on a number of bad apples: 'It has become far too easy for the public to confuse the true pilot with real fire in his belly with the rotter who, in airfield parlance, "has no guts". . . . I am sure that . . . any [pilot] who believes the role of aviation is to launch new fashions and cause a sensation will soon be returned to his original arm of service.' The 'true' pilot was advised to ignore these 'elegant aviators cluttering the boulevards, theatres and bars in their tan boots and extravagant uniforms' and model himself instead on the taciturn Adjudant René Dorme (C94/CRP/N3): 'It's a waste of time trying to spot [this ace] in the street. In fact, you never see him on the boulevards or at the theatre. And if, by chance, he should venture out and about, his tunic bears [just] three inconspicuous ribbons: the *Légion d'honneur*, the *Médaille militaire* and the *Croix de guerre*.'

One anonymous chasseur summed up the feelings of his pals: 'Muddy and miserable, huddled in the bottom of his trench, the poilu reads his newspaper and spies a whole column devoted to the latest exploit of one of our aces. "You'd think these aviators are the only ones with any mettle," he protests. And flyers enjoy much more than individual renown. Unlike the men in the ranks, they get hours of complete rest and relaxation between the hard knocks. They get comfortable billets near to big towns, with *pinard* and civilians – male . . . and female.'

Having spent time in 21st Colonial Infantry before qualifying as a pilot in April 1917, Louis Lelandais also thought aviation a cushy number: 'You had smart uniforms, it was easier to get leave, you could go sauntering round Paris. Not like the infantryman, emerging from the trenches lathered in mud, filthy, uncombed, unwashed and unshaven. His existence was pure penal servitude. . . . "We've nothing to complain about," I used to tell any grumblers. "I think we live like kings."' Marcel Brindejonc des Moulinais (DO22/N23) would have found few grounds for disagreement. 'Yesterday I ate wild duck,' he wrote to Jacques Mortane. 'Today it's partridge for lunch and probably pheasant this evening. I rose at half past eight this morning and I've just had breakfast: a big bowl of milk, two fried eggs and a duck breast.' And Captain Z. was equally well found: 'Thanks to the legendary sixth sense of the aviator on campaign . . . the squadron almost always contrived to find a billet close to a village with welcoming homes and shops well stocked with a wide variety of provisions.'

For off-duty pilots Paris was a magnet. 'Any good aviator has to spend plenty of time on leave,' commented Lieutenant Jean Pastré (BR7), tongue firmly in cheek. 'How else can he keep abreast of the latest fashions, find out whether cross-belts are in or out, or even learn the latest tricks of his trade over a chat in his preferred training schools, Fouquet's or Maxim's. Demonstrating a spin in the Place de la Concorde or the Café de la Paix: how's that for combining the horrors of war with the pleasures of the days to come, the serious and the frivolous, for preserving the style – sadly long gone – of the tourneys of old?'

'"Leave" without "Paris"', reckoned William Wellman (N87), 'was no leave at all.'

Manufacturers like Voisin, Nieuport and SPAD courted the pilots who flew their planes. 'Leave was introduced in 1915,' recalled aircraft manufacturer Gabriel Voisin, 'and the first chaps were expected to arrive in Paris thirsting for liberty . . . In 1914 I had bought a little house on the Boulevard Lannes previously owned by a famous mystic, Sâr [Joséphin] Péladan. I held the house-warming in 1915 and all my guests were aces: Nungesser, who'd scored his victory in a Voisin; my brother's friend Garros; my chum Audemar; Léon and Robert Morane, recently recovered from an accident. All the best bomber and fighter pilots were there.'

The large number of young ladies in attendance soon made Voisin's house on the Boulevard Lannes *the* social centre for off-duty pilots, as well as attracting police attention. But when the *flics* came calling, it was Charles Nungesser (V106/V116/N/SPA65), '*l'hussard de la mort*' (Death's Hussar), who took control: 'With his blonde hair, battered face, china-blue eyes, mocking smile and scarred chin, he had the bearing, the self-confidence and the voice.' He calmly drew the gendarmes aside and within minutes had them drinking a toast to fighter pilots. Furthermore, confessed the owner, 'when dawn [finally] crept upon us, the ladies were wearing the policemen's uniforms.' Nungesser – whose personal insignia was a skull and crossbones, a coffin and two candles, all enclosed within a black heart – later attempted to defend the roistering: 'They're not women. They're pals. You have a good time together. All aviators are playboys. We fly fighter planes. We hunt down a Boche or fly a mission (no more special missions, by the way, they're no good for your health). You come home and head to Paris for a couple of days. That's all there is to it.'

An ace was particularly prized as a companion. 'Of course I'm a godmother,' states a character in *La Guerre, Madame*, Paul Géraldy's contemporary comic novel about *marraines de guerre*, the 'godmothers' who 'adopted' individual soldiers at the front. 'I really wanted an aviator but all the girls are chasing them.' Rumour had it that actress Yvonne Printemps had abandoned her lover, actor/director Sacha Guitry, to join Georges Guynemer at his usual Paris hotel, the Édouard VII, on the Place de l'Opéra. 'To be honest, everyone knew about it,' recalled the actress Arletty. 'People said how lucky she was – an air ace, the youngest, the most famous. She'd have been a fool to turn him down.'

Sous-lieutenant Philippe de Forceville (MF33) spotted the pair together. 'When Guynemer picked up his *Légion d'honneur* [in July 1917], General Franchet d'Espèrey assembled an [entire] division for the ceremony. The whole aviation service was represented [and] I attended on behalf of 33rd Squadron . . . Afterwards, Guynemer invited us to dine. All the senior officers had left by then and we joined the pilots from Brocard's [N3] – favourites of ours because they provided our escorts . . . Who should turn up [but] Yvonne Printemps? That's when we discovered she was Guynemer's mistress. All the aviators stayed at the Édouard VII when they were in Paris, Guynemer included; the porter knew all the comings and goings. We always dined at the Café de Paris because it had heated seats and Yvonne Printemps liked a warm derrière. Guynemer never received a bill so I'm sure he never had to pay. Of course, we all used to get one. He'd ask us to pay then reimburse us later.'

Jean Navarre (N67) was also happy to profit from his fame. 'He never went anywhere expecting to pay,' claimed his comrade Lieutenant Alfred Rougevin-Baville (N67). 'He frequented the Café de Paris, a famous restaurant on the Avenue de l'Opéra. "I am Navarre," he would announce in restaurants and theatres. This was his "open sesame" and he never had to get out his wallet. One day, however, the maître d' gave him the bill. Navarre took his kepi – never hung up but always kept under his arm – and passed it round the restaurant, collecting coins and notes. He paid the maître d' and pocketed the rest.'

Fast planes, fast women, fine dining – and fast cars: many aces found it hard to resist the lure of the automobile. Among the motorists was Jules Védrines (DO22/MS/N3): 'Clad always in a black-and-white checked cap, worn back to front for flying, [and] a tight-fitting, white woollen roll-neck sweater, [he] set female hearts aflutter driving through the smart streets of Paris at the wheel of his fabulous bright red Hispano sports car. Védrines was a star.' Nungesser encountered trouble with the law again after borrowing a sports car from Pégoud and setting off, 'cigar in mouth, smiling broadly, frightening pedestrians to death and giving them a mouthful if they complained'. Meanwhile Guynemer was also stopped by a *flic* as he bowled along Rue Brunel in a Sigma sports car presented to him by the manufacturer. 'My name is Guynemer,' he declared loftily, refusing a request to produce his papers, 'and you, Officer 323 of the seventeenth *arrondissement*, will be hearing from your superiors about your rudeness.'

Guynemer and Nungesser both got away scot free, but not so Jean Navarre. After a premature return from convalescence and his twin brother's death in action, Navarre became increasingly erratic in his behaviour. On 9 April 1917, the worse for drink, he decided to take his Hispano-Suiza for a spin around town and ended up driving on the pavement. Ordered to stop by two gendarmes who shot at his tyres when he failed to comply, he roared back on to the road, ran into another two *flics* and punched one who tried to remonstrate with him. The pilot fled back to Vadelaincourt but was followed and arrested a short time later. After a brief spell in the Cherche-Midi military prison, he spent the next eighteen months in a sanatorium. Although released in September 1918, he was still at a training establishment when the armistice was signed and never saw action again.

Maxime Lenoir (C18/N23) enjoyed all the publicity and refused to believe anyone who claimed otherwise: 'Some feign modesty and say they don't give a damn [but] a fighter pilot's greatest thrill is to down his fifth plane and know he's entitled to a mention in despatches. Waking up one morning to find that your name is known all over the world, that it's in all the newspapers, is unforgettable.' However, the famously austere Captain Alfred Heurteaux (MS38/N/SPA3) was adamant that he had no time for the trappings of fame: 'We were irritated by all the letters we had to deal with, all the invitations . . . we were just like pop stars,' he recalled in the 1970s. 'We piled the letters on the squadron table. Each of us knew which letter or letters he was looking out for. We opened the rest together. You wouldn't believe the kind of stuff we received. We were fed up with all the fuss. I went to a restaurant with Guynemer. When we left, we found pieces of jewellery with addresses in our overcoat pockets. What sort of nonsense was that?'

Even Guynemer grew weary of the constant adulation. Journalist Jeanne Tournier bumped into him in the lift of the Édouard VII: 'We all stared at the face so familiar to us from the newspapers. We were worried about him. We thought he looked pale. We were particularly struck by his eyes: staring straight ahead, very black, very bright, rather feverish in their intensity. . . . The lift boy finally recovered from his confusion and opened the door. The gallant aviator stepped back to let us pass. But all the ladies hesitated. We couldn't bring ourselves to walk in front of him, to treat him like anyone else. We were also seeking the right gesture, the right sign, to show him how much we admired him. As if he was a mind-reader, the hero hung back, smiling. Our group included a ravishing young beauty and he gazed at her for a moment. We stood motionless as we watched the officer's slender form disappear down the long corridor. We were lost for words, rooted to the spot by his combination of frailty and courage. . . . Women don't go to war, but we reckoned quite a few of us were stronger than that young man.'

In August 1917 Adjudant Armand Viguier (VB107) was in Paris picking up a new plane. Strolling along the Avenue de l'Opéra, close to the Hotel Édouard VII, he too spotted Guynemer, just weeks before the ace was lost over the Ypres salient: 'Tan boots, red trousers with black stripes, medals all in a row. I could have gone straight up to him and said, "Hello, old chap. How are you?" The Parisians recognized him. How could they not when his picture was in all the papers? On the *grands boulevards*, the locals fell silent when he passed. They almost came to a stop. I followed him for some time. He was stooping slightly, tired of giving his all, marked out by death.'

'I was on an errand in Paris and met him on the boulevards just before his death,' recalled Major Louis Bernard-Thierry, former commander of the training school at Pau, where Guynemer had learned to fly. 'It was 7.00 pm so I invited my former fledgling to dine. We chatted briefly, then entered the Restaurant de la Madeleine. The room was full and the orchestra was playing at the rear. Guynemer was well known to the public and had an aviation major at his side, so we'd scarcely set foot through the door before he was greeted by a spontaneous ovation. Everyone stood up. The orchestra stopped for an instant, broke off the piece it had just begun and struck up a stirring *Marseillaise*. We searched for a modest little spot in the corner of the room. For the best part of an hour, an endless queue of diners came asking for a signature or a word or two on a menu or a postcard. It was almost impossible to eat. The women fawned over him, reaching out to touch him and to flirt. Some kissed his tunic or the long, palm-strewn ribbon of his *Croix de guerre*. When we finished our meal and left, the whole room rose again.'

Just a few days later Guynemer disappeared over Poelkapelle. Having created such an enormous national hero, the press could only seek to mythologize his death. 'No one saw or heard the crash,' wrote Henri Lavedan. 'Neither plane nor body has been found? What was he doing? What course did he set? Which wing did he use to glide into immortality? At what point in his zenith did he realize he was heaven bound. . . . He died in full flight, [a lark] ascending. We may eventually say: "One day the ace of aces flew so high in combat that he never returned to earth."'

Contemporaries tried to identify the characteristics that made Guynemer and his ilk so successful. 'Fighter pilots need more by way of special qualities than any other type of military aviator,' claimed Jacques Mortane. 'But some individuals have a real talent for it. That's the only reason for their rapid and frequent success.' For Paul Waddington (SPA154), innate daring was essential: 'You could say that anyone alive and kicking and without a victory after three or four months in a squadron was no fighter pilot. You always had to be ready to risk everything, and those unwilling to do so were the ones who never attacked at point-blank range, or indeed attacked at all. They didn't have the necessary "go". Speaking bluntly, any pilot without a victory after six months in a fighter squadron should have been transferred out.'

Equally important was a cool head. 'Unless a fighter pilot can disregard the danger, stay calm, identify and counter the slightest move on the part of the enemy – whether one or several – he may score a few lucky victories, but he'll never be the finished article and one day he'll meet his maker,' claimed René Fonck. 'I repeat, for real results you have to learn how to master your nerves, maintain absolute self-control and think rationally in tricky situations.' The pilot had to process a number of different variables in an instant – height, speed, angle, cloud cover, the position of the sun – and then react decisively and effectively. Natural talent certainly played its part, but experience also helped. Aerial combat did not become a regular feature of the conflict until February 1916, giving many of the aces plenty of time to learn their trade, accumulating hundreds of flying hours on reconnaissance missions (like Fonck, Georges Madon and Maxime Lenoir) or bombing raids (like Nungesser). Guynemer spent eight months from gaining his wings to the start of his real success; Nungesser, a year; Fonck, almost two years; and Madon (BL30/MF218/N/SPA38), nearly three. Then the victories came in a rush: 41 in 24 months for Madon, 42 in 33 months for Nungesser, 49 in 19 months for Guynemer and 74 in 21 months for Fonck.

'You need experienced aviators in a fighter squadron,' insisted Fonck. 'Beginners should never be posted direct. The intrepid will be downed within a matter of months while they're still new to the job, while the timid will be utterly useless for at least six months. . . . You only become a great "ace" after a long and difficult apprenticeship, littered with repeated disappointments and setbacks, during which you risk your life a hundred times over.' Maxime Lenoir agreed. 'You need plenty of flying hours to be a good fighter pilot,' he insisted. 'Some people think you run across a German every time you go up. That's ridiculous. Firstly, just finding one isn't enough, you have to make him accept combat. The sky isn't the Place de la Concorde. If someone is slightly ahead of you and wishes to get away, he can do so in perfect safety. You also need plenty of practice. Of course, some men score a victory their first time out. . . . I commend these upstarts but I don't envy them. They don't have the nous of the old hand with long experience over the lines. . . . "Slow and steady wins the race" applies more to aerial combat than to any other [area of aviation]. Without being too much of a Sancho Panza, I would also add "discretion is the better part of valour" and "patience is the best buckler against affronts". These are the general principles of fighter operations. I worked hard in my early days with N23; I was a grafter. My only ambition was to be a champion but I never assumed I could achieve it in a matter of days. I had plenty of frights en route to my first success.'

Yet novices *were* posted straight into fighter squadrons, especially after periods of heavy fighting. One such fledgling was Corporal René Fisch, who in July 1916 went straight from aerobatics school to N23: 'On the day I made my first flight over the lines, I was very proud, full of vim, but I came back empty-handed. I hadn't seen a thing. Adjudant [Maxime] Lenoir – though still not 28, the old man of the squadron! – was there to greet me. "Now then, young 'un, how did you get on?" he asked. "Spot any enemy aircraft?"

'"No," I replied. "I kept my eyes peeled but I didn't see a thing."

'"Tell me about wanting to blow your nose when you were over Les Éparges," he said. "You shouldn't carry your handkerchief in your flying-suit pocket, you know – particularly with the cold. It's better to keep it under your arm, like this. You spent at least five minutes looking for it. Fair enough, but you let the German get away. . . . Since it was your first time out I was 50 metres behind you the whole way."

'And I hadn't spotted him at all.

'"We're going back up right now," [he said]. "I'll teach you." And he passed on everything you should be learning in aerobatics school.'

Back in Paris in 1918 after three years in a German prison camp, Roland Garros returned to the offer of a staff post from Prime Minister Georges Clemenceau. But Garros rejected the idea: he wanted a front-line posting and instead joined the celebrated Storks as a lieutenant in SPA26. There, keen to catch up with all the latest developments in combat tactics, he set about picking the brains of his colleagues. 'He never stopped quizzing Captain [Xavier de] Sevin about fighting single-seaters and two-seaters, alone and in groups,' wrote René Chavagnes, 'and flew his first sorties with [the captain] without entering combat. Day after day he worked meticulously to get his plane in perfect running order and – because he's short-sighted – practised shooting his carbine in the spectacles he'd brought home from Germany.'

While de Sevin did all he could to help, Garros found it extraordinarily difficult to extract information from the rest of his comrades: 'When [they] did agree to abandon their exemplary reserve, it was usually to sing the praises of their perennial role models, the leading aces. But he had to make sure he approached them in the right way. Too direct a question was judged annoying or intrusive. Their horror of appearing to boast made them hide behind a façade of indifference, cynicism or detachment.' Charles Nungesser (V106/V116/N/SPA65) also used humour as a form of defence. 'It's quite simple . . . when I took on the enemy I was always afraid,' he claimed, tongue-in-cheek. 'I closed my eyes, never knowing if I would reopen them to see my opponent coming down in flames or me in a hospital bed.' So too, Maxime Lenoir: 'Entering combat is like diving. You shut your eyes and away you go. You reopen them and either the Boche is going down, or you've been hit, or – as is often the case – nothing has happened.'

Fresh out of training school in the summer of 1918, Sous-lieutenant Marcel Coadou (SPA88) found Gabriel Guérin (SPA15/88) slightly more forthcoming. 'After several unsuccessful attacks I approached the aces in the group,' confessed Coadou. "How did you gain your first victory so quickly?" I asked them. . . . Guérin [twenty-three confirmed victories] shared the secret with me. . . . "It's not difficult. You manoeuvre, position yourself directly behind [your opponent] and just when you think you're going to hit his tail with your propeller, you fire – but not before!"'

Similar tactics brought twenty-three victories for Adjudant René Dorme, who used aerobatics to place himself in his opponent's blind spot, then crept forward until he was within firing range. 'Opened fire from 6 or 7 metres,' he wrote of his first victory, achieved over Péronne on 9 July 1916. 'Observer killed, plane came down in a spin.' Guynemer admired him greatly: 'He shoots down [a Boche] a day! . . . His method is simple but not open to all. He spends six, seven or eight hours a day lying in wait. Then as soon as he spots a Boche flying towards him, he manoeuvres, puts on a bit of show, waits until his prey has wasted all his bullets, then opens fire. He's a fine shot, and three or four rounds are usually enough to produce the anticipated result. If not for the war, Dorme would have been an excellent man with rod and line.'

Alfred Heurteaux, with twenty-one victories, also stressed the importance of a keen eye. 'We never fired more than seven or eight rounds to bring down an aircraft,' he recalled. 'I even downed one with a single round.' Typically, Jean Navarre favoured the unexpected, sometimes flying into the attack upside down: 'Seeing me approach like this puts the German pilot off balance for an instant. Perhaps he's the one who's upside down? The key to the manoeuvre is to take advantage of this momentary pause for thought – aim, fire and try to come out on top.' René Fonck, however, spurned aerobatics: instead, he sought surprise. He lurked in the cloud at very high altitude, up to 6,000 metres, then he swooped down at top speed, took his shot and flew off before the enemy could react, whether or not he downed his opponent. 'Fonck . . . was an assassin,' said Paul Tarascon (N3/N31/SPA62). 'He simply dived, hit [his opponent] or brought him down within three or four rounds, then slipped away.' Guynemer, too, had no time for manoeuvring: 'I fly by the book. Aerobatics is my last resort. I stay right on my rival and once I've latched on to him I don't let go.'

Yet in other respects Guynemer and Fonck approached their task very differently: 'Guynemer seldom unleashed a surprise attack,' observed Sous-lieutenant Louis Risacher (SPA3). 'He gave his opponent a warning and offered him every chance. But unlike many pilots, Fonck included, once engaged in combat he never broke off. His technique was different. Fonck's method was admirable and I would never wish to criticize it, but he surprised [his opponent], made a pass at full speed and then flew off. In contrast, having unleashed an attack, Guynemer pursued it to the end.'

'I knew how to position myself in my attacker's blind spots, without ever really engaging in a duel,' explained Fonck. 'Guynemer fought differently and was regularly fired upon but his tactics were very risky and left the pilot vulnerable if his gun jammed. . . . A fine shot, certainly. A first-class pilot too. But a mad so-and-so. Like Lasalle, Murat or Marshal Ney during the First Empire, he charged straight at the enemy, sabre in hand. He charged machine guns firing at point-blank range, he charged groups, he charged anything. His superior shooting and iron will brought him a lot of success. Remember though: no other ace was brought down as often as this hero, not by a long chalk.'

'Fonck was an exceptionally good shot,' remarked Paul Waddington (SPA154). 'His plane never took a hit. He always attacked and fired on German patrols and aircraft on advantageous terms, corrected his aim in a way that was probably inborn, and scored victories inaccessible to others.' In contrast, '[Guynemer] returned after every sortie in a plane riddled with bullets. He attacked at absolutely point-blank range whatever the circumstances . . . so one day he didn't return at all. For example, if he attacked a German two-seater whose rear gunner was firing accurately with no need for correction, he took a lot of hits. It was Guynemer who went down every time.'

Whatever their tactical differences, the most successful pilots left nothing to chance. Prior to take-off, René Fonck always inspected his aircraft and loaded his own ammunition belts, personally inserting every round. Guynemer also checked his own machine, using engineering knowledge gained studying for the entrance exams to the École Polytechnique. He had entered aviation as a mechanic, knew his planes inside out, and was constantly suggesting improvements to the manufacturers. One set of sketches was accompanied by a note: 'The Boches are working flat out and so must we. If we don't, it's curtains.'

One of his particular projects was the new SPAD 12, the first single-seater to be armed with a 37mm cannon, a gun that – although heavy – occasionally produced spectacular results. On patrol with Albert Deullin (MF62/N3/SPA73) on 27 July 1917, Guynemer spotted an Albatros 'blipping his engine above a patrol of eight other Boches. He was acting the fool, escorting his chickens back to the coop. "Nothing to worry about," he seemed to be saying. "I'm here." I thought him a bit patronizing . . . though having been picked to escort such a large formation, he had to be an ace of sorts. I approached from the rear and got within a few metres. Boom! The impact was immediate. The plane split in two and burst into flames, the wings going one way, the fuselage the other. Bits were scattered everywhere and the braggart eventually burned up between Langemarck and Roulers.' The enemy pilot was Guynemer's forty-ninth victory, probably Leutnant Fritz Vossen of Jasta 33.

Maxime Lenoir was also working on a new weapon: 'Our plan was to load 60 metres of piano wire to be rolled out automatically as soon as a Boche came into view. The wire ended in four big hooks and we planned to let it dangle while we cut across the enemy's flight path and positioned ourselves so he would tangle himself up in it. Once contact was made, the shock would break the grappling iron and set off a charge, blowing up our victim in the air . . . On paper, this seemed an excellent plan with a promising future: fishing for Boches would be all the rage. But real life was another matter, and the tests I conducted with [Edwardes] Pulpe all showed just what a stupid idea it was. But I can vouch for the effort we put in. Imagine the impact on our opponents if our Machiavellian scheme had worked.'

Most of the aces took a similarly cold-blooded view of their work. 'Aerial combat is more of an ambush than a duel,' claimed Jean Morvan (SPA163). 'You seldom bring down an adversary who's manoeuvring. You murder the daydreamer – from the rear, before he suspects a thing, if possible from close in.' And these dreamers were not for the most part the enemy fighters of popular myth, but the slower, less manoeuvrable two-seaters, targeted on a strategic basis to stop them observing French lines, and also as an easy mark. For example, forty-one of the fifty-three victims registered to Guynemer, the so-called 'knight of the air', were two-seaters.

René Fonck was unabashed. 'We had to shoot down as many [Boches] as possible,' he insisted. 'I made no distinction between fighters, spotters and photo-reconnaissance planes. All were ripe for elimination! . . . [I often wished] to spare the life of an opponent who fought bravely, but it was seldom possible to extend quarter without betraying the nation's interests.' Albert Deullin took a similarly dispassionate view: 'I had an argument with two Aviatiks,' he reported. 'I finished one off. Then as I turned towards the other, I saw the first flip over, wheels uppermost, and jettison the observer from 3,600 metres. Take that! Magnificent.' So too, Guynemer: '[I was in] combat with two Fokkers,' he wrote to his sisters in 1916. 'The first was surrounded, the passenger dead, and it dived at me blind. Result: thirty-five rounds at point-blank range, then bang! Four other aircraft saw the fall . . . might get the *Croix* [*de guerre*] for this.'

When Sous-lieutenant Jean Peretti (N3) attacked a Fokker over Verdun on 28 April 1916, he fell victim to an equally single-minded German. Sous-lieutenant Albert Deullin described the incident to Antonin Brocard: '[Peretti] got off ten rounds before his gun started misfiring. Since his Quillien system gun-mount was very high at the rear, he couldn't clear the blockage without getting himself killed, so he decided to clear off. Flying to his rescue, Chainat saw him . . . side-slip left, pass beneath the Fokker and shoot off towards Verdun. The Fokker spotted him, followed and fired a strip from the rear from over 200 metres. One bullet hit Peretti in the kidneys and also broke his pelvis. He almost had strength enough to regain Verdun . . . but he crashed on landing . . . 200 metres from Thierville bridge. The plane was an unholy mess. Peretti was thrown forwards, fracturing his skull and his foot, but he suffered no disfigurement and his face was still wreathed in smiles.'

In the heat of battle pilots sometimes snapped. William Wellman 'saw red' after he and a comrade had forced down a Rumpler, and pursued the fleeing crew with machine-gun fire into some nearby shelter trenches: 'the

154 Kings of the Air

battle madness still held me in its grip,' he later admitted. Adjudant Lucien Jailler (N15) machine-gunned the downed pilot of an Albatros even though he was 'kamerading' in surrender, and on 8 July 1916, flying a barrier patrol at the southern end of the Somme battlefield, Lieutenant Raymond Lis (N15) targeted a German hospital plane: 'Over our lines at Harleville, [I] gave chase to a transparent German plane marked with red crosses. Fired a drum without hitting it. I could climb no higher in my 80hp Nieuport. The enemy did a U-turn and returned to its lines.'

Yet when passions cooled, vestiges of the old chivalry could still be found. On 2 September 1915 the German who shot down Sous-lieutenant Adolphe Pégoud (MS49) returned to drop an ivy wreath on his victim's home airfield. It was tied with a white ribbon bearing the inscription: 'The victor honours the French pilot Pégoud killed while fighting for his Fatherland.' Similarly, Louis Lelandais (SO104/BR287), who gained his wings in 1917, recalled 'a German pilot who fell behind our lines and was taken in by one of our squadrons. The captain invited him to dine and treated him like one of our own.' Much the same scene, with the nationalities reversed, later appeared in Jean Renoir's *La Grande Illusion*.

Squadrons might also drop messages about aircrew downed over enemy lines. After losing a bomber over Dunkerque in 1914, GB1 had been contacted by the Germans, and the following February the CO, Major de Goÿs, returned the compliment. 'I have the honour of informing you that, during a bombing raid on Verdun, our guns and aircraft shot down the plane flown by Lieutenant von Hidessen, with Lieutenant Müller as observer,' he wrote to the German aviation commander in Metz. 'Lieutenant von Hidessen is wounded. Both men are receiving all due care and attention at the Saint Nicholas hospital in Verdun. I am pleased to inform you that both officers did their duty. . . . P.S. Lieutenant Müller succumbed to his injuries before the opportunity arose to drop this message over your lines.' Major Siegert was quick to reply, 'The German squadron . . . has learned of the death of Lieutenant Müller, and of the injury and current condition of Lieutenant von Hidessen. The German officer-aviators acknowledge the courtesy implicit in the tone and content of this message. It is much appreciated and they convey their thanks to their French counterparts.'

GQG did not approve: 'The commander-in-chief has received reports that one of our pilots, acting as spokesman for his comrades, has dropped news of two German officer-aviators taken prisoner by our troops over enemy lines. Although mindful that, in similar circumstances, German aviators were the first to adopt this method of informing us of the death of

French pilots, an action likely to encourage our officers to behave similarly when the occasion arose, the commander-in-chief orders aviators henceforth to refrain from this sort of communication. [He] alone is entitled to communicate with the enemy using procedures laid down by international conventions and military law.'

Observer Auguste Heiligenstein and his comrades also incurred the wrath of GQG. After two German planes were downed in his vicinity, Heiligenstein 'went to see the sad sight with a few chums. The plane had exploded on hitting the ground, killing the two aviators outright. We thought that might be our fate one day. The [Germans] were carrying papers and money, and a few days later one of our fighters dropped a package containing what we'd found, plus a note saying where the two aviators were buried. Our gesture didn't go down well with GQG, and a note arrived ordering us not to resume paying our respects to the enemy dead.'

Yet messages were still being exchanged as late as the spring of 1917. Maréchal des Logis Denis Epitalon (SPA15) failed to return from patrol on 15 April, and eleven days later a German aircraft dropped a note. 'Did my duty to the last,' wrote Epitalon. 'I'm sorry I was forced down but there's nothing I can do about it. News of Lieutenants von Stieglitz and Fleischmann, downed close to Jonchery, is requested in return. I am unhurt.' Then on 6 May came news of two more pilots from the same patrol, Lieutenant Paul Bergeron and Sergeant Nicolas Buisson, requesting information on two more German fliers missing since 21 April.

Even in combat some pilots could still extend quarter to their opponents. In the skies above Verdun Jean Navarre dived on a flight of three German aircraft: 'All I could do was focus on the tail-ender who was clearly panicking. He called on the grace of God and dived. I didn't press the point: why kill a man just for the pleasure of it?' Meanwhile Georges Madon experienced similar generosity on the part of an enemy pilot: 'I touched down gently, avoiding the potholes. Feet back on the ground once more, I thanked heaven and saluted the German flying 1,200 metres overhead.'

'A squadron without aviation is a squadron lost' – naval aviation
The world's first successful seaplane flight had taken place on 28 March 1910, when inventor Henri Fabre piloted his floatplane on the Étang de Berre, immediately provoking interest from the French navy. Seven officers were despatched to earn their wings with the Aéro-Club de France and two aircraft were purchased: a Voisin floatplane and a Maurice Farman biplane.

Trials based around *La Foudre*, a converted torpedo-boat tender, were deemed a success, and on 20 March 1912 the Service de l'Aviation Maritime was formed under the command of Capitaine de Frégate Louis Fatou.

Three more bases were planned – at Brest, Cherbourg and Montpellier (soon changed to Saint-Raphaël) – and three aircraft types were recommended for purchase: a coastal seaplane, a land-based reconnaissance aircraft and a light machine for shipboard use. All were initially envisaged in an observation role: 'While the virtual impregnability and tremendous speed of aeroplanes make them eminently suitable for spotting and reconnaissance, they have little to offer offensively,' observed the chief of the naval staff on 15 May 1912. The naval manoeuvres of 1914 began to prove, to staff officers at least, that the machines might have some attacking potential, but sea officers remained sceptical. '[I was part of] a class of fanatical gunners,' recalled Aspirant Edmond Benoit, then training at the naval academy. 'In those days the gun was still the sailor's weapon of choice.'

In July 1914 the fledgling service was absorbed into the new Service Central de l'Aéronautique Maritime under the command of Capitaine de Vaisseau Jean Noël. With just twenty-six qualified pilots, *La Foudre*, the Saint-Raphaël base, and fourteen aircraft – six Nieuport 6H/M, six Voisins, a Caudron and a Breguet – it was a tiny affair, but the outbreak of war provoked its immediate expansion. Ten new seaplanes were purchased, two squadrons formed at Bonifacio and Nice, and two merchantmen requisitioned for conversion as seaplane carriers (plus two more in 1915). In December 1914 bases were established at Dunkerque and Saint-Pol-sur-Mer to control the southern North Sea and conduct anti-submarine warfare, and two months later FBA machines from Dunkerque began raiding the German submarine bases along the coast at Ostend and Zeebrugge.

The Nieuports were sent first to Bizerta (Tunisia), then to Malta and finally to Antivari (Bar) in Montenegro, but their performance did not impress and Vice-Admiral Boué de Lapeyrère, commander of the French Mediterranean fleet, thought them a complete waste of time. They were also dispatched to Port Said where, operating from the seaplane carriers *Anne Rickmers* and *Rabenfels II*, they helped repulse a Turkish attack on the Suez Canal in early 1915. Following Italy's entry into the war that May, a squadron of FBA Type B seaplanes was dispatched to Venice and a flight of Nieuport floatplanes to Brindisi, the latter aiming to bottle up the enemy U-boats in the northern Adriatic by blocking the straits of Otranto. But the Nieuports continued to underperform: 'These monoplanes have a top speed of 120km/h [and] take 55 minutes to reach their operational height of 2,000 metres,' reported Capitano di Fregata Ludovico de Filippi, of the Italian seaplane carrier *Elba*. 'Patrols normally last three hours . . . [and] each plane is equipped to carry small bombs. . . . They are rather fragile, temperamental machines and need perfect weather conditions to take off and land. I therefore consider them unsuitable for long-range missions at sea. And their only [other] weapon is an automatic pistol. . . . I believe the best use for these planes would be in one-off coastal patrols immediately preceding the arrival or departure of a friendly vessel . . . or liaising with our destroyers in anti-submarine work.'

By now enemy submarines had become the main focus of the naval aeronautical service. 'The growth of naval aviation was largely unplanned,' stated Edmond Benoit. 'It came in response to the urgent need to protect sea traffic.' A total of 1,000 flying boats – 500 Donnet-Denhauts and 500 FBA Type Hs – were ordered in 1916, to be distributed between twenty new aviation centres and a further fifteen satellite *postes de combat*, and by the end of that year 966 planes of all types were operational. Three separate geographical commands were created – [Eastern] English Channel and North Sea, Atlantic and [Western] English Channel, and Mediterranean – each composed of a number of smaller divisions, while a parallel administrative reorganization recognized the growing importance of the service, establishing it as a separate department within the navy ministry and ushering in substantial improvements in operational and logistical efficiency. At the same time research and development became the responsibility of a new technical section, created initially within the naval construction department but transferred in June 1917 to a new directorate of submarine warfare.

The FBA Type H soon proved ineffective in air-to-air combat, as Enseigne de Vaisseau Robert Guyot de Salins and Sergeant Jérôme Médeville discovered during a routine reconnaissance mission along the Belgian coast on 23 October 1916. Their outward journey from Dunkerque was uneventful, but a plane from SFS II climbed to meet them on their return. Two of the three-strong French patrol made off, leaving de Salins and his observer Médeville alone to face the enemy. De Salins dived in a steep spiral. 'I discharged one magazine, two, then a third,' recalled Médeville. 'We closed with him and kept right on his tail. Suddenly some rounds from above alerted us to the presence of a second adversary. I quickly swung the gun in this new direction and, through bracing wires, stays, floats and wings, peppered first one opponent, then the other. Bullets were raining down on all sides. One of my rounds partially severed a bracing wire. My pilot and I checked on each other from time to time. . . .

In mid-action I was hit on the head and slumped down [momentarily] while I gathered my senses. I loaded a fourth magazine while the pilot carried on manoeuvring. The enemy machines made some fantastic turns and all three of us had a number of close calls. . . . A collision seemed the most likely outcome of this duel. . . . [But] then the machine gun jammed . . . and the engine stalled. . . . Mechanical failure, our worst fear . . . We landed in enemy waters with the bullets raining down non-stop. We raised our arms in surrender but still they hunted us down . . . I think [the enemy pilots] had spotted us and were trying to kill us in cold blood.'

Fifteen minutes later the Germans finally broke off, leaving the two Frenchmen to the mercy of a boat coming out of Zeebrugge. Before the pair were captured, they jettisoned everything of use, camera included, and also managed to write a message to their unit, attaching it to the leg of one of their two carrier pigeons – their only means of communication – and releasing the bird. Médeville eventually escaped from captivity in January 1917; Guyot's fate is unknown.

In an attempt to compensate for the FBA's poor performance, the French devised new tactics: 'If you're attacked in the air, the odds are stacked against you. Touch down at sea straight away and fight from the water.' But this was equally ineffective. 'You Frenchmen call it heroic,' commented a bemused Oberleutnant Friedrich Christiansen, the German CO at Zeebrugge, after three of his Rumplers downed a patrol of four FBA machines from Dunkerque on 26 May 1917. 'I call it crazy.'

French bombing raids over the Flanders coast – small in number and payload even when reinforced with army Voisins – continued into 1917 against targets in Ostend, Zeebrugge, Gistel and Middelkerke. Their most significant success came in January 1917 with the blocking of the Bruges–Zeebrugge canal, yet they could never deliver a telling blow – unlike the enemy counter-raids. Dunkerque and Calais were targeted throughout the conflict by air, sea and land. A German raid on 23 December 1916 temporarily disabled the Dunkerque base, destroying three hangars and twelve FBA flying boats, while a further action on 2 October 1917 wiped out all the bombers in their hangar. The bomber squadron housed there was disbanded shortly afterwards, although the base continued to operate seaplanes until the end of the war.

Local civilians felt themselves defenceless. 'The situation is growing worse by the day,' wrote Félix Coquelle on 23 October. 'Yesterday evening brought more unwelcome visitors who caused serious damage. We must retaliate, whatever the cost.' Calais too was suffering: 'It's extremely distressing to see . . . a port so important to the allies – home to representatives from nearly all the belligerent powers and so many people working to defend our nation – so inadequately defended against Boche air raids. . . . These bandits can operate at night and return calmly the following morning to enjoy their work of destruction and plan their next outing. . . . Life . . . is a real nightmare at the moment and I'm not sure if we'll emerge safe and sound.' The ordeal would continue deep into 1918: Calais did not hear its final air-raid warning until 25 September; Dunkerque, 4 November. Both towns suffered considerable damage and a significant number of casualties: in Calais, 278 were killed (including 108 civilians) and 528 injured (206 civilians); in Dunkerque, the toll was higher still, with 575 killed (262 civilians) and 1,101 injured (345 civilians).

Dirigibles entered the order of battle in December 1915 for anti-submarine patrols, mine location and convoy escort work, while captive balloons first appeared in April 1917 for use in coastal observation and mine-watching. The first five dirigibles were obtained from Britain – three S.S. and a 'Coastal' by purchase, plus a Zodiac by gift – and were soon supplemented by home-produced Vedette and Escorteur types. Then in March 1917 the navy acquired the seven dirigibles released by the army: the *Lorraine, Capitaine-Caussin, Tunisie, Champagne* and *d'Arlandes* went to the naval bases in Paimboeuf, Bizerta and Corfu, while the older *Fleurus I* and *Montgolfier* became training machines at Saint-Cyr.

Anti-submarine tactics changed during 1917, favouring convoy escort work over attempts to destroy U-boat bases. Balloons and aircraft operated in partnership: a pair of flying boats preceded the convoy by some 25 kilometres, searching for mines or submarines, while a balloon guarded the ships from the rear. 'The submarines cruised at shallow depths,' explained Edmond Benoit, who in May 1918 was piloting Donnet-Denhaut flying boats on anti-submarine patrols out of Dunkerque, 'so the seaplanes could detect them easily enough, even in the foggy, rough waters of the North Sea. When we spotted a submarine, we attacked it with our bombs. It's very difficult to judge how effective this was. I don't think I ever managed to sink any. Naval planes in general sank a dozen confirmed. We acted more as a deterrent.'

On 6 September 1917 a British-built VA5 dirigible, based at Montebourg and commanded by Enseigne de Vaisseau Yves Angot, spotted a submarine stalking a schooner: 'At 10.30 am, exiting cloud, height 300 metres, my wireless and my mechanic both indicated a suspicious object ahead of us and to our right. . . . Parts of its superstructure were clearly visible, particularly its periscope and another vertical object, no doubt the [wireless] mast.' Angot dived into the attack but he was uncertain of the outcome. 'The pilot of this scout thinks it highly unlikely he sank the submarine,' reported his CO, Lieutenant de Vaisseau Dieudonné, 'but it performed its mission to perfection and almost certainly prevented the loss of a large coaster. The attack probably failed because [the balloon's] type-D bombs didn't work . . . It is scheduled to carry two British 75-pound bombs, but we only have British 100-pounders at the base and the bomb racks aren't strong enough to take them. Three men are needed to operate these 2,200m³ balloons, so you can't carry two 100-pounders even if you reduce all other weight to the absolute minimum. That's why I decided to try two type-Ds instead. With further modifications, I hope I can make this balloon even more useful.'

The new bases included one in Guernsey, opened in August 1917 – an obvious choice given the island's location. However, the harbour at St Peter Port was too small for the FBA H flying boats to take off, driving them out to the open sea. 'With the winds blowing from the South-East to West or North,' declared a local newspaper, 'the air is, under the lee of the islands, full of holes and waves just like the sea when it is rough. The machine tries its best to fly but it is buffeted about in all directions, and seems to be always on the verge of a side-slip, which is likely to be fatal when it does occur at a low altitude.'

On 31 January 1918 two Guernsey-based planes – a Tellier and an FBA – were patrolling south of the Les Hanois lighthouse when they spotted what they thought was a submarine. Aware that a French boat was operating in the vicinity, they approached the target carefully, but the submarine had already begun to dive by the time they had definitively identified it. Still they turned their guns on it and watched it struggle back to the surface before heeling over at 45 degrees and disappearing again amid patches of oil. The Guernsey base launched several more attacks on suspicious targets during the final summer of the war, including 'one greyish object, elongated in form, with spray at the front', but all were inconclusive.

Over the course of the war the navy trained some 1,500 pilots and observers. Candidates attended the military flying schools for basic pilot training, but in 1917 specialist wings were introduced for seaplane pilots, and schools were opened at Hourtin and Saint-Raphaël to provide additional training for naval pilots and observers. Schools were also established at Brest and later Corfu for captive balloon crews, and at Saint-Cyr (transferred to Rochefort in 1918) for dirigibles. Flying qualifications were open to all: unlike the army, however, officers were few. At the La Penzé base in 1918, for example, only three of the twelve pilots and two of the twenty observers were officers, with the remainder all petty officers or leading seamen. Naval aircrew also tended to be older than their army counterparts: naval promotion was slow even in wartime and any volunteer was required to have some years' prior sea service. 'The crews? They were almost all navy men, with relatively few officers and petty officers,' confirmed Edmond Benoit. 'They were experienced types who could be relied upon.'

Aspirant Benoit had first volunteered in 1914 while serving on the protected cruiser *d'Entrecasteaux*, based at Port Said: 'What made me do it? Novelty was the main attraction . . . I was mad about flying and applied straight away. I requested a transfer on several occasions, but I had to wait until 1917 before I was accepted.' After basic training at Ambérieu, Benoit moved on to the naval school at Hourtin for specialist seaplane work: 'The lake was 17 kilometres long and, with an instructor and a seaplane to myself, I could practise taking off and landing non-stop. After forty-eight hours they decided I deserved my wings.' From Hourtin, Benoit proceeded to the bombing and air gunnery school at Saint-Raphaël and within a fortnight was a squadron commander at Bizerta.

Flying-boat crews faced a particular risk: if forced down, they landed at sea. With no wireless, their only option was to release their carrier pigeons or hope to catch the attention of a passing vessel. On 3 October 1918 Maître Guillaume Kerambrun had just returned to La Penzé after a four-hour patrol in poor weather when he was scrambled again: a German submarine had just been spotted off the north coast of Brittany. 'The conditions are lousy,' he was told. 'You're the senior pilot. It's your job to get out there.' He and observer Lieutenant de Vaisseau Latard de Pierrefeu took off in their Tellier, only for the engine to fail in mid-air. They managed to touch down safely but spent a further twenty-four hours in rough seas before a warship arrived to take them off.

Yet their ordeal was nothing compared to that endured by Enseigne de Vaisseau Jacques Langlet and Second Maître Maurice Dien, pilot and observer of FBA flying boat H.4. With their comrades in H.48, they left Toulon-Saint-Mandrier at 10.00 am on 2 July 1918 to escort a convoy inbound for Marseille, but ninety minutes later, some 30 nautical miles south of the Île de Planier, their engine began playing up. '[It] kept missing, then restarting,' recalled Langlet. 'We tried using the hand pump to repressurize the tanks but eventually it stalled.'

All they could do was touch down in the heavy seas, release one of their two pairs of carrier pigeons, each bearing a note of their position, and watch H.48 fly off to seek help. But the north-westerly mistral was growing stronger, driving them further from land and carrying off their sea anchor in the swell. They jettisoned as much as possible – bombs, radiator, magnetos – used rudder and ailerons to keep the nose facing into the wind and took it in turns to steer. Finally they opened their emergency rations. What a disappointment, recalled Langlet: 'two mouldy ship's biscuits (in pieces), a tin of pâté (spoiled, as we later discovered), two 20oz tins of corned beef (in good nick), two bars of chocolate (mouldy) and a bottle of rum. I was seasick until that night and Dien until the following day.'

By then the wind had strengthened further. 'A dreadful sea with troughs at least 8 metres deep,' reported Dien. 'We'd taken on some water, but the lieutenant used the first-aid box as a baler. . . . We'd been drifting very rapidly south-east since 2 [July]. We hoped towards Corsica or Sardinia.'

Day three was just as bad: 'Sea still rough. We took it in turns to sleep. . . . The bottle of rum slowly emptied. Very thirsty. No more biscuit. Just a few crumbs. All we had left were the two tins of "monkey".'

Day four brought a change in the weather: 'The wind eased and seemed to be backing west-southwesterly. But it was a variable breeze that drove us back over seas we'd already covered that morning. . . . I unscrewed the compass but the liquid inside was undrinkable. The lieutenant rinsed his mouth out with salt water. We each sucked a button, which produced a drop or two of liquid. By noon we were dying of thirst. The wind had dropped. The blazing sun burned the arms of my shirt, and a violent bout of sunstroke made me feverish. The compass [liquid] didn't look too bad. I tried a drop. It was ghastly, but it did quench your thirst a little. We couldn't be too far from land. There were butterflies round the plane.'

Throughout days five and six the calm and the heat continued unabated: 'No wind. Light breakfast. Nothing to drink. Smoked a cigarette which made us thirstier still. An awful day. Made drowsy by the sun, I dozed on one of the wings and burned my arms. Always the same impossible dreams: a boat, land, water!'

Langlet takes up the tale: 'That night we thought we could see fires twinkling. Thinking we'd spotted a lighthouse, we launched several rockets, hoping that torpedo-boats would come for us. It was all a mirage! They were stars! We finished off the last of the rum. We could no longer moisten our lips or swallow. But on the morning of 7 July we managed to rig up something to distil seawater. . . . The results weren't great, but gradually we increased the yield of each operation from a thimbleful to the size of a Madeira glass. That was how we survived, and it was all down to Dien's skill and ingenuity. He's a wonderful mechanic.'

With a breeze now picking up from the south, they rigged up sails using canvas torn from the upper wings. Day eight . . . day nine . . . steady progress northwards. Insects everywhere. Surely they must be nearing land? Hearing an aircraft engine, they lit a small fire and fired a Véry light – but no response. Then at 2.00 pm on day ten they finally sighted land. 'The lieutenant pointed out a brown mass among the clouds that didn't change shape as you looked at it,' recounted Dien. 'Definitely land. I piled on the sails. The wind was pushing us towards it, though not flat out, but things were definitely looking up. We'd fashioned a rudder out of an aluminium panel from the fuel-tank housing and we were almost sailing landward. . . . A fire, three bangs, no question this time. But then the wind veered and started pushing us parallel to the coast. I was too restless to sleep and watched the fires recede from view. At daybreak we could see a headland [Capu Rossu on the west coast of Corsica].'

Day eleven – and rescue at last. 'Activity on the mountainside, then a small boat pulled out and drew alongside us. "Are you French?" was the lieutenant's first question. We'd hauled down the flag from the upper wing just in case. They dragged us on board and ferried us ashore [where] intrepid Corsicans immediately surrounded us, lavishing upon us their island's famous hospitality. . . . It was over! My strength failed me. I collapsed on the sand and woke to find myself surrounded by weeping women . . . fussing over me to an almost embarrassing degree. Then we were loaded on to donkeys and taken to Piana and a good bed where we slowly regained our strength. . . . The plane was dragged on to the beach. Poor old thing. We owed it a real debt of gratitude. It had carried us for 267 hours, the first three days in a terrible sea. I still wondered if it had all been a dream. If I wasn't being cared for in Ajaccio and my burned arms weren't hurting so much, I'd have thought it was just a nightmare.'

Back at the base the mood was sombre. At Toulon cathedral that morning their comrades had attended a memorial mass, and by evening the CO, Lieutenant de Vaisseau Samy Fournié, was busy drafting letters of condolence. Then an urgent telegram arrived: 'Seaplane reported drifting 2 July reached land Gulf of Porto 13 July. [Pilot] and observer both safe and well.' Champagne was poured and toasts drunk. 'Should they have been getting the off-base subsistence allowance?' asked the paymaster dryly. 'Half-rate only,' joked Fournié. 'They already had accommodation!' After the war Langlet went on to captain the merchant vessel *Peiho*; Dien pursued a distinguished career in civil aviation.

By November 1918 the naval aeronautical service contained 11,000 officers, petty officers and men – around a tenth of all navy effectives – operating some 700 seaplanes, 200 captive balloons and 37 dirigibles from thirty-six centres and satellite posts, with several hundred more in reserve.

The balloons were eventually credited with locating sixty U-boats and destroying over a hundred mines, while the service as a whole was delivering bomb and torpedo attacks, attaining local air superiority in some sectors, and impressing many officers with its offensive potential, particularly in anti-submarine warfare. 'A squadron without aviation', concluded Capitaine de Frégate Henry de l'Escaille, later a leading figure in the aircraft manufacturing industry, 'is a squadron lost.' But the costs were high, with 195 deaths recorded among the 1,500 pilots and observers trained during the course of the war.

Chapter 5

'Masters of the Air' –
1918

'Setting foot on French soil again' – prisoners and internees

In February 1918 two outwardly disreputable characters turned up at the door of the French embassy in The Hague. They were the celebrated aviator Roland Garros (MS23) and his comrade Anselme Marchal (C66), newly escaped from captivity in Magdeburg. Garros had tried to escape several times over the previous three years – by tunnel, sea and even air. Consequently, he had been moved back and forth across the country, from Küstrin [now Kostrzyn] to Trier, Gnadenfrei, Magdeburg and Burg, before finally returning to Magdeburg. Marchal had been a prisoner since 20 June 1916, when the engine of his specially modified Nieuport 12 seized up over Austrian-occupied Poland after a daring leaflet raid on Berlin. This time the pair had succeeded by disguising themselves as German officers and simply walking out through the gates. Marchal spoke German, so rather than head across country they took the train to Aachen and eventually swam to freedom across the river that marked the Dutch border.

Another escaper was Maréchal des Logis André Seigneurie (N103), who had been forced down and captured behind enemy lines on 2 July 1916 after a dogfight with Oberleutnant Ernst Freiherr von Althaus (KeKV) while on reconnaissance near Péronne: 'I was sent to work at my own request on a farm in a village of 1,200 people . . . [and] on 10 September [1916] an infantry sergeant and I managed to escape. We walked for sixteen nights in a row before problems with my left foot, which I'd injured in 1914 before transferring to aviation, forced me to surrender just 28 kilometres from the Dutch border. I couldn't take another step. The German police locked me up for two days while they waited for a guard to take me back to the camp. Back at Giessen I spent thirty days in a cell on black bread and water, with soup and a palliasse every four days. I passed the winter with my company preparing another escape attempt and, whenever I could, buying items I was going to need [censored]. On 15 March 1917 I again requested permission to work outside the camp, and on 28 March they sent me to [censored] Arbeitskommando. At 8.00 pm on 7 April – the time we normally returned to our huts – my comrade and I found ourselves alone. We cleared off and covered 40 kilometres that same night. At dawn we hid in a pine forest and . . . in the evening we set off again for the Dutch border. At 3.00 am on 10 April, after a twelve-night march, we ran into some German sentries who opened fire [and] my comrade fell wounded at my feet. I ran on across the fields and eight minutes later was surrounded by Dutch soldiers. I was very well received. The officer gave me an escort to the nearest town [censored] and a hotel where I found a comfortable bed, a bite to eat and best of all the chance to tidy myself up a bit. On 12 April a Dutch NCO took me to the French consulate in Rotterdam. I did all right for myself there: they bought me a new set of clothes since mine were in tatters. On 2 May I sailed for England, then I carried on by train via Folkestone to Boulogne. Setting foot on French soil again was the happiest moment of my life.'

Seigneurie was granted leave, but just a month later he was back at the front, first with his old squadron and subsequently with SPA90 and SPA314.

Airmen who came down in neutral territory were held as internees. In June 1915 Eugène Gilbert (MS23/49) had left Fontaine in his MS Parasol on a solo mission to bomb the Zeppelin sheds at Friedrichshafen. Returning home after dropping his payload on target, he suddenly noticed a problem with his fuel system. 'I checked the valve on the rear tank to see if it was open. No. I looked everywhere and finally identified [the problem]: the tap had blown off. Damn and blast! I searched the fuselage, but without any luck.' Gilbert's engine cut out, forcing him down in Switzerland, where he was interned in a hotel in Hospenthal, in the heart of the Alps. Two months later Gilbert and his fellow internee Bontemps took advantage of wet and windy weather to make a bid for freedom. With Gilbert in a false beard and wearing a coat over his uniform, the pair walked the 5 miles to the main line station at Göschenen, bluffing their way past a patrol. 'We should have been arrested twice more,' remembered Bontemps, 'but [the checks] were little more than a formality and they didn't bother to question us. It was still pouring down as we neared the station and the train wasn't quite yet due, so we sheltered in an outhouse. We were pretty relaxed, confident the worst was over, when the staccato thump of footsteps outside hinted that we weren't completely out of the woods. Faster than my pen can write, Gilbert hid inside a barrow and I crouched behind a cart. A patrol passed, moved away, and we set off again for the station. We were still too early, leaving us with another anxious few minutes. A policeman was pacing the platform. Would he recognize Gilbert? Apparently not. When the train arrived, we jumped straight into the front carriage and with luck found two seats in semi-darkness: they might have been waiting for us.'

From Lucerne, they went by train to Geneva and then by tram across the border to Annemasse. Bontemps continues the tale: '"France," Gilbert said to me. Neither of us could say another word. It meant everything to us.' But Gilbert had a shock in store – he was sent straight back to Switzerland. As a condition of his internment he had given an assurance not to abscond, and at the time of his escape the Swiss had not yet received the official letter releasing him from his parole. Gilbert finally fled for good on 26 May 1916; he returned to France and became a test pilot at Villacoublay, only to be killed in an accident in May 1918.

Some of the successful escapers felt forgotten on their return. Surely more could be done to acknowledge their bravery? Led by Garros, a group of pilots met at the Aéro-Club de France in May 1918 to form a society for aviation escapers. 'Once back in France, our escapers vanish into the crowd, with no recognition for their deeds,' he claimed. 'It's a crying shame. Any prisoner who manages to escape has achieved something worthy of celebration.'

'War, German style' – the raids on Paris

From January to September 1918 Paris fell victim to a number of air raids conducted by German heavy bombers, popularly known as the 'Gotha' raids after the type most frequently used. These were just the latest in a series of attacks first launched at 12.45 pm on 30 August 1914, when a Taube overflew the city at a height of 1,000 metres and dropped five bombs, killing one civilian and wounding four others before flying off untouched by the guns of the city's garrison, the Camp Retranché de Paris. Four armed Farmans operating as HF28 were immediately allocated to the CRP, but to little effect, and the raids continued over the next three months, killing eleven and wounding fifty. On 2 September one Farman did manage to get within range, but its machine gun jammed on the tenth round and the intruder got away unscathed.

Paris was also under threat from enemy Zeppelins, whose exceptional range required the capital's air defences to be reinforced in all directions. '[Artillery and searchlights should be] located at key points outside the capital and linked by telephone, via the armies, to various posts distributed along the front,' Joffre advised the minister of war. 'This should give sufficient warning of the bearing of enemy dirigibles for our batteries to take the necessary action.' General Gallieni favoured mobile motorized AA units but the lack of available chassis made his plan unviable. Instead, an outer ring of listening posts was set up about 100 kilometres from the city, with an inner ring of fifteen fixed batteries – each deploying two 75mm field guns, four machine guns and some searchlights – placed on the most likely access routes. As soon as the alert was sounded, a complete blackout would be imposed across the city. A second line of listening posts was soon added in a semicircle some 20 kilometres north and east of the centre, but all these dispositions remained untested until 21 March 1915, when two Zeppelins bombed the city with relatively little damage. The early warning system worked well enough, the artillery less so – the guns struggled to find the right range and tended to fire indiscriminately. An extra seventeen planes were added to the strength but during a raid on 28 May 1915 not a single CRP machine made it into the air. Standing patrols were then introduced, again with little impact. Details of the enemy bearing could only be conveyed via cloth panels laid on the ground, messages could take up to an hour to travel from listening post to airfield, and the latest and most powerful aircraft types always went to the front. In consequence, the planes seldom had time to reach interception height.

On 21 October 1915 Paris was cloaked by a thick blanket of fog: 'We'll cop it if we have to go up in that,' remarked Adjudant Marcel Duret (CRP) to his observer Tavardon. But a Zeppelin was reported approaching the city and Duret received orders to mount a standing patrol. His comrade Sergeant Paul soon crashed, disoriented by the mist. However, Duret struggled on: 'I was lost as soon as I left the ground,' he later claimed. 'I wanted to turn back after a near miss with a Voisin, then the drama began. I climbed to 2,200 metres, circling so I didn't stray too far from the airfield. The pale moon cast an eerie light on my machine. It felt like the last dawn of the condemned man. I was starting to worry. "We've had it, old man," I said, leaning towards Tavardon. "There's nothing else I can do. I'll try to hang on until we run out of juice."'

Duret had plenty of fuel in the tank, time enough to find a landmark if he could. The lake at Enghien-les-Bains, just north of Paris, was the first obvious target. Then he spotted more lights. Convinced it was the centre of the city, he descended into a fog bank and promptly lost all vision: 'My final recollection is of pulling back hard on the joystick. The next thing I was pinned beneath a pile of splintered wood. I called out twice without reply so I was pretty sure Tavardon was dead. I couldn't breathe. I was choking. I couldn't move. I thought, "If we've come down in the back of beyond, that's it. I'll suffocate before help gets to me." Fortunately, a brave woman and two or three others came to my rescue just moments later.'

German planes penetrated the defences twice more, on 29 and 30 January 1916, when heavy fog again stopped the guns and searchlights from engaging the enemy. Twenty-six aircraft braved the weather on the first night, five spotting the intruder but none able to match it for height or speed. The following night a dozen planes went up, but the fog was thicker still, forcing them back to the airfield. 'No use complaining!' proclaimed *La France illustrée*. 'It's war. War, German style! Our enemies have handed us another lesson. We may equal them in will to win, but do we match them in our determination to develop weapons of war, acquire the technical superiority required to counter the threat of their evil genius, find new applications for science, or make new discoveries, however small?'

On 24 April 1916, a dark and cloudy night, several Farman MF.11 took off in search of a Zeppelin (probably LZ.97) returning from a raid on London. Their pilots included Captain Maurice Mandinaud (MF36/N81): '[Suddenly I spotted] a point, a long way off and very high in the sky. A point not of light but of darkness, more solid than the surrounding blackness. A cloud? No, it was moving too quickly. I thought at first it was a fellow pilot heading for home. I kept my eye on it. It seemed to be coming towards us, heading for the Belgian coast. Then another point appeared to its right. No sooner had I decided they were two of ours than I realized the first was a Zeppelin. It was very small, not much bigger than my finger end, so it was still a long way off. And it seemed very high. I circled to gain height, keeping my eyes trained upon it. It was still heading towards us and now we were both at the same altitude. At 2,000 metres it was clearly still oblivious to our presence. By the time it spotted us, we were at 300 metres, almost upon it, and my observer Lieutenant [Pierre] Deramond was preparing for combat. Then, to our astonishment, the gigantic airship reared up at an angle of at least 30 degrees and began to climb at . . . frightening speed, far beyond anything we could match. . . . Fortunately the Zeppelin stopped moving forwards while it climbed . . . so we could circle again to reach its new height.

'By now the enemy was on the alert [and] we joined combat. We were close enough to obtain an excellent view down on to the envelope. Machine guns were mounted on platforms aft, right and left, and they opened fire. Our 130hp Farman only had seventeen bombs and a machine gun with a few tracer bullets, [but] we made seventeen passes around 100 metres above the enemy, returning fire each time. We were pretty certain we'd hit the target every time but we could see no outward signs of damage. With every pass came the same awful surprise. . . . It was no holds barred. We fired all our rounds from point-blank range without ever seeming to deliver the knock-out blow. But . . . the seventeen bomb holes must have compromised the airship's buoyancy and produced a serious loss of gas. In an abrupt, daring and undoubtedly perilous manoeuvre, the huge mass began to dive towards the ground, zigzagging at speed before eventually crashing on to the Belgian plain. The ground was still swathed in darkness, but we were able to watch the Zeppelin fall by the first light of dawn. I wanted to spend longer observing its death throes, but the dense fire of the AA batteries and the state of our plane forced us to put safety first.'

Mandinaud had to put down in the neutral Netherlands, where he and Deramond were interned for a time before later escaping back to France. The Zeppelin survived the crash.

Night flying required particular skills, researched over the summer of 1917 by Captain Henri Langevin, CO of N313, from his base in the Dunkerque suburb of Coudekerque. He correctly identified the operational height of the German bombers (about 3,000 metres), so improving the accuracy of French anti-aircraft fire. He also demonstrated the effect of moonlit nights on visibility: aircraft silhouetted against the moon's reflection in the water could be spotted over the sea but disappeared from view as soon as they crossed the coast. Impressed by his work, GQG transferred N313 to Avord to work up as a dedicated night-fighter squadron, an ill-timed move that removed it from the line just as the Germans stepped up their bombing campaign against Dunkerque. The French eventually set up a dedicated night-fighter school at Pars-lès-Romilly in September 1918, but only a handful of men had completed the course before the armistice.

The German Gothas first appeared over the front in the late summer of 1916 and began raiding London the following year. Maxime Lenoir (C18/N23) was patrolling the front lines when he encountered his eleventh and final victim on 25 September 1916: 'No ordinary opponent . . . but a three-seater [Gotha] equipped with two machine guns, each with its own crewman . . . How did I ever manage to defeat this flying house? How was I not blinded by the explosive bullet that brushed my eye . . . ? How did I struggle home despite all the damage inflicted on my Nieuport Bébé? How did I, a mere David, eventually come to see Goliath strewn in pieces across the sky? I don't know. But I do know the delight I experienced on witnessing the eventual outcome of this encounter. My victim crashed close to Fromezey, the wreckage burying the mangled bodies of the three Boches who'd tried to shoot me down – and very nearly succeeded. My engine had holes in two of its cylinders. The bullets had passed clean through the tank, thankfully without igniting the fuel inside, severing a strut and two cables. What's more – and this shows how close we came in combat – my plane was drenched with German blood. It was streaming down the wings and the engine cowling.'

Georges Guynemer (MS/N/SPA3) also found the Gotha a tough nut to crack: 'On 8 February [1917] I set off on patrol with my comrade [André] Chainat. Of course, the Boches still thought themselves untouchable and were planning a brazen attack on Nancy, but we were keeping our eyes peeled. Suddenly we spotted a huge plane with two Mercedes 200hp engines and a three-man crew firing in all directions. It was a Gotha, a truly formidable aircraft, but relatively unknown [at the time]. Without hesitation, we both attacked full tilt from opposite directions. I wasn't worried about Chainat. He was very easy to work with – brave, skilful and cool. The [Gotha] offered a number of blind spots for a counter-attack and we quickly sought them out. It really would have been harder to miss [them]. We fired off entire strips and managed to silence the enemy guns. We forced the *aérobus* down behind our lines at Bouconville with a hole in its radiator. All three members of the crew were taken prisoner. Their plane had taken 180 rounds.'

Between January and September 1918 the Germans flew 483 separate sorties over Paris. The capital's air defences had been strengthened with extra weapons, sound locators and searchlights since 1914, and decoy cities were also planned for Conflans and Villepinte to try to fool the raiders. So intense was the defensive barrage that less than a tenth of the enemy raids reached the city centre; eleven victories were claimed and many planes elected to drop their bombs on the heavily industrialized northern suburbs instead. The French hailed this as a moral victory, but the many factories in the area suffered significant damage, as did the important railway junction at Creil.

'Everywhere – if one looks for them – large white cards are hung on doorways,' wrote American Mildred Aldrich, visiting friends from her home near Meaux. 'On them are printed in large black letters the words *"ABRIS 60 personnes,"* or whatever number the cellars will accommodate, and several of the underground stations bear the same sort of sign. These are refuges designated by the police, into which the people near them are expected to descend at the first sound of the *sirènes* announcing the approach of the enemy's air fleet. More striking than these signs are the rapid efforts being made to protect some of the more important of the city's monuments. They are being boarded in, and concealed behind bags of sand. . . . Sandbags are dumped everywhere, and workmen are feverishly hurrying to cover in the treasures, and avoid making them look too hideous. They would not be French if they did not try, here and there, to preserve a fine line.' One night the alarm sounded: 'My hostess and I tumbled out of our beds, unlatched the windows so that no shock of air expansion might break them, switched off all the lights and went on the balcony just in time to see the firemen on their auto as they passed the end of the street, sounding the "*garde à vous*" on their *sirènes* – the most awful, hair-raising wail I have ever heard – like a host of lost souls. Ulysses need not have been tied to the mast to prevent his following the song of this siren! We were hardly on the balcony when, in an instant, all the lights of the city went out, and a strange blackness settled down and hugged the housetops and the very sidewalk. At the same instant the guns of the outer barrage began to fire, and, as the night was cold, we went inside to listen, and to talk. I wonder if I can tell you – who are never likely to have such an experience – how it feels to sit inside four walls, in absolute darkness, listening to the booming of the defence, and the falling of bombs on an otherwise silent city, wakened out of its sleep. It is a sensation to which I doubt if any of us get really accustomed – this sitting quietly while the cannon boom, and now and then an *avion* whirs overhead, or a venturesome auto toots its horn as it dashes to a shelter, or the occasional voice of a gendarme yells angrily at some unextinguished light, or a hurried footstep on the pavement tells of a passer in the deserted street, braving all risks to reach home. I assure you that the hands on the clock-face simply crawl. An hour is very long. This raid of the 17th lasted only three-quarters of an hour. It was barely half-past eleven when the *berloque* sounded from the hurrying firemen's auto – the B-flat bugle singing the "all clear" – and, in an instant, the city was alive again – noisily alive. Even before the berloque was really audible in the room where we sat, I heard the people hurrying back from the *abris* – doors opened and banged, windows and shutters were flung wide, and the rush of air in the gas pipes told that the city lights were on again.'

On 23 March 1918 the Germans also opened up with the 'Paris Gun', the so-called 'Big Bertha' – actually two weapons, both 210mm railway-mounted cannon, based near Crépy-en-Laonnois, 121 kilometres from the capital. The first shell landed at 7.15 am in the Place de la République; the second, fifteen minutes later in the Rue Charles V; and the third, in the Boulevard de Strasbourg. Over the next twenty-four hours a total of twenty-one shells landed in the city itself, and one in Châtillon. Only by reassembling the fragments did the French work out that they were dealing with artillery and not aircraft. René Fonck (C47/SPA103) was at the front that day. 'We received a telephone message during the afternoon telling us they were shelling Paris,' he recalled. 'The news seemed so improbable that everyone burst out laughing. I preferred to keep my own counsel. How could a gun sited more than 120 kilometres away drop a shell close to the Gare de l'Est? Everyone thought the idea quite frankly ridiculous. But then, how could aircraft possibly conduct a daylight raid, pass unseen through a swarm of SPADs all positioned to stop them, and drop bombs all morning? The gun hypothesis offered the only possible explanation. Simply the range remained unexplained.'

Sound location gave the French the approximate position of the guns, quickly confirmed by the aircraft of SPA62. 'Then we were over the Boches,' recalled Lieutenant Jean de Brettes. 'Nobody had fired at us yet. Not a good sign, it must mean that enemy patrols were around. North-east of the Saint-Gobain forest, the Germans suddenly opened up with anti-aircraft fire. The shells were all bursting at my exact height and I had to dodge to avoid them. My observer began taking photographs. Now we were over Crépy, the batteries still going hammer and tongs. The SPADs never left me for an instant. At one point they dived across me towards six German fighters. The [Boches] shot down one of our chaps, then headed towards Marie. Someone came spinning down. A Boche or a Frenchman? I got my answer five minutes later [when] just three SPADs followed me across our lines. I hoped our comrade had only been wounded. The mission was over: I was first to land and as each aircraft followed we all ran over in search of news. Once we were all down, we found out the missing pilot was Lieutenant Lecoq. We later discovered he'd been the one shot down over our lines by the six Boches. He'd taken a number of hits to the body. Although our photos weren't great, they did show the exact location of the "Berthas", so we could start correcting the fire of the guns detailed to destroy the enemy "colossi". During the flight my colleague Adjudant [Charles] Quette spotted a flash that proved to be one of the Crépy guns firing. A few days later new photographs were deemed necessary to complete the information gathered during our first trip and to confirm the effects of our fire. I was picked again, with Lieutenant [Paul] Brousse as my observer. A second crew accompanied us: Adjudant Fabien Lambert (pilot) and Lieutenant [Robert] des Allées (observer). Despite adverse weather conditions, sustained and accurate anti-aircraft fire, and the continual presence of enemy fighters, we got [our] new photographs.'

French counter-battery work began immediately, but to little avail. The site lay hidden deep within woodland and was protected by a smokescreen as well as anti-aircraft guns. According to the authorities, 367 shells landed on Paris between 23 March and 9 August 1918, the most lethal attack taking place on 29 March, when the ancient church of Saint-Gervais-et-Saint-Protais in the fourth *arrondissement* took a direct hit during the Good Friday service: 91 worshippers died and 68 more were wounded. French artillery and bombers were all unable to halt the shelling, and only the allied advance during the second battle of the Marne in July prompted the Germans to withdraw the massive guns out of range.

'Berthas by day, Gothas by night,' proclaimed *l'Illustration*, 'the dull rumble of the guns at the front, the uhlans just "five marches" from the boulevards . . . things should be pretty grim in Paris just now! [Yet] everyday life continues, no airs, no graces and no faint hearts. This is our Paris in wartime: no fuss, no panic, no bravado. A model of steadiness and self-control.' Writing for the magazine *Everyweek*, Marie Harrison described the bombardment as a period of 'acute unpleasantness' because the shells arrived unpredictably, unlike an air raid which at least had a definite beginning and end. 'Yet,' she gushed, 'I found Paris brighter than London, I found it more alive, more interested and so more interesting.'

Mildred Aldrich also detected few signs of panic: 'Every one hates it. But every one knows that the chances are about one in some thousands – and takes the chance. I know of late sitters-up, who cannot change their habits, and who keep right on playing bridge during a raid. How good a game it is, I don't know. Well, one kind of bravado is as good as another. Among many people the chief sensation is one of boredom – it is a nuisance to be wakened out of one's first sleep; it is a worse nuisance to have proper *saut de lit* clothes ready; and it is the worst nuisance of all to go down into a damp cellar and possibly have to listen to talk.'

Charles-Édouard Jeanneret, a Swiss national and trainee architect better known as Le Corbusier, was an unrepentant night owl. In February, when bombs fell close to his home and office, he stayed out on the Pont des Arts, 'enthralled' by the action overhead. He eventually decided discretion was the better part of valour. But, he boasted, he remained calm, unlike the females of his acquaintance: 'The women are another set of bombs about to go off. They make such a fuss. [The raids] don't worry me, although after the unusually lively events of the past few days I've decided to weave my way past the cellars each night. I'll say it again. Danger doesn't bother me . . . I'll make a damn fine soldier.'

'When will it be my turn?' – injury and death

The simple act of flying put aircrew under enormous physical stress. A ground temperature of 15° C falls to –42° C at 6,000 metres, and at –34° C, the temperature found in the upper air even in mid-summer, the body loses 75 per cent of its efficiency. The cold was recognized as a problem from the start, prompting Le Matin into urgent action to encourage its readers to donate warm clothing for the aviators. Sadly, its campaign was rather more enthusiastic than helpful, distributing woollen gloves and scarves that froze after absorbing water from clouds and rain. 'I give mine to my mechanic,' one pilot told James Hall (N124). 'He sends them home, and his wife unravels the yarn to make sweaters for the children.'

'[No one] was daft enough to wear clothes straight from a freezing locker,' recalled André Duvau (BR29). 'You took care to lay out your flying suit and fur-lined boots reasonably close to the mess stove. Once you were warm, you put on a big woollen jumper over your tunic, "slipped" into your flying suit and pulled on your overboots, making sure to tighten the belt and the wrist- and ankle-tabs. On your head went a silk stocking, then a silk balaclava, a woollen balaclava and a fur-lined leather pilot's helmet. You turned up your flying-suit collar and wrapped a muffler round your neck, fixing it at the back to stop the wind from whipping the ends in your face. A pair of good goggles completed the outfit, along with two pairs of gloves – paper, then fur-lined. We lumbered about like deep-sea divers.'

Jacques Boulenger (F223) paints a vivid picture: 'Here comes the pilot, swaddled in his fur-lined rubberized-canvas flying suit, tan leather helmet making his skull look smooth and ovoid, balaclava narrowing his face like a nun's wimple, sheepskin-lined overboots turning his feet into paws.' The whole outfit was so cumbersome that many a flyer could only get dressed with the help of his mechanic. 'Ouf!' said Bernard Lafont (V220). 'The ceremony's over. It followed the customary rite and everything went according to plan. I'm stifled in all these layers. I need to be up in the air, out in the chill of the slipstream.' Jean Navarre (N67) adapted the gear to his characteristically individual taste, scoring his sixth victory on 2 March 1916 in an outfit topped off with 'an unkempt bearskin'. But bearskin or no bearskin, nothing could completely counteract the freezing temperatures. 'I've never been so cold in my life,' remarked André Quennehen (MF5) after a raid in February 1916. 'I couldn't get out of the plane when I landed. My legs and feet were completely numb. Still, I was happy. I'd completed my mission.' Flying in a Blériot two-seater the previous winter, observer Lieutenant Henri Sabouret (BL9) had sought extra help. 'I became aware of a strong smell of burning and spent several minutes anxiously searching for its source,' said his pilot Jean Bourhis. 'Then my observer shouted, "It's on fire! It's on fire!" I cut the engine and dived, but the lieutenant could still feel the heat. The lining of his leather jacket was burning. He removed his leathers and muffler and threw a little pocket hand warmer, the cause of all the fuss, over the side. I flew home slowly . . . delighted to see Sabouret shivering without his warm clothes!'

As planes flew higher and higher, so aircrew faced ever tougher conditions. In the winter of 1917/18 Sous-lieutenant Léon Bourjade (N/SPA152) was patrolling the skies above the Vosges. 'During my last patrol at 5,000 metres, the temperature was –23°!' he reported. 'I could feel it through all my furs. I've lost some skin off my nose and cheeks. They were exposed to the air and suffered a touch of frostbite.' Bourjade quickly found an answer – for his feet, at least: 'Now I'm flying in electrically heated overboots. They're working well and I really like them.'

At a height over 3,000 metres the effects of oxygen starvation begin to make themselves felt, but pilots were reluctant to carry cylinders because of the extra weight incurred. In August 1917 Adjudant Adolphe Lemelle (SPA73) set off from 2,500 metres in determined pursuit of a German who had been attacking a French observation balloon. On reaching 6,500 metres he began to feel ill: 'I felt sure it was my breakfast. Never mind, I'd survive. I carried on trailing my Boche on this devil of a climb. A few minutes later my symptoms were getting worse. I'd started hiccoughing like mad. With every passing second my head seemed to be swelling more and more. I couldn't breathe and I thought I was about to faint. My balance had gone, my reflexes were slowing. Everything was shutting down. I recovered enough to realize I'd put the plane into a spin. I pulled out, then woke again to find myself spinning the other way. I never actually blacked out, I just felt light-headed, and descending in an uncontrolled spin was making me dizzy. I no longer had control of my faculties but instinct took over and I began to prepare for landing. A jolt, then shell-bursts all around me: enemy guns, shrapnel, shells. I had to be on the wrong side of the lines. I'd started to feel a bit better and worked out that I must be between Nieuport and Ostend. I banked immediately and headed out to sea. The gunfire had done me good. I'd rallied enough to know that to return to our side I had to keep the sea on my right and the land on my left. I found my route and headed home. After that, I don't remember a thing. I landed. Where? How? I don't know. I woke up in a hospital bed. Apparently, I'd been found out cold in my plane. Our group doctor had provided first aid and then sent me here.'

The intense concentration demanded by military flying and the constant exposure to danger also placed crews under immense psychological pressure. 'Flying has a way of ageing you very quickly,' declared writer Jacques Duval, while Colonel Paul du Peuty described the tactics of continuous offensive action planned for 1916 as 'a draining process for pilots and observers alike'. Maréchal des Logis Marcel Viallet (N67) thought the solitude of flying only added to the burden: 'When danger strikes,' he argued, 'an infantryman has his comrades beside him; men are yelling, the officers barking out orders. In the excitement of the counter-attack . . . he scarcely has time to think. But we're on our own up there. All we can do is wait. There is almost nothing we can do to avoid it.'

'You rapidly learn to shield yourself behind an armour of indifference,' observed one bomber pilot, 'and your memories more often focus on some minor irritant – your tie was too tight or your windscreen was rattling – than a critical moment during one of [our] four-hour battles.' Only a week into the war, flying two reconnaissance missions a day during the battle of the Frontiers was already weighing heavily on Marcel Brindejonc des Moulinais (DO22/N23): 'It was a good job I slept well because I was growing increasingly demoralized, physical tiredness compounding the frayed nerves of someone whose vision and judgement were being tested to the limit. We were responsible for others, you see; heaven knew the repercussions of any mistake. We had to keep our eyes peeled at all times!' Even a routine artillery spotting mission took a heavy toll. 'Back in the tents, I stretched out in an armchair, exhausted,' wrote Bernard Lafont (V220) from Verdun. 'My body was tired from all the rapid changes of height and constant changes of pressure. My ears were buzzing and my head still full of the rumble of the engine. But above all I was weary from the continual strain on my mind and senses . . . constantly risking my life to . . . observe some distant object on the ground or in the vast void of the sky.'

Bomber commander Major Maurice Happe (GB4) displayed zero tolerance towards pilots displaying 'mental weakness', returning them to the GDE or even to their original regiment, but some commanding officers considered it part of their duties to care for the well-being of their men. Captain Jean Personne (F25), for example, tried to give his crews some sort of outdoor occupation as relaxation, including gardening or raising chickens. Nevertheless many pilots eventually succumbed to exhaustion, among them Brindejonc des Moulinais who, 'dead in spirit' was hospitalized in June 1915. 'Two doctors had already examined me and advised plenty of Vichy water, sodium sulphate [a common laxative], calomel [mercuryl chloride], cacodylate etc,' he wrote to his parents. 'It sent my system haywire and I finally decided that I'm just dog-tired. It's this lousy war!'

Many airmen in Brindejonc's situation were treated at the Hôpital Complémentaire VR75, a convalescent establishment at Viry-Châtillon, originally set up under the auspices of the Ligue Aéronautique de France. Surrounded by a 'magnificent 10-hectare park, whose fountains and harmonious design are reminiscent of the gardens at Versailles', it was open to men 'who ha[d] risked their lives and given unstintingly of their patriotism'. One patient had fond memories of his time there: 'The pilots called this hospital Squadron VR75. We had plenty to eat and lots of English cigarettes. We always slipped a few packets in our pockets when we went off to enjoy ourselves in Paris. A big twenty-five- or thirty-seater diligence, drawn by four horses, took us to Juvisy station, [and] the chief MO, a colonel called Mougin, would watch us leave. "Anyone with a pass, climb in!" he'd say. "The rest of you . . . sort yourselves out!" Some men hauled themselves up next to the driver, others clambered on to the running boards. The convoy looked like a bunch of human grapes. I left the hospital after a month, wearier than when I went in – hardly surprising given our rather rackety existence.'

Convalescent pilots were given non-operational duties before they flew missions again. Brindejonc des Moulinais (DO22/N23), for example, was promoted to sous-lieutenant and sent to the schools as an instructor before returning to front-line service in the spring of 1916.

Up to a fifth of those who earned their wings in wartime were killed, with the majority of casualties occurring among the novices. 'The young chaps suffered an enormous number of deaths and losses,' claimed Paul Waddington (SPA154). 'It wasn't unusual for a young fighter pilot to arrive and be dead within a fortnight due to inexperience. After a certain amount of flying time and extricating yourself from tight spots, then fine! You'd every chance of staying the course.' In a two-seater, of course, the death of the pilot normally doomed his observer as well. 'Could any situation be more ghastly, any agony worse, than that of the observer who's seen his pilot killed and knows he's going to die from ignorance of what to do next?' pondered Jacques Mortane. 'How many fatalities have occurred because an observer lacked the necessary coolness and couldn't react quickly enough?'

The loss of friends and comrades also affected the survivors. 'In January 1917 [I was] one of the ten pilots who formed the initial nucleus of [N]81, under the command of Captain Mandinaud,' recalled Adjudant Pierre de Cazenove de Pradines. 'I had the honour of being the first member of the squadron mentioned in despatches. I later suffered the sorrow of witnessing the tragic end of nearly all my valiant comrades from the early days

[Mandinaud, Rivière, Caillou, Boiteux-Levret, Reymond, Sauvat], first-class pilots, all with such promise. We had to avenge our comrades and press on without allowing gaps to appear. It was a challenge, but the memory of their deaths was the only spur we required, and this very difficult task was accomplished with aplomb. Almost all those who replaced the dead now figure among the ranks of the aces, and all have at least one victim to their credit.'

The previous year Bernard Lafont (V220) had watched as a Caudron staggered back to the airfield at Lemmes, behind Verdun. The observer was dead, but the pilot was physically unharmed: 'He was standing by his plane, gabbling away, badly shaken and very distraught. He told us about the dogfight: a Boche had surprised them, a few rounds and it was over. The pilot's face and clothes were covered with the blood pouring from the observer's wound. The draught from the engine had sprayed it all over him and he'd been forced to descend under this ghastly shower. He managed to land but he was obviously very emotional, every now and then his limbs began to tremble. I stood in front of the plane, abandoned on the airfield. The panels of the fuselage were red, so too the struts and the engine housing.'

Some pilots openly admitted their fears. 'Your first flight is a picnic,' claimed Marcel Viallet. 'Do you think about coming under fire? Your aircraft breaking up in mid-air? The controls malfunctioning? Not on your life. The first time you climb into a plane, nothing can rattle you . . . [Then one day the enemy] side-slips and spears you from the rear. By Jove, you mind your step then.' Jacques Ehrlich (SPA154) was an experienced balloon-buster, a task requiring a cool head and a steady hand on the controls. He was also a successful one, shooting down eighteen 'sausages' (and one aircraft) between June and September 1918. But he was always afraid. 'I touched wood the whole time,' he admitted. 'I was scared of the Boches attacking me from the rear, of being shot down by the guns and machine guns protecting the balloon; I was scared of technical trouble stopping me getting back. When my mission was over I immediately pulled off my glove and frantically touched wood again until I got home. But as soon as my feet hit terra firma my fears vanished. I roared with laughter, wild with delight. I could have been at the music hall.' Pierre Violet was equally superstitious: 'two days ago I was flying at 800 metres over the Boche lines [above Verdun] when a shrapnel ball hit me full in the chest. It pierced my flying suit, fur lining and jacket, but my leather belt stopped it and it's just left me with a bruise. I found it eventually. Everything's fine, so I've kept it. You can't be too careful.'

For fighter pilots, accepting what was in effect single combat could require a major effort of will. 'It's hard to quell the innate sense of self-preservation that screams at you to sheer off and get away from the planes with the sinister black crosses,' observed Marcel Viallet. Indeed, some men were unable to do so: 'There were plenty of fighter pilots who never attacked,' recalled Paul Waddington (SPA154). 'Sometimes because they didn't know how, [but] often because they allowed the patrol leader, who generally had more experience, to take the lead.' Adjudant André Chainat (SPA3) experienced exactly this phenomenon while on patrol in 1917: 'I ran across two comrades with the group insignia. "Follow me," I signalled to them. They did so half-heartedly. I put myself between them and pushed them back towards the Boches. I worked out a plan and signalled "I'm attacking". I was up against the last in line, thank goodness, and sent him down in flames. I looked round for my comrades. Both had disappeared . . . Some are true and some false; some will enter [combat], some will not [and] others just pretend to do so . . . Some disappear from view until all sign of . . . danger is past. Their engine began to sputter, their gun jammed, they were attacked by an enemy superior in number and don't know how they got away . . . if they go out on their own they never meet [an enemy plane].'

For Edmond Genet (N124), Chouteau Johnson was unquestionably one of the false. Johnson spent fourteen months as a volunteer with the Lafayette Escadrille but never impressed his comrade. 'Am mighty well disgusted with one of the fellows here whom I have mentioned before,' grumbled Genet. '[Johnson] is not an enthusiastic fighter and takes every possible chance to shirk, while we break our necks and risk our lives to maintain the good name of the Escadrille. I'm certain [he] will see the finish of the war, return to America, and pose as the hero of the Escadrille and be received by everyone – who will know the difference?'

Others, however, managed to conquer their nerves. 'The first time I came under fire I desperately wanted to flee, to return quickly to the airfield,' admitted Marcel Brindejonc des Moulinais. 'But my second clash was completely different. I knew what to expect. Only five rounds hit my plane where it mattered. Just knowing it was possible to escape was enough to give me the courage to continue.' Georges Guynemer was initially indifferent to the danger. 'No particular impression, except one of curiosity satisfied,' he noted after his baptism of fire, although after he was wounded over Verdun in March 1916 even he was beset by doubts. He overcame them by manoeuvring close to an enemy two-seater without attacking it: 'That's how you break yourself in,' he wrote to his sister. 'I've got my nerves completely back under control again. The Boche fired 500 rounds at me while I manoeuvred. It didn't bother me. It was just what I needed. . . . This morning decided my future. Without it, I was finished.' Raoul Lufbery (VB106/N124) acknowledged the part played by adrenalin: 'Opening fire is mildly intoxicating for the pilot. Our worst imaginings fade away and we give each other a real peppering.' So too did Adjudant Célestin Sanglier (N62): 'That little shiver as the first rounds whistle past your ears, then the thrill of combat, and you forget everything, even that a round from your opponent might hit you.'

'Just keep telling yourselves that flying is no more dangerous than driving a motor car,' René Dorme (C94/CRP/N3) encouraged his parents. Indeed, the leading French ace, René Fonck (C47/SPA103), never suffered a scratch. In contrast, Charles Nungesser (V106/V116/N/SPA65) accumulated a frightening catalogue of injuries: skull fractures, concussion, internal damage, multiple fractures to the jaw, collarbone and wrist, shrapnel in the right arm and mouth, dislocated knee and right foot, and withered tendons and muscles. Seriously wounded on 29 January 1916, Nungesser was back flying missions over Verdun only two months later. After returning to hospital for more treatment in December 1916, he refused a medical discharge, used a period of convalescence in May 1917 to shoot down another six aircraft, and was eventually forcibly readmitted with exhaustion. Gaston Partridge (VB101) tried to remain sanguine about the risk of injury: 'Flying solo, being wounded – they're nothing to worry about. You just have to accept them as unavoidable necessities.' Sergeant René Mesguich (MS12) was of similar mind: 'The bullet penetrated the fatty layer of flesh, good old flesh that never did me any harm,' he wrote, after he and observer Robert Jacottet shot down an Albatros from FA12 on 26 May 1915. 'It missed the nerves, so it didn't affect my movements, but it did send a trickle of warm blood down my arm, annoying me intensely. It was just enough to make me seem interesting and give me a few days' rest, without stopping me moving my arm and walking around as normal.'

Adjudant Maxime Lenoir (N23) was eventually shot down over Verdun on 25 October 1916: 'The best thing about all [my] official accolades is they say I don't care a jot for my own mortality. I didn't call my plane "*Trompe la mort*" ["The Death Defier"] for nothing. . . . I make light of death. It doesn't scare me. Life can be sweet, but a good death is no less fine.' Captain Albert Auger, CO of N3, sought comfort in patriotism: 'Awareness of his own mortality is what allows a man to live his life to the full. A readiness to die for one's country is the measure of a man.' Aspirant Pierre

Gourdon (MF201) put his faith in God. 'Don't live your life, live a dream, an ideal,' he advised. 'Death is an everlasting dawn where the soul resides in eternal glory, no longer afraid of the day. Heroes today will tomorrow be angels. All true sacrifice is welcome unto God.' André Steuer (N103), who flew on after his brother Pierre (C46) was killed in action, also found solace in religion: 'I'm off to strafe the trenches this afternoon and may not return,' he wrote six months later. 'I hope God will protect me but I believe that whatever happens will be for the best. I go without fear.' Steuer survived the mission but ten days later he collided in mid-air with his comrade Sergeant Romans (N103); both men were killed.

The sheer fickleness of fate only added to the strain: 'When will it be my turn?' wondered André Quennehen (MF5), after his former observer, the son of General de Maud'huy, was reported killed while serving with MF63. 'Death seems deliberately contrary,' affirmed Jacques Mortane, 'playfully striking its victims when they least expect it or just when they think themselves safe and sound. . . . Brindejonc des Moulinais often survived when he thought his end was nigh. [Then] a wing shears off during a completely routine flight – a stupid accident, scarcely believable – [and] a hero is lost.' Similarly, Corporal Rolland Longueteau (MF29) returned safely from strafing a German train, skimming along only 5 metres off the ground, only to lose his leg in an explosion when his mechanic slipped loading a new bomb into the aircraft. 'There's nothing we can do about it,' remarked Captain Pierre Poisard (C28). 'We volunteered to give our lives [for our country]. We must do our duty and suffer the blows of fate in silence.'

Many pilots were less afraid of death than the manner of their dying. 'If his luck's out, even the best pilot can be killed the first time he has an accident,' observed one anonymous aviator. 'If fortune is smiling on him, a bungler can walk away unscathed from a disaster.' No pilot wanted to die in an accident – certainly not Adjudant Gilbert Triboulet (N57), killed behind the front lines on 11 December 1917: 'The young hero would have proudly welcomed death in combat, a glorious sacrifice consummated in the clear blue skies, a mortal blow from a stronger, more agile opponent, the vertiginous fall of the downed eagle. Instead fate condemned him to die in the only way he would have despised.'

Nor did pilots want to die at the hands of 'friendly fire' – and no one was immune. Guynemer's plane was hit by bullets from a British DH4, cutting his longerons, shortly after he had claimed his fifty-third victim over Poperinghe on 20 August 1917. The ace responded immediately. 'I thought he was a Boche so I shot the observer,' he reported. 'The DH4 dived towards enemy lines and climbed again, manoeuvring just like a Boche. Low on fuel. Had to break off.' Jean Navarre heard the ominous rattle of machine-gun fire while escorting a Farman near Châlons in 1916: 'I lifted my head to see a magnificent twin-engined Caudron weaving about above me, firing his Colt non-stop. If this was a joke, it was in pretty poor taste. The little twerp thought I was a Boche. To give him a scare, I manoeuvred, passed behind him and easily got the upper hand. Increasingly angry, he carried on peppering me. The idiot didn't get anywhere near me, so it was all just for show, but it was still damn annoying. He was becoming a real pest. I lined him up and let him hear my gun snap. That did the trick and he went into a vertical dive.' Navarre was beginning to enjoy 'this all-French encounter' and decided it was 'time to show off a bit'. He stunted around the Caudron until the crew recognized his roundels, then escorted it back to its home airfield where he promptly crashed on landing. 'I went looking for my antagonist and gave him a real mouthful. He couldn't apologize enough. Everyone made fun of him. I continued my lecture and left him to stew.' Navarre returned to Le Bourget by taxi and train, picked up a new aircraft, and by early afternoon was back again on front-line duty.

'The aviator isn't afraid of certain kinds of death, a direct hit from a shell or a bullet, a swift fall and a crash into the ground,' remarked *La Guerre aérienne illustrée*. 'What he really dreads is seeing his plane on fire, realizing the gravity of the situation and being burned alive.' Raoul Lufbery (VB106/N124) and his comrades had discussed just this prospect: 'I should always stay with the machine,' advised Lufbery. 'If you jump you're done for. But there's always a good chance of side-slipping your aeroplane down in such a way that you fan the flames away from yourself and the wings. You can even put the fire out before you reach the ground. It has been done. Me for staying with the old bus, every time!' But when actually faced with this awful dilemma he chose to jump. Like many of his fellow Americans, Lufbery had transferred to the US Air Service in 1918, and on 19 May he joined combat with an Albatros. Eddie Rickenbacker (94th Aero Squadron) watched him fall: 'Luf fired several short bursts as he dived in to the attack. Then he swerved away and appeared to busy himself with his gun, which evidently had jammed. Another circle over their heads and he had cleared the jam. Again he rushed the enemy from their rear, when suddenly old Luf's was seen to burst into roaring flames. He passed the Albatros and proceeded for three or four seconds on a straight course. Then to the horrified watchers below there appeared the figure of their gallant hero emerging in a headlong leap from the midst of the fiery furnace! Lufbery had preferred to leap to certain death rather than endure the slow torture of burning to a crisp.'

Marcel Viallet chose differently. With no parachute to provide escape from a stricken plane, his greatest fear was falling: 'The panic and confusion induced by watching the ground rush towards you as you fall is so great that my pen has gone on strike. Even if, by extraordinary good fortune, the hero of the drama survives to tell the tale, imagine the willpower needed to fly again.' When enemy bullets set light to his fuel tank during a dogfight, Viallet heeded Lufbery's advice, surviving the experience and the war: 'I dived like a madman, a dramatic manoeuvre that undoubtedly saved my skin.'

The task of writing to – and sometimes visiting – the families of the dead fell to squadron COs like Captain René Roeckel (F7). When Lieutenant Marcel Vernes was killed alongside pilot Sergeant Jean Peinaud close to Folemprise Farm on the Chemin des Dames on 24 March 1917, Roeckel went to pay a condolence call on his family. 'Captain Roeckel has just left,' Mme Vernes wrote to her son's fellow officers. 'He presented us with [Marcel]'s crosses . . . He talked of his friendship with Marcel and his confidence in him, and his words comforted us. . . . I have a profound need to know more of the men who were part of [Marcel's] life, who loved him, liked him and join us in mourning his passing. . . . You made sure that his years with the colours were happy ones. May God bless you and keep you.' Some unfortunate families did not even have a body to mourn. The disappearance of Georges Guynemer left his grieving father convinced that the enemy had deliberately concealed the details of his son's fate. 'The Germans have misled us over the burial site at Poelcapelle [sic],' he wrote angrily to the minister of war. 'We have not yet received a reply to the request for information made by the president of the Republic via the king of Spain. . . . I demand that we refuse to accept either Germany's silence or its lies.'

Lieutenant Rémy Grassal (C13) spoke for many aircrew: 'I stare Death in the face every day. It doesn't frighten me. Any friends who survive will tell you that I always did what was asked of me, regardless of the danger, and gave my all in the performance of my duty.' The words of Sous-lieutenant Raymond Havet (N77) also provide a fitting memorial. Havet was shot down over Chambly on 16 March 1917, probably in combat with an aircraft from FA39. He left a note on his bunk before setting off that day, describing how he wished to be remembered: 'This Boche was no better than the rest. I made a mistake and beg your forgiveness. No tears, no wreaths, no flowers. Just a drop of champagne, later . . . when the time is right.'

'The decisive arm' – the battles of 1918

The release of enemy troops from the Eastern Front in 1917, following Russia's October Revolution and subsequent withdrawal from the conflict, had led the Allies to expect a major German offensive in the spring of 1918, and Pétain believed air power could play a crucial role in first stemming the attack and then turning the tide. 'If the aviation service can paralyse the enemy supply lines effectively enough for long enough, it could be the decisive factor,' he wrote to General Pershing, commander-in-chief of US forces in France, on Christmas Day 1917. 'While our reconnaissance aircraft should remain proportionate in number to other types, there should be no limit on fighters. We need to turn out as many as possible. By depriving the enemy of intelligence, crippling his lines of communication and sapping his morale, they can play a vital role.'

By March 1918 an enormous industrial effort had doubled the number of bomber and fighter squadrons available. GQG aviation commander Charles Duval now had the means to create a powerful air reserve for use *'en masse'*, supporting Pétain's plans for limited attacks backed by overwhelming firepower. He first combined the fighter groups and bomber groups in larger formations, the Escadres de Combat and Escadres de Bombardement, all under the direct orders of GQG. In early March he then assembled the fighter groups and day bombers – a total of 585 machines – in two massive mixed temporary *groupements* named after their respective commanders, Major Victor Ménard and Major Philippe Féquant, while placing the night bombers in two separate formations, each 100 machines strong. Nor did he neglect the cooperation squadrons, allocating a number of fighter groups directly to the armies and tasking them specifically with ensuring complete freedom of action for the cooperation squadrons over the front.

For Pétain and Duval alike, the needs of the infantry remained paramount. The battle, they believed, would be won on the ground, and the ultimate purpose of aviation, directly or indirectly, was to support the land war. 'All available squadrons will act to increase the impact of our guns,' instructed Pétain in February 1918. Fighters and bombers were ordered to intervene against enemy ground troops: 'harass[ing] marching columns, convoys, bivouacs and parks with bombs and machine-gun fire night and day', while army group commanders 'secure[d] a sufficient concentration of aerial resources to guarantee the complete demoralization of the follow-up waves'. The bombers were also to target the enemy front lines to a depth of 20 kilometres, adding ammunition dumps, stations and important rail junctions to their list of objectives. Meanwhile the fighters would seek out and destroy enemy aircraft above and across the front lines. 'This ultra-offensive role has so far been undertaken by provisional formations brought together under a single command only on the eve of battle,' explained Duval. 'With no prior opportunity to train together, these formations have lacked cohesion and consequently have taken time to reach full operational effectiveness.'

The fighters were to operate *en masse*, or in mixed sorties as bomber escorts. Unable to ignore the bombers, the Germans would be drawn into combat – and the fighters would pounce. 'I was convinced our fighter squadrons could play the pivotal role if converted into a true offensive arm,' claimed Duval. 'Two things were required to effect this transformation: suitable materiel and a change in the individualism and combat techniques of our pilots. The kind of offensive formations I envisaged were squadrons of two- and three-seaters, operating in groups, with top cover provided by patrols of single-seaters. The nucleus of this kind of aviation, the school in which were developed the appropriate tactics and materiel, was the bomber squadron.'

Orders were given to construct the new airfields required to turn this reserve into a truly mobile offensive force, and GQG also emphasized the benefits of flexibility, reminding pilots that 'Reconnaissance machines may be forced to engage in combat, while fighters can sometimes bring back valuable intelligence.'

To counter the expected German offensive, the Groupements Ménard and Féquant, plus one night bomber group, were temporarily allocated to Northern Army Group (General Franchet d'Espèrey), and when the attack finally got under way on 21 March the squadrons moved by night along the threatened front, committing dozens of planes to the skies at a time. The Germans achieved notable early gains using aircraft in close support of their infantry, but the French quickly acquired air superiority over the whole of the Picardy front, deploying their air power to stall the enemy and relieve threatened Amiens by striking at the rear in formations up to eighty strong, disrupting supply lines and preventing the advance of reinforcements.

On 27 March GC19 was active in the skies east of the city. A group of three fighters set off to attack columns around Péronne and Rosières-en-Santerre, but engine trouble soon forced the return of Sergeant Jean Sers, while Sergeant André Courtieu became separated in the mist, to be pounced upon by five German single-seaters and chased 5 kilometres back to safety. Left to cross the lines alone at 500 metres, Sous-lieutenant Albert de Kergorlay (SPA96) descended to 200 metres to strafe troops crossing the bridge at Villers-Carbonel, then flew on. 'Attacked a *drachen* at Chaulnes, ground fire (plane hit six times) forced him down to 200 metres,' recorded the squadron war diary. 'Dogfight at Avretours – attacked by five Boches – forced landing at Mesnil Saint-Georges. Germans still advancing. Had to burn plane.' Two days later de Kergorlay was back in the air again, this time as part of a joint patrol with SPA73, strafing German troops around Hangest-en-Santerre.

Pilots from GC13 were also busy, among them Sous-lieutenant Antoine Cordonnier (N57/SPA15). 'You know what's asked of us when the enemy must be halted to give our reinforcements time to move up,' he wrote to his family. 'We have to fill the gaps and descend almost to ground level to strafe the invader. I did my best, renewing my vow to make the ultimate sacrifice if need be.' Nearby was René Fonck (C47/SPA103): 'We were flying so low we were almost on the tips of their bayonets, and our machine-guns rattled at point-blank range on the solid mass below. The more heavily laden bombers dropped their cargo among the marching troops, on the columns and convoys. Our assault spooked the horses and they tossed their harness into the ditches, producing absolute pandemonium. [But] surprised by this totally unexpected success, our battalions were uneasy to find nothing but empty space ahead of them. They declined to press home their advantage and vital hours were lost.'

By early April the German offensive was running out of steam. 'The enemy seems to be sleeping now,' continued Cordonnier, 'but I'm sure he's concealing his hand and preparing to strike again. There are plenty of planes about, looking for a weak spot to report to the German infantry. We are also putting our fighters up again and are planning to do so several times a day if the weather stays fine. I spent nearly all last Sunday in the air, except when I nipped down to the village between patrols for mass. It was just a brief respite. And I still need the prayers of my comrades.'

GQG was delighted with the performance of the air reserve: 'Uncertainty over the exact location of the expected German offensive forced us to distribute our squadrons right along the front line, if not evenly, at least in large formations wherever enemy action seemed likely,' it reported in May. 'Once the direction of the attack became clear, we had to act quickly to concentrate our planes in Picardy, especially as the ferocity of the enemy assault suggested we might be facing an intervention *en masse* by a large number of aggressive, energetic squadrons. The necessary orders were executed with a speed and precision that exceeded the most optimistic of expectations. . . . The extreme mobility of our squadrons quickly produced results, and from 25 March we were able to assert our air superiority right across the battlefield.' Duval, too, was pleased with his new formations: 'Our fighter pilots have worked tirelessly to sweep the skies, preventing enemy aircraft from reaching our lines and clearing a path for our bombers to the German lines. [Our pilots] have been trained in this tactic and are more than ever convinced of its value.'

On 9 May 1918 leading ace René Fonck achieved six victories in one day – an incredible feat. 'Downing five opponents in twenty-four hours had long been a dream of mine,' he admitted. 'I thought it a record that would take some beating. The sun was shining brightly at daybreak, but a thick fog blew in and soon halted any reconnaissance. At 10.00 am the mist began to lift and forty-five minutes later I was able to take off alongside Captain Batlle and Lieutenant Fontaine.

'Just across the lines we ran into a reconnaissance plane on patrol with a pair of two-seater fighter escorts. In a prearranged manoeuvre, I immediately gave the signal to attack and scored a direct hit on the enemy with my initial machine-gun bursts. I abandoned him to his fate, then effected a rapid split-S followed by a side-slip to avoid being hit in my turn. This put me under the wing of a second Boche whose gunner was trying to get back at me. But he wasn't quick enough; I opened fire again and my opponent went tumbling down. Meanwhile a third Boche was busy giving my comrades the slip. He saw me turn, decided I was in no position to follow, and went into a vertical dive – an error that led to his downfall. In seconds, I was on his tail and ready to fire. I immediately made the most of my advantage. His plane broke up in mid-air and fell to the ground in pieces: he had shared the same fate as his compatriots.

'The entire dogfight had lasted no more than forty-five seconds. All three two-seaters were found close to our trenches, near Grivesnes, no more than 400 metres apart. We were scarcely back on the ground before the telephones began reporting my triple exploit.

'On reflection I decided the enemy would definitely panic, so I refuelled quickly. Everyone was cheering like mad but I didn't have a moment to lose. Around 5.30 pm I took off again, alongside Sergeant Brugère and Lieutenant Thouzelier. Some light cloud was blowing in and giving us plenty of screening cover.

'At 6.20 pm I spotted a Boche manoeuvring above Montdidier and headed straight into the bank of mist between us. It enveloped me completely like cotton-wool. Shooting down an enemy as you come out of the fog is easy. I emerged at a distance of 30 metres and surprised the observer, who was leaning out of the fuselage and doing a bit of artillery spotting. A burst of fire soon brought [the Boche] down. I'd lost visual contact with my companions but I wasn't too bothered. I preferred to manoeuvre alone among my opponents without needing to worry about my comrades. Camaraderie obliges us to fly to the rescue of any compatriot who finds himself outnumbered and I always tried not to let anyone down. But freedom of action was my real love – that was the key to all my victories. Then four Fokkers appeared, with five Albatri almost directly above them. One against nine: pretty tricky. I thought twice about attacking but I wanted to reach my target, so I threw caution to the winds and decided to risk combat. The Fokkers were flying in a V and from my very high altitude I rapidly devised a plan of attack. Keeping an eye on the Albatri, I dived vertically at a speed of at least 240km/h, slipped between the two squadrons and arrived on the last of the Fokkers. I fired my first burst from the rear at 30 metres and immediately saw the Fokker fall. Hearing the rattle of my machine gun, the two nearest Boches turned simultaneously in my direction, but I was travelling at 68m/s [245km/h] and managed to slip between them before they had time to complete their manoeuvre. They would need eight seconds to return to the line, enough for me to close with the patrol leader and bring him down. Now it was the turn of the Albatri to dive at me. The boldness of my manoeuvre had caught them on the hop but they had recovered. I flew like a meteor. I could feel them snapping at my heels. I turned my head and saw them forming a great arc in the sky, all converging on me. But I was also pleased to see two distinctive streaks of flame in the far distance. The gap between us carried on growing and as soon as I was safe from attack I set course for my airfield. The reception awaiting me was incredible. The cheering never stopped – they even carried me in triumph for a short way – and the bar stools saw plenty of action.

'At 8.00 pm my sextuple success was ratified. I was delighted. I'd beaten the target I'd set for myself prior to take-off.'

By mid-May Duval was experimenting again, seeking 'better coordination . . . and a basis for any future mass offensive formations' by combining the fighters and day bombers of the Groupements Ménard and Féquant in a single Air Division some 600 machines strong. Less than a fortnight later the new formation faced its first big test. On 27 May the Germans renewed their offensive, this time targeting the Chemin des Dames, making significant inroads into French positions with their opening attack. The night bombers were immediately despatched to raid the German rear, and within two days three *groupements* of Breguet 14 day bombers – under Major Joseph Vuillemin, Major Armand des Prez de la Morlais, and the influential Major Louis de Goÿs, recently escaped from captivity in Germany – were attacking enemy columns around Fère-en-Tardenois. Losses quickly mounted as the Breguet squadrons penetrated deeper and deeper behind German lines, moving beyond the effective range of their SPAD escorts. Even so, by the time the French counter-attacked south of Montdidier on 11 June, 600 aircraft had been assembled to cover a 130-kilometre front.

Duval was ever the pragmatist, prepared to tailor his formations according to the situation, and on 15 June he redivided the Air Division into two Mixed Brigades – each composed of one Escadre de Combat and one Escadre de Bombardement – under the command of de Goÿs and Féquant. He also created a specialist photo-reconnaissance formation – the Groupement Weiller – combining BR45 and BR220 under the command of Captain Paul-Louis Weiller (MF22/MF40/C21/BR224). Earlier photo-reconnaissance missions had penetrated no more than 25 kilometres behind enemy lines, but trials conducted by Weiller had shown the Breguet 14 was capable of venturing much further. Weiller stripped a Breguet of all surplus weight, including its defensive armament, added oxygen equipment for the crew, and supplemented the normal combination suit, boots, gloves and balaclava with a 'wire-mesh lining. It was powered by a small generator mounted on the wing and its temperature was controllable via a rheostat placed within reach of the pilot'. Thus equipped, Weiller's Breguets could carry a camera 1½ to 2 metres in focal length, operate at altitudes between 6,400 and 6,700 metres and travel up to 120 kilometres behind enemy lines.

Lieutenant René Dreyfus and his observer Lieutenant Louis Servanty (BR220) set out on one such long-range mission on 28 February 1918. 'We took off at 1.00 pm in very good weather,' recalled Servanty. 'We were only meant to be covering 40 kilometres but our plan was to push on for another 25 kilometres to reconnoitre a sector reportedly of considerable interest to the staff. I couldn't see anything unusual, but the big railway hub of Mariembourg was visible some distance across the Ardennes. Dreyfus [confirmed] we had enough petrol, so we decided to go and take photographs. We crossed the Ardennes [where] I took a picture of Rocroi and then we arrived over Belgium. A strong easterly wind was pushing the plane slightly off course and I realized I didn't have a photograph from directly above the target. The petrol situation was a bit of a concern, but there was no point coming all this way and leaving the job half done. My pilot took me round again. Perfect, this time the photographs were fine. The return journey was rather edgy: any problem would prevent us from making our lines. Lieutenant Dreyfus kept his eyes glued to his petrol gauge and watch. We had just enough juice to fly straight back. A dogfight would mean a forced landing! More than three hours after take-off we finally spotted our trenches again. We encountered heavy gunfire but not enough to stop us from touching down.'

The role of his new formation, explained Weiller, 'was to produce, if possible daily . . . a detailed photographic map of the enemy rear to a depth of 20 to 100 kilometres. Our Breguets were fitted with twin machine-guns at the rear, on mounts constructed by our own mechanics. Their firepower gave us some defence against the enemy fighters, which could easily outstrip us and attack in force. . . . We began in groups of three, combining our firepower to scare off the enemy fighters. We suffered some losses, but six machine-guns were certainly enough to inflict some damage of their own, and we took pretty good care of ourselves. Lack of materiel subsequently forced us to change our tactics to one plane flying as high as possible. Our main objective was to take photographs, not get into a scrap.'

Crossing the lines at 6,000 metres, Weiller's aircraft did their work and got out fast. The prints were developed on the airfield, then passed to a team of interpreters who compiled a daily list of changes for Foch's situation map. 'The Germans helped us considerably by marking their hospitals with very visible red crosses, which allowed us to track their movements,' added Weiller. 'The hospitals set off several days before the troops, so we knew which sectors the Germans were planning to attack.'

Air superiority enabled the French to resist the attacks of late May and early June, but the sheer effort of maintaining their position was taking an enormous toll of men and machines. 'Most of our victories came during 1918 but we also suffered heavy losses,' admitted Paul Waddington (SPA154). 'We enjoyed clear air superiority over the Germans from late spring onwards. It was hugely important. It gave us a lot of confidence, enabling us to attack on favourable terms with the minimum of risk. Still, we suffered almost daily losses. A fighter group of four squadrons contained around sixty to eighty pilots, all of them acquainted with each other, and at least five to ten were killed every month.' Yet Gabriel Pallier (SPA15) was enjoying himself too much to worry. 'I loved being part of the squadron,' he recalled. 'The camaraderie was extraordinary. The best moment was the day the Germans cut and ran. We felt ourselves kings of the air. In 1918 the Germans were refusing combat. We were cocky. We thought we were conquerors. Risk? What risk? The squadron had a complement of eighteen [which] was replaced twice over. [But] I was lucky. I had the insouciance of youth. I was having a whale of a time.'

New squadrons were created throughout 1918, normally by drafting up to half the strength from an existing squadron or squadrons and filling the gaps with men taken from the depots. SPA164, part of GC21, was formed around a core of experienced pilots at Somme-Vesles in September 1918. All five had transferred from other squadrons within GC21: the CO, Lieutenant Henri Barancy, and pilots Sous-lieutenant Marcel Robert and Sergeant Charles Vauquelin from SPA124, Sous-lieutenant Paul Barbreau from SPA154, and Russell McCormick from the US Aviation Service. Two more pilots were drawn from the pool at the GDE, but eleven were straight out of flying school: the oldest was 30-year-old Sous-lieutenant Marcel Borne, a pre-war cavalryman who had been recalled to serve in transport before transferring to aviation in 1915; the youngest, 20-year-old Corporal Simon Heiné, was part of the class of 1918. '[The squadron] was composed almost entirely of young chaps straight from the schools,' recalled Robert, 'so we had to finish off their training, teach them to shoot, drill them in formation flying and familiarize them with the sector. And until we could throw them into battle without too much risk we had to think twice about involving them in combat. . . . The weather in September 1918 was particularly bad and the end of the war was nigh, which explains the lack of dogfights. We registered some probable victories but none confirmed. By the time of the armistice, SPA164 had suffered only one loss – a success in itself.' That loss was the unfortunate Heiné, shot down between Condé-lès-Autry and Cernais-en-Dernois on 30 September 1918, probably by Vizefeldwebel Alfons Nagler of Jasta 81.

But SPA159 – formed around a draft from N90 at Malzéville in January 1918, and later part of GC20 – met a very different fate. Only Captain Albert Roper, the CO, and Sous-lieutenant Victor Esperon du Tremblay had any recent experience; the rest of the pilots had come straight from the pool. In May 1918, just as the German Aisne offensive was in full swing, the squadron moved to Villeseneux, where it was pitted against the Jasta aces of JG1, von Richthofen's old unit. On 30 May Roper was seriously wounded. On 9 June Sergeant Adrien Villard was shot down and killed, as was the new CO, Lieutenant Jean Dehesdin, only three days after taking command. Two days later Sous-lieutenant du Tremblay and Sous-lieutenant Pierre Cramoisy were killed, and Sergeant Élie Le Roy wounded; on 28 June Lieutenant Maurice Patret, Sergeant Pierre Lafargue, Sergeant Frantz Divoy and Corporal Camille Javet were all killed; and on 20 July the new CO, Lieutenant Georges Mazimann, formerly of SPA57, was shot down and killed over Soissons.

Without a single victory to its name, SPA159 had lost nine men killed and two wounded, including three COs, inside two months – an unenviable assignment for the next CO, Captain Henri Hay de Slade (SPA86), and his deputy, Sous-lieutenant Louis Risacher (SPA3). Risacher's transfer was nothing unusual. 'After racking up a certain number of victories you were posted to squadrons that might lack a bit of "go",' said Paul Waddington (SPA154). 'Capable pilots were drafted in to improve performance.'

'I was the only officer apart from my fine comrade, Captain Hay de Slade,' recalled the sous-lieutenant. 'The rest of the unit were all novices who didn't have a clue. I had to teach them everything. Absolutely everything.' Sharing the instruction work, Hay de Slade began by painting bold red stripes down the side of his SPAD so his pilots could recognize him easily in the air. 'I restored their self-confidence and taught them how to shoot down Boches again,' he maintained. 'How did I do it? First I went up on patrol with each pilot in turn. "We're going for a jaunt along the front," I said. "We'll run across some Boches. I'll show you what to do. Take no action yourself and don't fire your machine gun." That was all it needed. I showed them the Boches weren't the ogres of their imagination and that all you had to do was manoeuvre. When you came out of your manoeuvre you were in combat. They were so badly scarred by their previous experience they thought they'd had it whenever they spotted a Boche.'

Certain pupils learned their lesson only too well. On 18 October Hay de Slade took one of his novice pilots over the front: 'This crackpot spotted five or six Fokker D.VIIs below us. I'd seen them too. We weren't in any position to attack, but he dived on them immediately. I could do nothing but follow and watch his back. I dived to help him out, landing myself with all the Boches on my tail instead. They sniped at me for five to ten minutes. Suddenly a SPAD appeared, firing. The Germans saw him too. One of them passed to my left, followed by the SPAD, which fired and tore him to shreds. It was Claude Haegelen of SPA100. Simultaneously a second SPAD – I knew he was American from his roundels – came hurtling towards another of the Germans and shot him down too. "God bless America," I cried, picking up speed in my old SPAD and catching a third Fokker D.VII right at the top of a loop. [The pilot] turned and looked at me, then his plane broke up and crashed. The others all made a run for it.'

Hay de Slade shot down six aircraft and two balloons during his time with SPA159, taking his final total to nineteen. Despite his individual tally, and his success with the squadron's fledglings, his superiors were hard to impress: 'This officer is brilliant in action but less than satisfactory in command,' read a post-war personnel report. 'He should be given a post befitting his particular talents.' Nevertheless Hay de Slade remained with the post-war Armée de l'Air, eventually retiring as a colonel.

On 15 July the Germans launched yet another offensive, this time around Reims. East of the city the French halted the offensive on the opening day, but to the west the Germans fared rather better, establishing a bridgehead on either side of the river at Dormans. The fighters of the Air Division were ordered to clear the skies of German fighters and balloons, while the bombers attacked the enemy on the ground, in particular the makeshift bridges thrown up around the town. Defending the crossing at Châtillon-sur-Marne, the troops of 317th Infantry were virtually cut off in the park and chateau at Vandières. Despite a pioneering attempt at large-scale aerial resupply – 250 tins of meat, 200 loaves and a supply of biscuits were dropped on 17 July, and the same again, with extra ammunition, the following day – the remaining handful of men were forced to withdraw. By then, however, the German advance had stalled and the French went on to the counter-attack.

'I've been feeling really tired recently,' said Sous-lieutenant Antoine Cordonnier (SPA15), 'but resuming the offensive has given me fresh energy.' Just as well, for another huge effort was demanded of the Air Division, and Cordonnier soon found himself facing eight German fighters. 'Around 10.00 am I was at 3,000 metres over enemy lines when I spotted eight little German monoplane fighters attacking four French biplanes. Two other pilots were following me, so I signalled the attack and hurled myself between the Fokkers and the poor biplanes. The [Fokkers] abandoned their prey and the spotters made for home. But that still left the three of us grappling with eight Boche monoplanes 8 kilometres behind enemy lines. We continued fighting all the same. We tried to get above them, but more Boches arrived to bar the way. One of my comrades was shot down in front of me. While he was falling, my other colleague pulled off an incredible manoeuvre to dodge the fire coming his way. They'd separated us, leaving me alone against five Boches, plus another pair who had put themselves between me and the French lines to block my retreat. I was in a real pickle [but] . . . instead of trying to defend myself, I attacked. I dived on my nearest pursuer. A short burst, a few rounds and my adversary went down in flames. The others seemed to hesitate briefly. Taking advantage of their momentary confusion, I pushed my engine [to the limit] and turned my plane towards our lines. A frantic five-minute chase and the Boches flew off.'

Cordonnier's victory was never confirmed, perhaps because the combat took place too far behind German lines to be spotted by French observers. And less than a fortnight later, he too was dead. On 28 July he failed to

return from a patrol over Arcy-Sainte-Restitue, probably the victim of
Leutnant Erich Löwenhardt of Jasta 10.

Denying the enemy any sight of the build-up was vital to the success of
the French counter-attack, so the German observation balloons were a
particular target. Paul Waddington downed six between June and August
1918: 'You had to cross the German lines, staying very low because the
balloons were winched down as soon the observers spotted you. You had
to beat them to it, so in general you opened your attack at a height of say
2,000 or 3,000 metres and crossed the German lines at 300 metres. You
also had to fire at point-blank range. Getting home again . . . meant
covering 15 or 20 kilometres behind enemy lines, where you could be
pretty sure you'd be hit by the screening machine-gun fire. . . . I made
about twenty attacks on 'sausages', shooting down six, and never returned
without bullet-holes in my machine. I remember the first time I attacked a
German balloon. I fired at point-blank range and my gun jammed after
three rounds. But one of those rounds was an incendiary and the balloon
exploded. One in every seven bullets in our ammunition belts was an
incendiary. That type of victory had the advantage of always being
confirmed. There was a huge explosion in the sky, visible from a long way
off, including the French lines, so you always had the witness statements
you needed.'

But one dawn raid alongside Jacques Ehrlich, himself the buster of
eighteen balloons between June and September 1918, almost brought about
Waddington's downfall: 'I was patrol leader, with my comrade Ehrlich to
my left. We were putting ourselves in the sun and giving the Germans
plenty of trouble, but it was a pretty risky tactic because it also put you in
the sun in relation to your colleague. Ehrlich bumped into me, taking half
my lower wings into the bargain. Fortunately his propeller just missed my
bracing wires . . . [but] I still went into a spin. I immediately cut the engine,
brought myself out of the spin and landed safely in a little vineyard near
Reims. My comrade returned to the squadron. "I've hit Waddington," he
said. "He must have dropped like a stone." And he was the one who
returned to look for me.'

Sous-lieutenant Léon Bourjade (N/SPA152) took particular delight in
his work, shooting down his first balloon over Vaxy on 20 February 1918:
'Two years behind a trench mortar had left me with such unhappy
memories of the *drachen* that the day I watched my first victim come down
in flames wasn't just a victory, it was revenge. . . . I swooped, I dived, I fell
on my prey. . . . A little red spot appeared. The flames spread very quickly
and the ['sausage'] completely disintegrated.' On the Champagne front in

July Bourjade shot down five balloons in ten days and he was eventually credited with twenty-seven balloons (as well as two aircraft) – the highest-scoring French 'balloon buster'. 'To counter the considerable risks involved in my work, I needed more than the simple ambition to win a palm for my *Croix de guerre*. Two things sustained me. Firstly, a sense of military duty: like Clemenceau, I wanted to "wage war". But more important was my faith in God, in Our Lady of the Sacred Heart, and especially in Sister Thérèse of the Infant Jesus, to whom I confided my fate completely.'

The armistice came as a blessed relief to the trainee priest: 'At last, no more lunatic attacks on a balloon defended by twenty machine-guns,' he reportedly quipped on 11 November 1918.

Throughout August and September the Mixed Brigades continued their attacks. Even after four years of conflict the squadrons were still at risk from friendly fire. 'Target only those planes clearly marked with crosses,' ground troops were urgently reminded. The orders for the counter-offensive had also reauthorized the fighter and bomber groups to harass the retreating Germans, licensing them 'to launch an all-out assault as soon as enemy troops can be seen clearly withdrawing across a broad front'. During the battle of Le Santerre on 11 August, for example, 133 bombers from de Goÿs' Brigade shot down six enemy fighters and dropped 24.7 tonnes of explosives on the villages of Guiscard and Beaurains-lès-Noyon alone.

After dropping their bombs, many pilots turned for home without waiting to see if they hit the target. 'Once we'd played our prank, our fear that the coppers would catch us far outweighed our curiosity,' claimed André Duvau (BR29). 'We looked right, left, up, down, front and rear for any approaching enemy fighters. We were fair game. The engine drowned out any noise, so we could only make a visual identification . . . you had to look, look and look again and you were still in danger of being taken by surprise.'

Ideally, the Breguets of the day bomber squadrons would receive dual protection: top cover from SPADs, using their superior speed and manoeuvrability to counter the enemy fighters, plus close support from the Caudron R.11, which was capable of accompanying the bombers all the way to the target, and whose five machine guns with their overlapping fields of fire offered considerable firepower without any need to manoeuvre. However, the SPADs remained limited in range, while the full entry into service of the R.11, completed in prototype in 1916, had been delayed by production difficulties, with only six squadrons formed by November 1918. Consequently, the Breguets were often forced to fend for themselves – and without full protection they remained vulnerable.

On 14 September, escorted by five Caudron R.11 from C46, Major Armand des Prez de la Morlais led twenty-three Breguet 14 from EB13 to raid the marshalling yards at Conflans-en-Jarnisy, near Metz, some 30 kilometres behind German lines. The French were organized in three waves and flew in and out by the same route. The first two waves, both from BR131, got through relatively unscathed, losing one Breguet and one Caudron, but the full weight of the German riposte fell on the third wave – eight machines from BR132 under Captain Jannekyn, plus a single Caudron. 'A westerly wind was blowing at over 20m/s [i.e. 72km/h],' reported EB13. 'Our fighters could not escort us all the way so we were anticipating some tough fighting with the enemy aircraft which have been very aggressive in this sector. . . . A slight delay on take-off meant the squadrons crossed the lines too far apart to assist each other. The enemy fighters spotted us and we came under heavy fire. One patrol, then two, then three – twenty-five planes in all – attacked each flight in waves. Our aircraft held their ground and continued towards the target. The fighting was fierce . . . . Our aircraft arrived over the target. The enemy planes flew off, clearing the way for the anti-aircraft batteries, which battled hard, but in vain, to defend Conflans station. Our planes flew over [the station] then turned for home into a headwind. The enemy fighters were lying in wait for us. Progress was slow and our planes spent another half hour under relentless attack above the enemy lines. It looked as if the Germans had all agreed to meet around our bomber flights. It soon turned into a real free-for-all, tracer bullets criss-crossing the sky in all directions. From time to time a plane abandoned the field after a mortal blow: a vertiginous spin, fire on board . . . the awful death always awaiting those who crash. Our ranks thinned out and the survivors closed up to fill the gaps . . . Eventually we regained our lines, and the Fokkers – which had also taken heavy losses – withdrew. We took stock on landing: six crews missing, one gunner dead, and a pilot and observer wounded. All the missing had been seen to fall – four in flames and the other three in hopeless circumstances. One gunner, Corporal Valat, was spotted wreathed in flames, frantically firing his machine guns. One pilot, Corporal Mestre, stood in the cockpit of his blazing plane and saluted his comrades before leaping into the void: a wave betokening farewell . . . and his willing embrace of the glorious death awaiting him. How many similar acts of heroism will remain for ever unacknowledged due to the modesty of survivors? . . . In this difficult situation every man went above and beyond the call of duty. The nine enemy planes downed by our bombers give ample demonstration of the courage and high morale displayed by all during this tough test. Our dead were splendidly avenged.'

That same night the Capronis of CAP115 followed up the attack, striking again at Conflans, some aircraft making two separate sorties, while US railway artillery simultaneously bombarded the town and its infrastructure.

Like Weiller's Breguets, the robust, well-armed Salmson 2 A.2 machines of the cooperation squadrons normally operated across the German lines in groups of three or four – one photographic aircraft accompanied by two or three escorts from the same squadron. They were also authorized to call on 'immediate support from the fighter groups, especially for long-range reconnaissance missions'. But Marcel Jeanjean (MF/AR/SAL33) doubted the effectiveness of his fighter escorts: 'The SPAD's Hispano [engine] is nowhere near as reliable as the sturdy Canton-Unné in our Salmson,' he claimed. 'And then there are all the "infernal" temptations our fighter escorts find so hard to resist. As soon as they spot an enemy dawdling in the clouds they completely forget about their protégés and dash over. Who'll be next to add a victim to his tally?'

By late September, as the allied advance continued, the Germans were largely confined within their own lines – but still they posed a threat. 'Permanent enemy patrols are active in strength ahead of our front,' reported II Colonial Corps. 'Our planes come under attack as soon as they cross the lines.' And while the Salmson could look after itself, it was not invulnerable. 'At 11.40 am, in the Chambly sector, six Fokker D.VII attacked a photo-reconnaissance mission flown by four planes from Squadron SAL47,' reported II Colonial Corps on 25 September. 'After a dogfight lasting several minutes, one of the Salmson escorts – flown by Sergeant [Alfred] Chauffour, with Maréchal des Logis [Raymond] Alby as his observer – was shot down by close-range enemy fire and broke up around 1,000 metres.'

Sidelined for a month after crash-landing in the trenches in August, Ernest Maunoury returned to the fray by downing a *drachen* unopposed from 800 metres. But he still had the German guns to contend with: 'The artillery was off target, though as usual they were firing at anything and everything. But one gun-layer [must have] miscalculated and just as I spotted a huge explosion, I felt a real jolt. My ears were ringing and I rubbed my eyes to make sure the engine was still running. My lower left wing had been completely shredded and now had a 60-centimetre hole in the middle. Obviously, I was rather shaken! Very gently I tried the controls and got a response. What a relief. The lines were still some distance away, so all I was bothered about after that was getting home. I'd felt the full force of a 105mm shell which had snapped one of my struts in passing and cut three-quarters of the way through my aileron control.'

After that close shave Maunoury had one more fright in store: 'During the final attacks on the Aisne we were strafing the trenches on a morning of dreadful weather. Suddenly I was blinded by flames. My plane was on fire. No ifs or buts, I was done for. I shut everything down and landed immediately. No time to bother about trenches or barbed wire. I jumped from my soon-to-be funeral pyre, tore off one of the access panels and realized it was the only thing burning. The exhaust pipe had set it alight.' Maunoury had landed within French lines and ended the war with a total of eleven victories, eight of them balloons. He later became an instructor, before dying in an accident at Cazaux on 15 September 1921.

On 26 September 1918 René Fonck repeated his astonishing feat of six victories (numbers sixty-one to sixty-six) in one day. Still he was left dissatisfied: 'I could have had another eight if my gun hadn't jammed,' he grumbled. Fonck had devised a highly effective method of solo combat appropriate to this era of group manoeuvring. After three years in a German prison camp, Roland Garros (MS23/SPA26) had not – yet old habits died hard. On 5 October 1918 Garros was part of a patrol that encountered a group of seven Fokker D.VII over Vouziers, 10 kilometres inside the German lines. His CO, Captain de Sevin, ordered him to stay in formation, but the ace had other ideas: '[he] darted straight into the Fokkers, followed by [de Sevin], who fought for a few seconds with several opponents. Eventually [the CO] managed to break off – but Garros, with a huge number 30 painted on the upper wing of his aircraft, had disappeared. There was no sign of him.' SPA 48 had several pilots in the vicinity, one of whom had spotted a SPAD taking on three Fokkers: 'Two of them banked, while the third waited calmly for the attack. Suddenly, at point-blank range, the SPAD broke up into fragments small enough to have been playing cards scattered on the wind.' Ironically, given his role in its development, Garros may have shot off his own propeller after his synchronizer gear malfunctioned. Leutnant Hermann Habich of Jasta 49 probably administered the coup de grâce.

The Air Division had proved a powerful weapon in this final year of the war, showing itself capable of decisive intervention in the land battle. In September 1918, for the battle of the Saint-Mihiel salient, some 1,500 allied aircraft took to the air under the overall command of the US general Billy Mitchell, so impressing Pétain with their performance that he was planning a second Air Division for his operations in Lorraine in 1919. But Duval had a tough time keeping his squadrons together until he was promoted to become Pétain's chief of staff that same month. He faced criticism from all sides: from the armies, from fighter commanders like Victor Ménard, and from the bomber enthusiasts led by de Goÿs. 'One can with some justification ask why [Duval] rejected the lessons of 1917,' complained Ménard after the war. 'GQG was obsessed with the idea of the aerial battle. It used the bombers as bait to provoke the enemy and devoted considerable resources to their protection. The armies protested vehemently, but daylight bombing raids escorted by the Air Division's single-seater fighters continued until the armistice. The aerial battle never came to pass, and most of these combined fighter/bomber missions failed in their stated objective. Nine out of ten were completely futile. In 1918 we had a formidable reserve of 600 fighters at our disposal, nearly all of them squandered in pursuit of an independent air war.'

'The armies misunderstand the role of the Air Division,' commented Duval in response to his detractors. 'In general they view it as no more than a pool from which to draw the extra cover they require for their reconnaissance machines. They cannot grasp the concept of an army group commander ordering squadrons from the Air Division to fly offensive missions over their front, in liaison with the armies, but not under their control.'

At the other extreme, de Goÿs and his parliamentary allies wanted a return to strategic bombing and reprisal raids. Duval, however, was unconvinced. Despite the provocation of the enemy attacks on Paris, he refused to participate in the British Independent Force set up in June 1918 to bomb German cities: 'Aviation is capable of much more than the subsidiary role it has so far played as an offensive force in the land battle,' he argued. 'Adopting British ideas would require us to divert at least some of our bomber force away from [that] battle. It would also require us to redirect resources towards the production of bombers instead of fighters and reconnaissance machines, so undermining or halting the development of aircraft directly employed in ground operations. Our overriding objective is to win the land battle. If we lose that, there is little point in bombing Cologne. . . . Our current bomber force is too small to divide and still provide effective cover for long-range and battlefield targets.'

The French remained aloof until the autumn, when a joint allied bombing formation was created under the direct orders of Marshal Foch, although it was scarcely operational by November 1918. To further appease the bomber lobby, the Mixed Brigades were broken up on 22 September and replaced by specialist bomber and fighter brigades, under de Goÿs and Duseigneur respectively.

In the post-war period the aviation service remained an integral part of the army, thwarting any movement towards independence and serving only to emphasize its role in supporting land-war objectives. 'In practice, the air service has to operate in conjunction with the armies,' argued Colonel Duval. 'It would be impossible to give it complete autonomy.' Bomber enthusiasts like Pierre-Étienne Flandin felt this hampered development: 'Participation in land and sea operations clearly determines the role played by the military and naval aviation services,' he complained. 'Those responsible for these operations cannot possess the vision to conceive, prepare and execute an air plan completely independent of land and sea operations and the aerial operations conducted in their support.' The army and the navy successfully blocked a plan to create an independent third force in 1929, and it was 1934 before the Armée de l'Air eventually came into being. Its first commander, in his final three months before retirement, was General Édouard Barès – such a key figure in the wartime service and for so long a proponent of an independent force.

The last confirmed victory achieved by any French fighter pilot came during a patrol over Reims on 4 November, when Sous-lieutenant Jean Morvan, Lieutenant James Connolly and Lieutenant Cook (SPA163) surprised a flight of four Fokkers and shot down two of them. But the final confirmed French victory of all was the work not of a pilot but a gunner, Sergeant Pierre Raveneau (SAL277), who shot down one confirmed (and one unconfirmed) enemy aircraft over the Vosges on 5 November. The unfortunate German was probably Sergeant Gustav Albrecht (Jasta 64w).

A few days later Lieutenant Gustave Minier (BR35) was at Tergnier: 'On the night of 10/11 [November] the phone finally sounded in the tent I shared with the squadron commander and another comrade, a pilot lieutenant like me. "Bravo!" shouted the captain. "It's over, lads. They've signed an armistice."' But Minier still had one last duty to perform: '[The captain] addressed himself to me. "A German envoy [Captain von Geyer] is coming from GQG. You're to fly him out as soon as he arrives. Go and get yourself ready." Dawn broke, dull and dismal, and the hangars opened. My plane was quickly pulled from its hangar and prepared for take-off. The news had flown round the airfield and a crowd of off-duty aircrew from every squadron had flocked to catch sight of the envoy. He arrived by car from GQG around 7.30 am, accompanied by a gendarmerie captain. The cloud ceiling had lifted somewhat since daybreak, so I could follow my orders and climb to around 800 metres. Approaching the lines, rain and low cloud forced me to descend and I crossed at scarcely 300 metres. None of the usual gun- or rifle-fire to greet me. Big white flags were streaming from the tips of my struts. I don't know if they protected me somehow, or if the enemy was too busy retreating to bother firing on an aircraft flying so low.'

On landing at the German airfield at Morville, von Geyer was whisked away. But to Minier's enormous embarrassment, his engine refused to restart, forcing the pilot to stay the night while the German mechanics worked to get his plane going again.

At the Lycée Sainte-Elme, a converted school in Arcachon, observer Jacques d'Arnoux (F55) was still recovering from a spinal injury sustained when he was shot down over the Chemin des Dames on 6 September 1917. '7 November [1918]: I got out of bed today and stood on my own two feet for the first time in fourteen months,' he confided to his diary. 'I walked a few steps virtually unsupported, deliriously happy. No dizziness. I'm improving. . . . 11 November: Victory. More stomach problems, more bedsores. Your personal battle is definitely not over yet. But have courage, have confidence, your victory will come. Until then – Vive la France! Vive la France! Vive la France!'

Pierre de Cazenove de Pradines (SPA81) flew his final patrol on 10 November. 'My abiding memory is one of joy,' he claimed. 'I fought with might and main to liberate my country but I can't say I ever bore any real hatred for my opponents. I thought they too were serving their country . . . [although] I tried to destroy as many as possible. As for the rest, it was just magnificent sport. Our planes – for the most part – were wonderful machines. We had a degree of independence unknown these days [and] comrades of the highest calibre whom we all too often had to mourn. It was a life that placed an incredible amount of responsibility on the shoulders of a 20-year-old. Happy days!' De Pradines was not alone in his views. 'Over the past days, months and years – through times of danger, grief and joy lived shoulder to shoulder – we've forged iron bonds of friendship that will only grow stronger with the passage of time,' believed Marcel Jeanjean. And René de Lavaissière de Lavergne (C11) never regretted his transfer: 'The war is meant to have cost me five years of my youth, provided moments of great physical and mental anguish, and at times brought me close to death. [But] in fact the aviation service gave me instants of great exhilaration that compensated for my dark days in the artillery.'

Indeed, some pilots found they missed the adrenalin rush of combat flying. 'Sometimes, deep down, in the calm that follows the storm, I find myself rather regretting that all danger is past,' admitted René Fonck. 'Constant peril can be particularly satisfying to anyone prepared to accept the challenge. Occasionally, we really miss it and that's when we embark on some lunatic enterprise or other.' Aged just 21, with twenty-five victories to his name, Pierre Marinovitch (N38/N/SPA94), 'the baby of Great War air aces', was killed at a flying display in Brussels in 1919; Jules Védrines lost his life that same year in a flying accident, some months after landing his aircraft on the roof of the Galéries Lafayette department store in Paris; while Jean Navarre died rehearsing his attempt to enliven the first official Armistice Day commemorations by flying through the Arc de Triomphe – Charles Godefroy successfully took up the challenge, his Nieuport 11 giving him just 3 metres clearance each way.

Throughout the 1920s former aces tried to earn a living from their fame and flying skills. Albert Deullin (MF62/N3/SPA73) was killed in a crash while testing a prototype at Villacoublay in 1923, while Georges Madon (BL30/MF218/N/SPA38) died a hero's death at an air show in 1924, deliberately crashing his plane into a house to avoid ploughing into a crowd of spectators. Nungesser recreated some of his dogfights in displays in the United States, but he and co-pilot François Coli (N/SPA62) disappeared without trace in 1927 while trying to cross the Atlantic. Even Fonck crashed while attempting the same feat: he lived to tell the tale but his two crewmen were both killed. Yet not every ex-pilot was a thrill-seeker. Léon Bourjade, the terror of German observation balloons, resumed his religious vocation after the war, entering the priesthood and serving as a missionary in Papua New Guinea. And after his daredevil deeds in 1919 Charles Godefroy never flew again.

The armistice was signed only fifteen short years after the Wrights first took to the air in powered flight. In that time aircraft reached levels of power and sophistication unimaginable in 1903, and the aeronautical service of 1918 had grown into a force capable of decisive impact in the land battle. Problems and false starts abounded as the service struggled to devise appropriate tactics and training in an era of rapidly changing technology, a creative process that in France provoked an intense debate that continued to dog the aeronautical service, and its successor, the Armée de l'Air, until the Second World War. Yet what caught the popular imagination was not the controversy but the thrill of flying and the fame of individual pilots. Every squadron contributed to victory, but it was the legendary 'knights of the air' of the fighter squadrons who inspired future generations and continue to dominate popular and professional memory. Guynemer, not the higher-scoring but coolly efficient Fonck, is the role model of the modern Armée de l'Air. His are the exploits that lie at the heart of its traditions: an account of his achievements is read out each year on the anniversary of his death, 11 September, while his family motto, *Faire face*, has been adopted by the academy, the École de l'Air.

'Flying had a bit of an aura,' recalled General Charles Christienne, who was commissioned in the Armée de l'Air in 1939. 'Aviators were something special. They displayed qualities that were particularly attractive to a young man: love of danger, because the risks then were considerable, or at least the public thought them so, plus a taste for adventure. And the international threat was growing. We all knew that peace couldn't last and there'd be another war one day. War, my God! How exciting it seemed to a boy of 15 or 16.'

The aces certainly inspired future general Léon Cuffaut: 'I spent my youth in Burgundy, near Auxerre . . . and used to watch the planes from the side of the valley. They belonged to the flying club set up by Jean Moreau, who was a future minister of aviation, a colonel in the reserves and a fighter ace with five [sic] victories in the 14–18 war. I made my first flight with him. The uniform, Jean Moreau and his lace-up boots, kepi a little askew, the sound of the engine: I was flying daft and used to spend whole days just cleaning aircraft windscreens.' Cuffaut naturally became a pilot, and a fighter pilot too, serving with the Normandie-Niemen Group in the Soviet Union during the Second World War.

Another future general, Jean Jardin, gained his wings in 1921: 'At the age of 16, at Montpellier airfield, I met the famous pilot Dieudonné Costes, a former ace during the 14–18 war. Afterwards he left the army and took a fairly humdrum job as a pilot with Aéropostale, carrying the post. That day in Montpellier – Palavas, in fact – he caught me staring and knew that I'd recognized him. "Do you want to go up for a spin?" he asked. . . . It was a real thrill to be up so high, above the clouds, with the engine thrumming and the wind whistling in my ears . . . it really opened my eyes. "I know what I want to do," I told myself that day. "I want to be a pilot."'

Appendix 1

Equivalent French and British Ranks

Army

Maréchal de France	Field Marshal
Général de division	General; commander of a division, army corps, army or army group
Général de brigade	Brigadier General
Colonel	Colonel
Lieutenant-colonel	Lieutenant Colonel
Commandant	Major; group commander
Chef de bataillon	Major in a chasseur battalion; group commander
Chef d'escadron	Major in a cavalry regiment; group commander
Capitaine	Captain; squadron commander
Lieutenant	Lieutenant; squadron commander
Sous-lieutenant	Second Lieutenant
Aspirant	Man having passed officer's exams and serving as an officer while awaiting full commissioned status
Adjudant-chef	Warrant Officer 1st class
Adjudant	Warrant Officer 2nd class
Maréchal des logis-chef	Sergeant in a mounted unit (i.e. cavalry, artillery, transport)
Sergent-major	Sergeant in charge of administration
Sergent	Sergeant
Maréchal des logis	Sergeant in a mounted unit
Sergent fourrier	Quartermaster sergeant
Caporal	Corporal
Brigadier	Corporal in a mounted unit
Caporal fourrier	Quartermaster Corporal
Soldat de 1re classe	Lance Corporal
Soldat	Private

Navy

Amiral de France	Admiral of the Fleet
Amiral	Admiral
Vice-amiral	Vice Admiral
Contre-amiral	Rear Admiral
Capitaine de vaisseau	Captain
Capitaine de frégate	Commander
Capitaine de corvette	Lieutenant Commander
Lieutenant de vaisseau	Lieutenant
Enseigne de vaisseau	Sub lieutenant
Aspirant	Midshipman
Premier-maître	Warrant Officer
Maître	Chief Petty Officer
Second-maître	Petty Officer
Quartier-maître	Leading Seaman
Matelot breveté	Able Seaman
Matelot	Ordinary Seaman

Appendix 2

Leading Fighter Aces and Squadrons

Pilots	Squadrons	Victories
René Fonck (d.18.6.1953)	C47, SPA103	75
Georges Guynemer (KIA 11.9.1917)	MS3, N3, SPA3	54
Charles Nungesser (d. on or after 8.5.1927)	N65, SPA65, V106, V116	45
Georges Madon (d. 11.11.1924)	BL30, MF218, N38, SPA38	41
Maurice Boyau (d. 16.9.1918)	N77, SPA77	35
Michel Coiffard (KIA 29.10.1918)	N154, SPA154	34
Léon Bourjade (d. 22.10.1924)	N152, SPA152	28
Armand Pinsard (d. 10.5.1953)	MS23, N26, N78, SPA23	27
René Dorme (KIA 25.5.1917)	C94, CRP, N3	23
Gabriel Guérin (KIA 1.8.1918)	SPA15, SPA88	23
Claude [Marcel] Haegelen (d. 24.5.1950)	F8, SPA89, SPA100, SPA103	23
Alfred Heurteaux (d. 30.12.1985)	MS38, N3, SPA3	21
Pierre Marinovitch (d. 2.10.1919)	N38, N94, SPA94	21
Albert Deullin (d. 29.5.1923)	MF62, N3, SPA73	20

Squadrons

N/SPA3	175
VB/N/SPA103	111 (incl. 3 balloons)
N/SPA65	108
MS/N/SPA38	98
N/SPA81	88
REP/MS/N/SPA15	80 (incl. 7 balloons)
N/SPA57	79 (incl. 14 balloons)
MF/N/SPA62	75 (incl. 7 balloons)
N/SPA154	63
N/SPA93	59
MS/N/SPA23	59
N/SPA77	59 (incl. 25 balloons)
MS/N/SPA48	54 (incl. 7 balloons)
MS/N/SPA26	51
MS/N/SPA37	50
MS/N/SPA12	50 (incl. 7 balloons)
N/SPA124	49

Appendix 3

Squadron Prefixes

AR	A.R.1, A.R.2
BL	Blériot 11
BLC	Blériot Cavalerie
BM	Breguet Michelin
BR	Breguet
C	Caudron
CAP	Caproni
CEP	Caproni, licence-built by REP
CM	Caudron G.2
D	Deperdussin
DM	Deperdussin Monocoque
DO	Dorand DO.1
F	Farman F.40 or F.50
G	Caudron G.6
HD	Hanriot Dupont HD.3
HF	Henri Farman
LET	Letord
MF	Maurice Farman
MS	Morane-Saulnier
MSP	Morane-Saulnier Parasol (Type A1)
N	Nieuport
PS	Paul Schmitt Type 6 or Type 7
R	Caudron R.4 or R.11
REP	Robert Esnault Pelterie (REP) Type N
SAL	Salmson 2
SM	Salmson-Moineau SM.1
SOP	Sopwith 1½ Strutter
SPA	SPAD 7 or 13
SPA-Bi	SPAD 11 or 16
V	Voisin
VC	Voisin Canon (Type 4)
VP	Voisin Peugeot (Type 8)
VR	Voisin Renault (Type 10)

Bibliography

Manuscript Sources
Archives nationales, Paris
C 7502   Chambre des Deputés: Sessions: Commission de l'Armée
130 AP 13   Fonds Jacques-Louis Dumesnil, sous-secrétaire d'État
              chargé de l'Aéronautique militaire et maritime, 1917–19

Service historique de la Défense – Air, Vincennes
1 A 20/1   Aviation de corps d'armée, de corps de cavalerie et de
              division: organisation générale
1 A 26/1   Réunion des directeurs d'écoles, mars 1918
1 A 47/1   IIe Armée. Ordre pour l'aviation de combat, 29 février 1916
1 A 88/1   Groupe des armées du Nord: Aviation. Organisation, emploi
1 A 89/1   Albert Deullin. *Les Patrouilles de chasse*, novembre 1917
1 A 89/1   *Instruction sur les groupes de combat*, février 1917
1 A 89/1   *Principes généraux de l'aviation de combat*, 3 juillet 1917
1 A 277   Archives des services aéronautiques aux armées et des
              unités: Xe Armée
1 A 348   Services de photographie aérienne. Organisation et
              fonctionnement
1 A 350/2   Exploitations de la photographie aérienne. IVe Armée.
              'Rapport du lieutenant Pépin, commandant la Section de
              photographie aérienne sur la 2e position allemande et
              l'arrière-pays (leur étude par la photographie)', 16 octobre
              1915
Z 35433   Colonel Georges Bellenger, *Le Laboratoire d'aviation
              militaire de Vincennes*
Z 36106   Colonel Jean Dumézil, *Rapport sur l'emploi de l'aviation au
              profit des réglages des tirs d'artillerie*, 4 septembre 1911

Journaux des marches et opérations
1 A 271/1   Ve Armée: Direction de l'aviation, 3 août 1914–30 avril
              1916
1 A 284/1   GB1, 23 novembre 1914–11 novembre 1918
1 A 286/5   SPA15, 17 mai 1916–10 juillet 1919
1 A 287/2   SPA26, 17 octobre 1915–1 mai 1918
1 A 289/7   SPA96, 29 juin 1917–11 novembre 1918

| 1 A 289/8 | CEP puis CAP puis C115, 7 mars 1916–15 septembre 1918 |
| Z 26912/1 | GB4, 5 décembre 1915–9 mai 1917 |

Carnets de comptabilité

2 A 1/1	1re Compagnie d'aérostiers, 3e trimestre 1914
2 A 2/5	1re Compagnie d'aérostiers, 3e trimestre 1918
2 A 83/1	93e Compagnie d'aérostiers, 3e trimestre 1918
2 A 86/5	BL3, 3e trimestre 1914
2 A 89/1	MF5, 3e trimestre 1914
2 A 110/5	V24, 3e trimestre 1914
2 A 124/15	BR35, 4e trimestre 1918
2 A 218/9	SPA159, 2e trimestre 1918
2 A 218/10	SPA159, 3e trimestre 1918
2 A 220/2	SPA164, 3e trimestre 1918
2 A 242/3	SOP229, 4e trimestre 1917
2 A 242/4	SOP229, 1er trimestre 1918
2 A 254/4	SAL262, 4e trimestre 1918
2 A 285/9	21e Compagnie d'aérostation de défense contre avions, 3e trimestre 1918
2 A 289/1	Camp Retranché de Paris: Section d'aérostiers, 1er trimestre 1918

Archives orales. Témoignages. Interviews

002	Charles Christienne
008	Jean Carayon
020	Marcel Jauneaud
025	Pierre de Cazenove de Pradines
026	Paul Waddington
031	Alfred Heurteaux
035	René Fisch
048	Albert Caquot
059	Louis Lelandais
062	Robert Sarkis
064	Léon Cuffaut
070	André Luguet
083	Joseph Branche
146–1	Raymond Brohon
173	Alfred Rougevin-Baville
266	Louis Risacher
365	Jean Jardin
548	Joseph Batlle

Service historique de la Défense – Terre, Vincennes
16 N 1406   IVe Armée: contrôle postale, 11 mai 1917
16 N 1407   IVe Armée: contrôle postale, 23 octobre 1917

Journaux des marches et opérations
26 N 71/6   Région Fortifiée de Verdun: Direction Service Aéronautique,
             1 novembre 1915–19 février 1916
26 N 71/7   Région Fortifiée de Verdun: Direction Service Aéronautique,
             19–27 février 1916
26 N 108/11 3e Corps d'Armée: Groupe de Brancardiers
26 N 248/15 2e Corps d'Armée Coloniale: Secteur Aéronautique, 1 mars
             1917–4 octobre 1918

National Archives, Kew
AIR 1/997/204/5/1241   Air Ministry: Air Historical Branch: Papers
                       (Series I). Miscellaneous. Training of pilots and
                       observers 1915–17. Report of Captain Walser, 4
                       Squadron RFC, on French observer school

Magazines and Newspapers
L'Aéro
L'Aérophile
Air actualités
Avions
L'Express du Midi
Le Fana de l'aviation
La Guerre aérienne illustrée
L'Illustration
Journal de Rouen
Le Looping
Pays de France
Le Réveil de la Meuse
Var matin
La Vie aérienne illustrée

Books and journals
Ader, Clément, *La Première Étape de l'aviation militaire en France* (Paris:
    J. Bosc, 1907)
Ader, Clément, *L'Aviation militaire* (Paris: Berger-Levrault, 1913)
Albertini, Scilocca, *Jean Casale: un as corse de l'aviation* (Ajaccio:
    Albiana, 2008)

Aldrich, Mildred, *The Peak of the Load* (London: Constable, 1919)
Alloitteau, Jean, 'Les Zeppelins attaquent à Revigny', *Matériaux pour l'histoire de notre temps* 2 (1985), 32–5
André-Gillois, 'Souvenirs aéronautiques', *Pégase* 2 (1976), 3–13
Arnoux, Jacques d', *Paroles d'un revenant* (Paris: Plon, 1925)
Aubout, Mickaël, 'L'Émergence des premiers terrains d'aviation de l'aéronautique militaire française, 1909–1914', *Revue historique des armées* 264 (2011), 98–107
Aubry, Catherine, 'Un poilu pas comme les autres', *Var matin*, 10 novembre 1988
Bacconnier, Gérard, et al., *La Plume au fusil: les poilus du Midi à travers leurs correspondance* (Toulouse: Privat, 1985)
Barrès, Maurice, *Chronique de la Grande Guerre 12: 24 avril–7 août 1918* (Paris: Plon, 1938)
Baudouï, Rémi, & Dercelles, Arnaud, *Le Corbusier: correspondances, lettres à la famille, 1900–1925* (Gollion: Infolio, 2011)
Bédier, Joseph, *L'Effort français: quelques aspects de la guerre* (Paris: Renaissance du livre, 1919)
Bellenger, Georges, 'Témoignage du lieutenant-colonel Bellenger', *Icare* 85 (1978), 17
Bellenger, Georges, *Pilote d'essais: du cerf-volant à l'aéroplane* (Paris: Harmattan, 1995)
Benoist de Saint Ange, Henriette, *Léon Bourjade: aviateur-missionaire en Nouvelle-Guinée* (Cadillac: Saint-Rémi, 2009)
Benoit, Edmond, 'Témoignage de M. Edmond Benoit capitaine de frégate honoraire', *Icare* 88 (1979), 83–6
Beraud-Villars, Jean, *Notes d'un pilote disparu* (Paris: Hachette, 1918)
Berger, Luc, 'Henry Potez et Marcel Dassault, constructeurs aéronautiques de la Grande Guerre', *Guerres mondiales et conflits contemporaines*, 209 (2003), 45–55
Bernard, [Adjudant], 'La Capture du commandant de Goÿs (26 mai 1915)', *La Guerre aérienne illustrée* 31 (14 juin 1917), 495–6
Bernard, Philippe, 'La Stratégie aérienne pendant la Première Guerre mondiale: mythes et réalités', *Revue d'histoire moderne et contemporaine* (septembre 1969), 350–75
Biddle, Charles J., *The Way of the Eagle* (New York: Scribner's Sons, 1919)
Billard, Fernand, 'Histoire d'un as – XL', *La Guerre aérienne illustrée* 56 (6 décembre 1917), 64
Bonnefon, Paul, 'Les Carnets de Pégoud', *Les Annales* (15 avril 1917)
Bonte, Louis, *L'Histoire des essais en vol (1914–40)* (Paris: Larivière, n.d.)

Bordeaux, Henri, 'Le Chevalier de l'air Georges Guynemer IV: l'ascension', *Revue des deux mondes* 44 (1918), 54–97

Boulic, Jean-Yves, & Lavaure, Annik, *Henri de Kérillis (1889–1958): l'absolu patriote* (Rennes, Presses universitaires de Rennes, 1997)

Boyé, Alfred, 'Seul avec deux morts', *La Guerre aérienne illustrée* 39 (9 août 1917), 611–12

Branche, Joseph, 'L'Observation en ballon captif: extraits de l'interview de M. Joseph Branche', *Icare*, 85 (1978), 123–31

Breguet, Claude, '10 ans d'avions Breguet 1909–1919', *Revue historique de l'armée* hors série (1969), 99–113

Breguet, Emmanuel, & Breguet, Claude, 'La Reconnaissance aérienne et la bataille de la Marne (30 août–3 septembre 1914)', *Revue historique des armées* 166 (1987), 92–100

Brettes, Jean de, 'Les "Berthas"', *Le Pays de France* 231 (20 mars 1919)

Brindejonc des Moulinais, Marcel, 'Brindejonc des Moulinais raconté par lui-même', *La Guerre aérienne illustrée* 1 (16 novembre 1916), 3–4

Brindejonc des Moulinais, Marcel, 'Brindejonc des Moulinais raconté par lui-même', *La Guerre aérienne illustrée* 3 (30 novembre 1916), 10

Brindejonc des Moulinais, Marcel, 'Brindejonc des Moulinais intime', *La Guerre aérienne illustrée* 14 (15 février 1917), 211–12

Brocard, Antonin, *Conférence sur le matériel d'aviation faite . . . aux élèves des Grandes Écoles* (Paris: École Spéciale Militaire, 1920)

Cagny, J. de, 'Aérostiers de 1914–1918', *Revue historique des armées* 123 (1976), 69–90

Caquot, Albert, 'Extraits de l'interview du commandant Caquot', *Icare* 85 (1978), 119–21

Carayon, Jean, 'Extraits de l'interview du général Carayon', *Icare* 85 (1978), 49–53

Carlier, Claude, 'Ferdinand Ferber et l'aviation', *Guerres mondiales et conflits contemporains* 209 (2003), 7–23

Carls, Stephen Douglas, *Louis Loucheur, 1872–1931: ingénieur, homme d'état, modernisateur de la France* (Villeneuve d'Ascq: Presses universitaires du Septentrion, 2000)

Castex, Jean, Laspalles, Louis & Barès, José, *Le Général Barès: créateur et inspirateur de l'aviation* (Paris: Nouvelles éditions latines, 1994)

Chack, Paul, *Marins à la bataille 5: de la guerre à la paix* (Paris: Éditions du Gerfaut, 2002)

Chagnon, Louis, '1916 ou l'année de rupture en matière d'utilisation de l'arme aérienne', *Revue historique des armées* 242 (2006), 36–47

Champeaux, Antoine, 'Bibendum et les débuts de l'aviation 1908–1914', *Guerres mondiales et conflits contemporaines* 209 (2003), 25–43

Champonnois, Sylvain, 'Les Wright et l'armée française: les débuts de l'aviation militaire (1900–1909)', *Revue historique des armées* 255 (2009), 108–21

Chavagnes, René de, 'Quatre escadrilles de Cigognes de Guynemer à Fonck 1: la légende des Cicognes', *Les Archives de la Grande Guerre* 1 (1919), 513–44

Chavagnes, René de, 'Quatre escadrilles de Cigognes de Guynemer à Fonck 2: le groupe des Cigognes (GC12)', *Les Archives de la Grande Guerre* 2 (1919), 641–68

Chavagnes, René de, 'Quatre escadrilles de Cigognes de Guynemer à Fonck 3: l'escadrille de Guynemer', *Les Archives de la Grande Guerre* 3 (1919), 50–80

Chavagnes, René de, 'Quatre escadrilles de Cigognes de Guynemer à Fonck 4: l'escadrille de Garros (E26)', *Les Archives de la Grande Guerre* 3 (1919), 189–214

Chavagnes, René de, 'Quatre escadrilles de Cigognes de Guynemer à Fonck 5: l'escadrille de Navarre (E67)', *Les Archives de la Grande Guerre* 3 (1919), 337–66

Chevalier, J., 'Une "chouette" qui prend feu', *La Guerre aérienne illustrée* 33 (28 juin 1917), 524–5

Chevalier, Pol, *A Bar-le-Duc pendant la guerre* (Bar-le-Duc: Constant-Laguerre, 1935)

Chevillard, Maurice, 'Maurice Chevillard nous écrit', *La Guerre aérienne illustrée* 13 (8 février 1917), 197

Christienne, Charles, 'Ader et Mitchell, les penseurs aéronautiques', *Revue historique des armées* 146 (1982), 24–41

Cony, Christophe, 'Les Grands As de 14–18: Léon Bourjade et les "Crocodiles" de la SPA152', *Avions* 159 (2007), 36–49

Cunningham, Alfred A., *Marine Flyer in France* (Washington DC: US Marine Corps History & Museums Division, 1974)

Daçay, Jean, 'Avant l'aviation', *La Guerre aérienne illustrée* 14 (15 février 1917), 2

Daçay, Jean, 'Nos as ignorés: les mitrailleurs', *La Guerre aérienne illustrée* 20 (29 mars 1917), 314

Daçay, Jean, 'Un français, tueur de zeppelin: le capitaine Mandinaud', *La Guerre aérienne illustrée* 22 (12 avril 1917), 339–41

Daçay, Jean, 'Les Frères Steuer', *La Guerre aérienne illustrée* 40 (16 août 1917), 627–8

Daçay, Jean, 'Un début d'asphyxie à 6,500 mètres', *La Guerre aérienne illustrée* 50 (25 octobre 1917), 799

Dassault, Marcel, *Le Talisman* (Paris: J'ai lu, 1971)

David, René, 'Notes posthumes de René David', *La Guerre aérienne illustrée* 10 (18 janvier 1917), 154

Davilla, James J. & Soltan, Arthur M., *French Aircraft of the First World War* (Stratford: Flying Machines Press, 1997)

Debay, Capitaine, *Organisation de l'armée, génie, aéronautique, cavalerie, artillerie d'assaut, alimentation en campagne, service de santé, marches et stationnement* (Fontainebleau: École Militaire de l'Artillerie, 1920)

Decoin, Henry, 'Tué en plein ciel: Havet', *La Guerre aérienne illustrée* 37 (26 juillet 1917), 589

Delacommune, Charles, *L'Escadrille des éperviers: impressions vécues de guerre aérienne* (Paris: Plon, 1918)

Delporte, Christian, 'Les Pertes humaines dans l'aviation française (1914–1918)', *Revue historique des armées* 172 (1988), 68–79

Detrez, Lucien, *L'Hécatombe sacrée de la Flandre française 1914–1918* (Lille: Desclée, de Brouwer, 1921)

Deullin, Albert, 'Lettre de sous-lieutenant Deullin au capitaine Brocard', *Icare* 85 (1978), 74

Diesbach, Louis de, *Souvenirs de Louis de Diesbach, pilote de chasse de la Grande Guerre* (Fribourg: Intermède Belleroche, 2005)

Dorme, René, 'Dorme raconté par ses lettres', *La Guerre aérienne illustrée* 62 (1918), 164

Dubreuil-Villatoux, Marie-Catherine, 'Joffre: père méconnu de l'aviation militaire?', *Revue historique des armées* 206 (1997), 3–16

Du Plessis de Grénedan, Jean, 'L'Aéronautique maritime', *Revue Maritime* (1920), 373–96

Duval, Jacques, *L'Armée de l'air: l'avion; les aviateurs; aviation d'observation, de bombardement, de chasse* (Paris: L'Édition française illustrée, 1918)

Duvau, André, *'Br. 29': souvenirs d'escadrille* (Vincennes: Service historique de l'Armée de l'Air, 1976)

Esnault, François, 'Les Zeppelins sur Paris', *La France illustrée* 2149 (5 février 1916)

Esnault, Gaston, *Le Poilu tel qu'il parle* (Paris: Bossard, 1919)

Etévé, Albert & Caquot, Albert, *La Victoire des cocardes: l'aviation française avant et pendant la Première Guerre mondiale* (Paris: R. Laffont, n.d.)

Étoile bleu, 'Deux ans après: souvenirs du GB1', *La Guerre aérienne illustrée* 56 (6 décembre 1917), 54–5

F., Captain, 'Un bombardement en dirigible', *La Guerre aérienne illustrée* 31 (14 juin 1917), 490–2

Finck, Lucien, 'Les Premiers Jours', *La Guerre aérienne illustrée* 52 (8 novembre 1917), 822–3

Finnegan, Terrence J., *Shooting the Front: Allied Air Reconnaissance in the First World War* (Stroud: History Press, 2011)

Fisch, René, 'Extraits de l'interview de M. René Fisch', *Icare* 85 (1978), 55–9

Fonck, René, *Mes combats* (Paris: n. pub., 1920)

France. Ministère de la Guerre. État-major de l'Armée. Service historique, *Les Armées françaises dans la Grande Guerre* (Paris: Imprimerie nationale, 1922–37)

Franks, Norman L.R., *Over the Front: a Complete Record of the Fighter Aces and Units of the United States and French Air Services, 1914–1918* (London: Grub Street, 1992)

Fromentin, Bernard, 'Souvenirs de guerre du sergent-mécanicien Fromentin de l'escadrille 86bis', *Icare* 85 (1978), 97

Gaillard, Jean de, 'La Bataille d'escadres', *La Guerre aérienne illustrée* 29 (31 mai 1917), 463

Garet, Marcel, 'Les Héros disparus: Marcel Garet', *La Guerre aérienne illustrée* 11 (25 janvier 1917), 172–3

Garros, Roland, 'Quelques souvenirs', *La Guerre aérienne illustrée* 71 (21 mars 1918), 299–303

Genet, Edmond Charles Clinton, *An American for Lafayette: the Diaries of E.C.C. Genet, Lafayette Escadrille* (Charlottesville: University Press of Virginia, 1981)

Gerau, Jean, 'Ce que le poilu pense de l'aviation', *La Guerre aérienne illustrée* 19 (22 mars 1917), 290

Goubert, Louis, 'Les Mémoires de l'inventeur Denhaut', *La Vie aérienne illustrée*, nouvelle série 21 (25 décembre 1920), 323–4

Goya, Michel, 'Le Complexe d'Achille: les as français pendant la Grande Guerre', *Inflexions* 16 (2011), 1–7

Goya, Michel, *L'Invention de la guerre moderne: du pantalon rouge au char d'assaut, 1871–1918* (Paris: Tallandier, 2014)

Goÿs de Mézeyrac, Louis de, 'Lettre du commandant de Goÿs de Mézeyrac au capitaine Do-Huu-Tay', *Icare* 85 (1978), 33

Gr., Sergeant [i.e. Grès, Émile], 'La "saucisse"', *L'Illustration* 3821 (27 mai 1916)

Grahame-White, Claude & Harper, Harry, *The Aeroplane in War* (Toronto: Bell & Cockburn, 1912)

Grand Quartier général des armées du Nord et du Nord-Est. État-major. 3e Bureau et Aéronautique, *Instruction sur l'organisation et l'emploi de l'aéronautique aux armées 2: aviation de combat* (Paris: Charles-Lavauzelle, 1918)

Grégoire, Jean, 'La Ravitaillement par avions', *La Guerre aérienne illustrée* 110 (19 décembre 1918), 943

Grégoire, Jean, 'Les Reconnaissance-records', *La Guerre aérienne illustrée* 110 (19 décembre 1918), 938

Guttman, Jon, *SPAD XIII vs Fokker D.VII, Western Front 1918* (Oxford: Osprey, 2009)

H., [Captain] Ch., 'Les Héros disparus: l'adjudant Gilbert Triboulet', *La Guerre aérienne illustrée* 70 (14 mars 1918), 286–7

H.-C., 'Chasse et chasseurs', *La Guerre aérienne illustrée* 53 (15 novembre 1917), 3–4

Hall, Bert, *'En l'air!': Three Years on and above Three Fronts* (New York: New Library, 1918)

Hall, James N., *High Adventure: a Narrative of Air Fighting in France* (Boston: Houghton Mifflin, 1918)

Harrison, Marie, 'An Englishwoman in Paris', *Everyweek* (25 avril 1918)

Heiligenstein, Gérard, *Mémoires d'un observateur-pilote: Auguste Heiligenstein (1912–1919)* (Paris: Officine, 2009)

Heurteaux, [Alfred] Joseph, 'Extraits de l'interview du général Heurteaux', *Icare* 88 (1979), 43–4

Hodeir, Marcellin, 'La Photographie aérienne: "de la Marne à la Somme", 1914–1918', *Revue historique des armées* 203 (1996), 107–18

Hodeir, Marcellin, 'Vincennes, berceau de l'aéronautique militaire', *Revue historique des armées* 251 (2008), 85–93

Hoeppner, Ernst von, *Deutschlands Krieg in der Luft* (Leipzig: K.F. Koehler, 1921)

Huisman, Georges, *Dans les coulisses de l'aviation 1914–1918: pourquoi n'avons-nous pas toujours gardé la maîtrise des airs?* (Paris: La Renaissance du livre, 1921)

Jeanjean, Marcel, 'Écoles de pilotage 1914–1918: souvenirs de quelques faux et usages de faux', *Almanach du combattant* (1969), 99–103

Jeanjean, Marcel, 'La Vie en escadrille pendant la guerre de 1914–1918', *Revue historique de l'armée* hors-série (1969), 39–49

'Jim', 'Jour de l'an tragique', *La Guerre aérienne illustrée* 32 (21 juin 1917), 499–500

Jobit, Marcel, 'Carnets de route du Sous-lieutenant Marcel Jobit', *Icare* 85 (1978), 19

Joffre, Joseph, *Mémoires du maréchal Joffre, 1910–17* (Paris: Plon, 1932)

Josse, R., 'Ferdinand Ferber 1862–1909, pionnier de l'aviation', *Revue historique des armées* 116 (1974), 112–32

Kerisel, Jean & Thierry, 'La Guerre 1914–18: le constructeur aéronautique', *Bulletin de la SABIX* 28 (2001), 15–26

Krempp, Thérèse, 'Le Commandant de Rose: un précurseur de l'aviation de chasse', *Revue historique des armées* 245 (2006), 82–94

La Frégeolière, Renaud de, *A tire d'ailes: carnet de vol d'un aviateur, et souvenirs d'un prisonnier* (Paris: Plon-Nourrit, 1916)

Lafont, Bernard, *Au ciel de Verdun: notes d'un aviateur* (Paris: Berger-Levrault, 1918)

Laouénan, Roger, *Les Coquelicots de la Marne* (Spézet: Coop Breizh, 1994)

Launouc, Pol, 'Pour prendre une photographie', *La Guerre aérienne illustrée* 34 (5 juillet 1917), 541

Launouc, Pol, 'Du haut d'un *drachen* en feu', *La Guerre aérienne illustrée* 42 (30 août 1917), 661

Lavaissière de Lavergne, René de, *Souvenirs d'un artilleur et pilote de la Grande Guerre, 1914–1918* (Paris: Officine, 2011)

Lavergne, Guy de, 'Extraits des souvenirs de guerre 1914–1918 du commandant de Lavergne', *Icare* 85 (1979), 60–6

'Le Breton', 'Le Réglage d'artillerie', *La Guerre aérienne illustrée* 38 (2 août 1917), 595

Le Roy, Thierry, 'Le CAM Penzé, ou la vie d'un Centre d'Aviation Militaire ordinaire', *Avions* 41 (août 1996), 37–40; 42 (septembre 1996), 40–4; 43 (octobre 1996), 32–8

Le Roy, Thierry, 'Jean Morvan, pilote de la SPA163 et dernier chasseur victorieux de la Grande Guerre', *Avions* 65 (août 1998), 30–4

Le Roy, Thierry, 'Le Personnel de l'aérostation maritime française: l'exemple des patrouilles de Bretagne et de la Loire, 1917–19', *Revue historique des armées* 252 (2008), 104–13

Lelandais, Louis, 'Extraits de l'interview de M. Louis Lelandais', *Icare* 85 (1978), 101–5

Lemercier, Robert, 'Le Nouveau Zinc', *Almanach du combattant* (1959), 103–9

Lenoir, Maxime, 'Mes combats', *La Guerre aérienne illustrée* 24 (26 avril 1917), 383–4

L'Escaille, Henry, 'De l'aviation d'escadre', *Revue maritime* (1923), 289–95

Lucas, Jean, *La D.C.A. (Défense Contre Aéronefs) de ses origines au 11 novembre 1918* (Paris: Baudinière, 1934)

Lufbery, Raoul, 'Mon premier combat', *La Guerre aérienne illustrée* 55 (29 novembre 1917), 35–6

Lufbery, Raoul, 'Un coup dur!' *La Guerre aérienne illustrée* 73 (4 avril 1918), 332–3

M., [i.e. Métairie, Auguste], 'Les Risques de la chasse', *La Guerre aérienne illustrée* 1 (16 novembre 1916), 14; 4 (7 décembre 1916), 63

Martel, René, *L'Aviation française de bombardement (des origines au 11 novembre 1918)* (Paris: Hartmann, 1939)

Mathieu, J., *Mémoires d'un observateur en ballon* (n.pl: the author, 1972)

'Mauricius', *Les Profiteurs de la guerre* (Paris: Ce qu'il faut dire, 1917)

McConnell, James R., *Flying for France* (Garden City: Doubleday, 1917)

Méchin, David, 'Georges Guynemer (1894–1917): chasseur de gloire', *Le Fana de l'aviation* 507 (2012), 18–29

Méchin, David, 'René Fonck (1894–1953): de la lumière à l'ombre', *Le Fana de l'aviation* 518 (2013), 18–34

Méchin, David, 'L'As qui tombe à pic', *Le Fana de l'aviation* 522 (2013), 32–9

Médeville, Jérôme, 'La Capture d'un hydravion', *La Guerre aérienne illustrée* 37 (26 juillet 1917), 586–7

Mercier-Bernardet, Fabienne, 'La France et l'organisation de missions spéciales', *14–18: le magazine de la Grande Guerre* 16 (2003)

Micelli, Corinne, 'L'Éclipse d'un astre', *Air actualités* 582 (2005), 48–63

Minier, Gustave, 'Le Vol de l'armistice', *L'Aéro* (11 novembre 1933), 1, 3

Mondet, Arlette Estienne, *Le Général J.B.E. Estienne, père des chars, des chenilles et des ailes* (Paris: Harmattan, 2010)

Morareau, Lucien, et al., *L'Aviation maritime française pendant la Grande Guerre* (Paris: ARDHAN, 1999)

Mortane, Jacques, 'Parlons d'ailes: l'héroisme de l'aviateur', *La Guerre aérienne illustrée* 1 (16 novembre 1916), 2

Mortane, Jacques, 'Parlons d'ailes: le bombardement d'Essen', *La Guerre aérienne illustrée* 2 (23 novembre 1916), 18

Mortane, Jacques, 'Parlons d'ailes: pilotes et poilu', *La Guerre aérienne illustrée* 6 (21 décembre 1916), 82

Mortane, Jacques, 'Parlons d'ailes: frivolité et héroisme', *La Guerre aérienne illustrée* 9 (12 janvier 1917), 130

Mortane, Jacques, 'Parlons d'ailes: to flying or not to flying', *La Guerre aérienne illustrée* 17 (8 mars 1917), 258

Mortane, Jacques, 'La Torche sublime', *La Guerre aérienne illustrée* 22 (12 avril 1917), 350–1

Mortane, Jacques, 'Parlons d'ailes: le civil a du bon', *La Guerre aérienne illustrée* 23 (19 avril 1917), 354

Mortane, Jacques, 'Les Grands Chefs: le capitaine Roeckel', *La Guerre aérienne illustrée* 27 (17 mai 1917), 419–20

Mortane, Jacques, 'Le Corsaire de l'air: le commandant Happe', *La Guerre aérienne illustrée* 29 (31 mai 1917), 458

Mortane, Jacques, 'Nos morts: Paul Hatin', *La Guerre aérienne illustrée* 31 (14 juin 1917), 493

Mortane, Jacques, 'En terrain reconquis', *La Guerre aérienne illustrée* 32 (21 juin 1917), 509–10

Mortane, Jacques, 'Au pays des as', *La Guerre aérienne illustrée* 33 (28 juin 1917), 515–18

Mortane, Jacques, ed., 'Le Carnet de vol de Guynemer', *La Vie au grand air* (15 juin 1919), 27–8; 29–30; 30–2

Mortane, Jacques, 'Missions spéciales', *Almanach du combattant* (1930), 277–85

Mortane, Jacques, 'Notes d'un engagé volontaire de l'aviation', *Le Pays de France* 43 (n.d.), 1–2

Mortane, Jacques & Daçay, Jean, 'Les mémoires de Dorme', *La Guerre aérienne illustrée* 57 (13 décembre 1917), 245–6

Moulin-Bourret, Annie, *Guerre et industrie: Clermont-Ferrand 1912–1922, la victoire du pneu* (Clermont-Ferrand: Université Blaise Pascal [Clermont II], 1999)

Nadaud, Marcel, *En plein vol: souvenirs de guerre aérienne* (Paris: Hachette, 1918)

Navarre, Jean, 'Mes aventures guerrières . . . et autres', *La Vie aérienne illustrée* 139 (10 juillet 1919), 435–8; 140 (17 juillet 1919), 451–3; 141 (24 juillet 1919), 474–5; 142 (31 juillet 1919), 483–5; 143 (7 août 1919), 499–501; 144 (14 août 1919), 523–6; 145 (21 août 1919), 533–4; 146 (28 août 1919), 551–3; 147 (4 septembre 1919), 565–6; 148 (11 septembre 1919), 582–3; 149 (18 septembre 1919), 597–9; 150 (25 septembre 1919), 619–20; 151 (2 octobre 1919), 637–8; 152 (9 octobre 1919), 652–4; 154 (23 octobre 1919), 677–8

Opdycke, Leonard E., *French Aeroplanes before the Great War* (Atglen: Schiffer Military History, 1999)

Orthlieb, Bernard, *L'Aéronautique: hier, demain* (Paris: Masson, 1920)

Pagé, Georges, *L'Aviation française, 1914–1918* (Paris: Grincher, 2011)

Parsons, Edwin C., *I Flew with the Lafayette Escadrille* (Indianapolis: Seale, 1963)

Péricard, Jacques, *Verdun* (Paris: Librairie de France, 1933)
Pernès, Bernard, *Verdun sans retour* (Paris: Publibook, 2009)
Pernot, François, 'Verdun 1916: naissance de la chasse française', *Revue historique des armées* 203 (1996), 39–50
Perrin de Brichambaut, Pierre, 'Aviation de guerre: feuillets de bord du capitaine-aviateur Perrin de Brichambaut', *Archives de la Grande Guerre* 8 (1922), 928–52
Petit, Edmond, *La Vie quotidienne dans l'aviation en France au début du XXe siècle (1900–1935)* (Paris: Hachette, 1977)
Petit, Jean-Jacques, *Les As de l'aviation* (Bayeux: Éditions Heimdal, 1992)
Pierrefeu, Jean de, *G.Q.G. secteur I* (Paris: Crès, 1922)
Poisard, Pierre, 'Poisard console ses parents', *La Guerre aérienne illustrée* 58 (20 décembre 1917), 104
'Pol', 'La Fin d'un 75 contre avions', *La Guerre aérienne illustrée* 11 (25 janvier 1917), 165
'Pol', 'L'Escadrille au château', *La Guerre aérienne illustrée* 13 (8 février 1917), 205
Porret, Daniel, *Les 'As' français de la Grande Guerre* (Vincennes: Service historique de l'Armée de l'Air, 1983)
R.C., 'Les Prêtres aviateurs: Antoine Cordonnier', *La Guerre aérienne illustrée* 111 (26 décembre 1918), 954
Renoir, Jean, *Ma vie et mes films* (Paris: Flammarion, 1974)
Renoir, Jean, *Correspondance 1913–1978* (Paris: Plon, 1998)
Reveilhac, J., 'Un aviateur exemplaire: Roland Garros (1888–1918)', *Pégase* 2 (1976), 25–35
Reymond, Émile, 'Le Journal du Dr. Émile Reymond', *Le Figaro* (12 janvier 1916), 1
Rickenbacker, Eddie, *Fighting the Flying Circus* (Philadelphia: J.B. Lippincott, 1919)
Robène, Luc, 'Les Sports aériens: de la compétition sportive à la violence de guerre', *Guerres mondiales et conflits contemporains* 251 (2013), 25–43
Robertson, Linda R., *Dream of Civilized Warfare: World War 1 Flying Aces and the American Imagination* (Minneapolis: University of Minnesota, 2003)
Rolland, Denis, 'Un ciel allemand?', in Offenstadt, Nicolas (ed.), *Le Chemin des Dames de l'évenement à la mémoire* (Paris: Stock, 2005), 121–36
Rossignol, Jean-Paul, '14–18: quand la France inventait le tir à travers l'hélice', *Avions* 149 (2006), 43–52; 150 (2006), 51–61

Roy, Jules, *Guynemer: l'ange de la mort* (Paris: Albin-Michel, 1986)

R.S., 'Souvenirs d'escadrille: le coup de vent', *La Guerre aérienne illustrée* 13 (8 février 1917), 202

Sandow, Jules, 'Les instruments du bord', *Le Looping* 2 (juillet 1918), 4

Seigneurie, André, 'L'Évasion d'un pilote-aviateur, raconté par lui-même', *Images de la guerre* (juillet 1917)

Thenault, Georges, *The Story of the Lafayette Escadrille* (Boston: Small, Maynard, 1921)

Thollon-Pommerol, Claude, *Le Concours d'aviation militaire 1911* (n.pl: the author, 2012)

Thollon-Pommerol, Claude, *'Donnez des aéroplanes à la France' (1912–1913)* (n.pl: the author, 2012)

Travet, Marcel, 'L'École', *La Guerre aérienne illustrée* 20 (29 mars 1917), 310–11

Un chasseur à pied, 'Ceux d'en haut jugés par ceux d'en bas', *La Guerre aérienne illustrée* 21 (5 avril 1917), 322

Verneuil, Max, *Aérostier, mon camarade* (Paris: Lavauzelle, 1933)

Viallet, Marcel, 'Pour nos jeunes', *La Guerre aérienne illustrée* 87 (11 juillet 1918), 564–5

Viallet, Marcel, 'Enquête auprès des as: leur peur, leur joie, leur émotion', *La Guerre aérienne illustrée* 116 (30 janvier 1919), 66

Viguier, Armand, 'Souvenirs de guerre du commandant Viguier', *Icare* 85 (1979), 60–6

Viguier, Armand, *Une vie avec le ciel comme horizon* (Lyon: Éditions des grilles d'or, n.d.)

Villatoux, Marie-Catherine, 'De l'inspection permanante de l'aéronautique à la direction de l'aéronautique: histoire d'une institution 1910–1914', *Revue historique des armées* 233 (2003), 15–26

Villatoux, Marie-Catherine, 'Léon Adolphe Girod (1872–1933): créateur des écoles d'aviation', *Revue historique des armées* 240 (2005), 67–74

Villatoux, Marie-Catherine, 'Charles de Rose, père de la chasse aérienne', *Chemins de la mémoire* 193 (2009), 13

Villatoux, Marie-Catherine, 'Le Renseignement photographique dans la manœuvre: l'exemple de la Grande Guerre', *Revue historique des armées* 261 (2010), 3–13

Villatoux, Marie-Catherine, 'Femmes et pilotes militaires dans l'Armée de l'Air', *Revue historique des armées* 272 (2013), 12–23

Viollis, Andrée, 'Les Femmes s'enrôlent', *Lectures pour tous* (15 juillet 1917)

Vitalis, Gaston, 'Un grand chef disparu: le capitaine Lecour-Grandmaison', *La Guerre aérienne illustrée* 42 (30 août 1917), 659–60

Voisin, André, 'Le Rendement de l'aviation française de bombardement de jour au cours de la guerre de 1914–1918', *Revue militaire française* 36 (1924), 109–28

Voisin, André, 'La Doctrine de l'aviation française de combat au cours de la guerre (période 1915–1917)', *Revue militaire française* 37 (1924), 113–26; 38 (1924), 257–80; 39 (1924), 403–23

Voisin, André, 'La Doctrine de l'aviation française de combat en 1918', *Revue des forces aériennes* 3 (1931), 885–90, 898–910, 1299–1301

Voisin, Gabriel, *Mes 10,000 cerfs-volants* (Paris: Table ronde, 1960)

Waddington, Paul, 'Extraits de l'interview du lieutenant-colonel Paul Waddington', *Icare* 88 (1979), 45–9

Walton, Liz, 'Seaplanes at the Castle Emplacement', *Journal of the Channel Islands War Study Group* 13 (2007), 4–16

Weiller, Paul-Louis, 'L'Aviation française de reconnaissance', in *L'Aéronautique pendant la Guerre Mondiale 1914–1918* (Paris; Brunhoff, 1919)

Weiller, Paul-Louis, 'Témoignages de M. Paul-Louis Weiller, ancien commandant du "Groupement Weiller"', *Icare* 88 (1979), 65

Wellman, William A., *Go Get 'Em!* (Boston: Page, 1918)

Winslow, Carroll Dana, *With the French Flying Corps* (New York: Scribner's Sons, 1917)

Z., [Captain], 'Ne méprisons point les rampants', *La Guerre aérienne illustrée* 73 (4 avril 1918), 338

Z., [Captain], 'Le Commandant du Peuty', *La Guerre aérienne illustrée* 77 (2 mai 1918), 397

Admissions dans l'aéronautique militaire française (Paris: Fournier, 1918)

'L'Aptitude physique des candidats à l'aviation militaire: les nouveaux procédés d'examen d'aptitude physique des docteurs Camus et Nepper', *L'Aérophile* (1–15 février 1917), 58–62

'L'As des as: l'adjudant Dorme', *La Guerre aérienne illustrée* 1 (16 novembre 1916), 9

'Les As disparus: l'adjudant Baron', *La Guerre aérienne illustrée* 1 (16 novembre 1916), 12

'L'Aviation militaire française en 1914/1915/1916', *Icare* 85 (1978), 11

'Les Bombardements-records', *La Guerre aérienne illustrée* 5 (14 décembre 1916), 74

'Compte-rendu de bombardement des usines de la Badische Anilin- und Soda Fabrik', *Icare* 85 (1978), 35

'Dans les airs, avec la mort', *La Guerre aérienne illustrée* 2 (23 novembre 1916), 19–20

'Enquête auprès des as', *La Guerre aérienne illustrée* 115 (1919), 51

'Extraits de l'interview d'un pilote qui désire conserver l'anonymat', *Icare* 88 (1979), 21–3

'Extraits du journal d'un pilote-bombardier tué au combat', *Icare* 85 (1978), 77–83

'Un grand as: Coiffard', *La Guerre aérienne illustrée* 93 (1918), 651

'Les Grands Chefs: capitaine Auger', *La Guerre aérienne illustrée* 50 (25 octobre 1917), 787–9

Guynemer: un mythe, une histoire (Vincennes: Service historique de l'Armée de l'Air, 1997)

'Héros anonymes: les régleurs de l'artillerie', *La Guerre aérienne illustrée* 2 (23 novembre 1916), 26–7

'Les Héros disparus: Pierre Gourdon', *La Guerre aérienne illustrée* 66 (1918), 223

'Les Héros disparus: Marc Pourpre', *La Guerre aérienne illustrée* 4 (7 décembre 1916), 55

'La Maison de convalescence de l'aéronautique militaire', *Bulletin trimestriel de la Ligue aéronautique de France* 1 (1916), 6

'N'oublions pas . . .', *La Guerre aérienne illustrée* 83 (1918), 503

'Nos héros disparus: Pierre Violet', *La Guerre aérienne illustrée* 35 (12 juillet 1917), 556–7

'Nos morts: André Quennehen', *La Guerre aérienne illustrée* 8 (4 janvier 1917), 123–4

'Un observateur: Remy Grassal', *La Guerre aérienne illustrée* 23 (19 avril 1917), 366

'Perdu la nuit dans la brume', *La Guerre aérienne illustrée* 3 (30 novembre 1916), 45

'Rapport du chef d'escadron Faure . . .' *Icare* 85 (1978), 21–2

'Le Remords de la fatalité', *La Guerre aérienne illustrée* 3 (30 novembre 1916), 39

'Le Sous-lieutenant le Bourhis', *La Guerre aérienne illustrée* 14 (15 février 1917), 215

'La Terrifiante Voltige aérienne', *La Guerre aérienne illustrée* 1 (16 novembre 1916), 13

'Un train-parc d'aviation', *J'ai vu* 127 (1917), 345–52

Internet

Berger, Luc, 'Marcel Dassault et Henry Potez: constructeurs aéronautiques de la Grande Guerre', in 1916: l'émergence des armes nouvelles dans la Grande Guerre, 1996, <http://www.stratisc.org/ EAN_7.htm>

Carlier, Claude, 'La Genèse de l'aéronautique militaire, 1892–1914', in 1916: l'émergence des armes nouvelles dans la Grande Guerre, 1996, <http://www.stratisc.org/EAN_3.htm>

Champeaux, Antoine, 'Michelin et l'aviation de bombardement (1911–1916)', in 1916: l'émergence des armes nouvelles dans la Grande Guerre, 1996, <http://www.stratisc.org/EAN_6.htm>

Jagielski, J.F., 'Une famille protestante dans la Grande Guerre: les Vernes. Deux correspondances de guerre', n.d. <http://crid1418.org/ doc/textes/temoignages/famille_vernes_.pdf>

aeroplanedetouraine.fr
albindenis.free.fr
www.archives13.fr
www.asoublies1418.fr
background.vibvib.fr/carnet_de_guerre.html
www.carnetdevol.org
cerfvolantancien.free.fr
www.corpusetampois.com
guy.joly1.free.fr
html2.free.fr/canons/canparis.htm
jmpicquart.pagesperso-orange.fr/Guynemer.htm
www.navarre-jean.com
pages14-18.mesdiscussions.net/pages1418
www.pionnair-ge.com
www.sabix.org
voisinrenault.free.fr

Index